# Master *your* Finances

Get out of debt • Create a budget • Invest wisely • Improve your credit • Plan for the future—today!

MICHELLE CAGAN, C.P.A.
KIMBERLY A. COLGATE
FAYE KATHRYN DORIA, C.F.P.
TERE DRENTH
CHERYL KIMBALL
BRIAN O'CONNELL
JUSTIN PRITCHARD, M.B.A.
PETER SANDER, M.B.A.

BORDERS®

Published by Adams Media, an F+W Publications Company
57 Littlefield Street
Avon, MA 02322
*www.adamsmedia.com*

ISBN 10: 1-59869-957-1
ISBN 13: 978-1-59869-957-9

Printed in the United States of America.

J I H G F E D C B A

# Contents

# Introduction

This book is chock-full of solid advice to help you reach your financial goals, no matter what your current financial situation is and no matter how lofty your goals are. Okay, so you may not be able to cash out your stock portfolio and retire to Aruba at age thirty-five, but you can live a life free from the stress of dodging creditors and wondering how in the world you're going to make your rent or mortgage payment.

Sound impossible? It's not. With strategic methods to eliminating debt, careful budgeting, wise investing, and smart planning for the future, you can be the master of your own financial future.

Inside this book, you'll find a great deal of information on how to keep wealth creation simple and how to use your smarts to secure your financial freedom. All you need to know is right here. There's no smoke, no fun-house mirrors, and none of the tricks Wall Street likes to use to keep you off balance. This is just straight information, presented in a way you can understand and geared to setting you on the path to financial security. Use it to the best of your ability, and take control of your financial life.

# 1 Money, Wealth, and Personal Finance

Mastering your personal finances isn't just about cashing checks, paying bills, and meeting your monthly obligations. It is about accumulating enough wealth to achieve family goals and aspirations through the application of sound financial principles and behavior.

## It's a Question of Money

According to the Bible, money "answereth all things" and the "love of money is the root of all evil." And, as the Beatles put it, money can't buy you love. So what is money? What does it mean to us? Is it good or evil? Does it give us happiness or misery? Is it something we should strive for or a goal in itself?

Regardless of your personal feelings and approach to money, at the very least you could hardly question that it is a means to an end. Unless you are able to build your own house, farm your own food, and make your own clothes, money is the vehicle to basic sustenance. Beyond that, we can all agree that money helps to achieve education, allow you to travel, and give you the ability to spend time doing things other than work. That is, money can make your life better and easier. And that's what personal finance is all about—managing money with an end in mind of achieving goals, while avoiding the problems that arise when there isn't enough money.

### *Money Is Not Wealth*

In economics, money is just a commodity. This may sound kind of strange—as if money could be traded around in bushels, barrels, or boxes; stored in silos and warehouses; or sold in lots and shipped in rail cars to the highest bidder. Well, that's actually true—though in a figurative, not a literal, sense. Money is "stuff" just like the "stuff" we buy with it. We use it to receive the value of what we produce (by working, selling, or investing) and to transfer that value to something else (food, transportation, clothing, shelter, or pleasure) that we need or want. Having money, by itself, doesn't really mean anything about wealth; as we know, you can have money in your pocket but owe $3,000 on your credit card bill.

## Take Charge of Your Personal Finances

There is a reason why you spent your hard-earned money for this book. Perhaps your finances are out of control, and you find there is always "too much month at the end of your money." You want to "get a rope" around your current finances, to stay afloat month to month, and to be prepared for those unexpected expenses—when your car breaks down or when you get those insurance bills (which shouldn't be unexpected anyway). Or perhaps you are in decent financial shape, financially "fit" as it were, and you want to fine-tune your finances and build wealth towards achieving some aspirational goals. The following are the most common personal finance issues:

- **Overspending:** Almost everyone succumbs to the temptation to overspend at one time or another, but chronic overspending is a serious problem. Debts pile up quickly and form a barrier to achieving other financial and personal goals.
- **Surprises:** Failing to plan in advance can give you an unpleasant surprise as you suddenly find yourself struggling to pay those "surprise" insurance and utility bills at the end of the month. Remember: Lack of awareness creates overspending—and debt.
- **Procrastination:** People tend to put things off, particularly for long-term goals and needs. Saving for retirement or college is more effective if you start earlier rather than later, even if you start in small increments.
- **Using emotion, not reason:** Allowing your emotions to cloud your mind can result in poor financial decision-making. Deals that look too good to be true usually are. Four-day weekends are fun and necessary at times, but are they really worth a thousand dollars? Reason must accompany emotions and feelings.
- **Financial personality clashes:** What do you do if you are a spender and your spouse is a saver? You build a workable financial plan that relies on each person's strengths to carry it out.

Whatever your issues, this book will help you solve them and to develop a personal finance system combining tools and techniques with habits and behavior to achieve your objectives.

## Knowing What You're up Against

To begin, you need to have a good working definition of what personal finance is. The objective of managing your finances is to reach your and your family's goals, in terms of both keeping what you have and obtaining what you want. When it comes to personal finances, your family is in charge—each family member is both the manager and the beneficiary. What does this mean? In a business situation, the managers and the beneficiaries (shareholders) are different parties. Managers manage business finance with the aim of achieving shareholder wealth. In government, officials manage finances for the benefit of the public. In the case of personal finance, you manage your own finances for your own benefit. Nobody does it for you. The process works better if everybody in the "entity" participates in this assignment. This means someone will have to take charge as a leader.

If you are in debt, you obviously have some work to do before you start accumulating wealth. Still, wealth should be the real objective of any personal finance-savvy individual or family. Active personal finance sets a mark, or goal, then provides the tools, techniques, and behaviors to reach that goal.

## Tools and Rules—And Beyond

Personal finance uses a system of tools and techniques to achieve financial reward. You are undoubtedly already familiar with many of them—banking, investments, insurance, and retirement plans. Information describing these tools and how they work is widely available. However, successful personal finance means being able to put all the tools together to build a solid financial plan. Successful personal finance also means having the right attitude and discipline in daily life to carry out your plan. Tools without a plan won't work, and a plan without execution won't work either.

### *A Few Basic Principles*

What is "personal finance" as a subject of study? A lengthy compendium of numbers, laws, and planning tools, tricks, and techniques? Yes—for the professional practitioner. This book, however, is not intended to prepare you for personal finance as a profession. It is intended to prepare you for personal finance in life. Three principles form the basic thread of personal finance:

1. **Money, income, and wealth aren't the same.** Personal finance isn't just about money or how much you make—it's about how much you keep. Personal finance is concerned with wealth and the accumulation, preservation, and distribution of that wealth.
2. **Personal finance isn't just about the tools—it's about behavior.** Again, it requires the right set of behaviors to make the tools and techniques work.
3. **Personal finance is a full-time job.** Personal finance is more than just sitting down once a month to pay bills. You must be aware of your responsibilities all the time—otherwise all that you strive for can be wrecked in an instant.

## Wealth and Financial Aspirations

Accumulating wealth means accumulating money beyond the obligations against that money. That is, wealth is having something left over after you pay all your bills and cover all your expenses. You will need this "something left over" to conquer long-term obligations, like your children's college education or your retirement plan. Beyond that, wealth can provide for your aspirations—goals wrapped around things you want, whether it's a bigger house, a nicer car, a better retirement, or starting a business.

### *But Isn't Income Important?*

No common financial scenario can succeed without it. But it's surprising how much income is overemphasized. Let's say that I ask, "How are you doing, moneywise?" Ninety percent of the time, the answer sounds something like: "I just got a raise, and now I'm making $80,000 a year." Okay, that sounds like a plausible answer.

But did it answer the question? Does the fact that you make $80,000 a year really tell me anything? What if you're spending $90,000? What if you have $20,000 in personal debt and a negative net worth? What if you have three kids, aged four years apart, the first of whom is about to start college next year? Income is a great thing, and if you can get more of it, so much the better, but it cannot serve as an indication of your financial health.

Most people can't control income on a day-to-day basis, but they can control their expenses. Accumulating wealth has as much (or more!) to do with how much you let out as how much you put in.

Your net worth is your assets (what you have) minus liabilities (what you owe or spend). Net worth is a bottom-line measure of wealth. Think of it this way: Money is accumulated into wealth, wealth achieves goals, net worth measures wealth. Do you know what your net worth is?

At the end of the day, personal finance is about strategies to accumulate, preserve, and distribute wealth. Accumulating wealth means putting in more than you take out and growing what you have through sound financial management and investing. Preserving wealth means controlling the outflow but also protecting your financial base. Finally, distributing wealth means managing the outflow towards achieving objectives—spending to meet goals.

### *A Brief Tour Through the Toolbox*

If you think personal finance involves more than balancing the checkbook and trading stock online, you're right. Conceptually, it's the planned application of tools and behavior toward a goal of accumulating, preserving, and distributing wealth. Let's look at a short list of some of the specific tools and strategies you will encounter as you manage your finances:

- **Budgeting and spending:** Budgeting is a short-term plan for managing financial flows. Closely related is spending. You ask: is "spending" a "financial tool"? Not really—but as already pointed out, the effective management of spending is critical.
- **Banking and credit:** These are tools to manage finances on a day-to-day basis; they may be used in wealth accumulation, preservation, and

distribution. To use these tools effectively, you need to be aware that the banking system can work for or against you.

- **Investing:** Investing is the other half of the accumulation game. Growing your accumulated wealth through productive investments augments your income contributions; investing may consist of in-tangible (securities) and real (property and collectibles) investments.
- **Insurance and risk management:** Insurance and risk management are preservation techniques. Once you have assets and income, you need to preserve and protect them from certain types of risk. Loss of income and assets resulting from death, disability, and casualty (fire, theft, and so forth) are some of the major areas of risk, and insurance products are a major—but not the only way—to manage these risks.
- **Contingency planning:** Aside from random, insurable events, personal life events can devastate finances. If you get laid off or have to care for a sick parent, what will you do? Minimize risks in advance, and have a ready plan to combat any problems you might face.
- **College and retirement planning:** There are several tools to help you accumulate the funds to send your kids to college and to prepare a retirement plan to meet financial needs in old age.
- **Estate planning:** The wealth that you do not consume in your lifetime will be left to others. It's important to know how to do this according to your wishes, providing for the needs of your heirs without paying too much in inheritance and gift taxes.

Good financial planning involves a combination of these tools, depending on your particular situation and the phases of life. In the earlier stages of life, accumulation is more important; as we get older, distribution comes more into play.

To borrow from Lincoln, you won't use all of the tools all of the time, but you can use some of the tools all of the time and all of the tools some of the time. It isn't just about the tools—they won't work without some cooperation from you.

## On Your Best Behavior

Financial principles, tools, and techniques won't work by themselves. Sure, they can help produce and preserve wealth, but no tool can work effectively if you aren't in charge. Good personal finance blends tools and techniques with attitude and behavior. Managing something implies watching it and controlling it when necessary. Awareness and control are part of what we call the financial "persona," or conscience, the part of you that watches everything and keeps it in order.

### A Financial What?

"Financial persona"—sounds funny, doesn't it? Like it might refer to greedy money people who prefer an in-depth reading of the stock page of the newspaper to a dinner with a best friend, those folks who think about money all the time. Fortunately, that's really not the case. The financial persona is a personality and a lifestyle, a set of attitudes and behaviors essential to achieving your financial goals and financial success.

> Avoiding injury in driving or in sports is as much a function of behavior and mindset as it is a function of devices and rules. The same approach should be applied to personal finance. There are dozens of excellent financial "devices and rules" that can help lead you to personal financial success, but they can't work if you don't develop the right mindset to go with them.

Next, let's review some of the characteristics of an effective financial persona:

- **Awareness:** You need to be aware of your current financial situation at all times. Somewhere in the back of your mind you should have a good notion of your net worth, debts, this month's expenses, current credit card balances, and income you can count on receiving. You don't have to write everything down, of course, and there is no need to keep a "mileage log" of all your minor purchases. However, you should be organized enough to know where to get that information if you do need it. A business CFO doesn't know the dollars and cents of every asset or income account in the business, but he or she could give you the highlights in an instant; in the same way, you should be aware of the highlights of your financial situation.

- **Control:** You should be able to control your expenses and financial transactions. If you buy that new shirt on sale, will you exceed the monthly personal allowance you have set for yourself? Maybe it's a good idea anyway, because you need a shirt and the price is 50 percent off. Eventually, you will begin to realize that without awareness there's no control, and without control, awareness doesn't help, either.
- **Commitment:** Commitment is the combination of diligence and persistence needed to get in control and stay there. Plans fail when you or your family members are only committed some of the time to achieving some of the results. Commitment implies agreement, follow-through, and rewards—when things go right.
- **Risk tolerance:** Everybody has a different tolerance for risk. While it always makes sense to keep some wealth in reserve to meet unexpected or unplanned contingencies, some people will naturally want a bigger cushion than others. This has to do with each individual's comfort level, security, and, to some extent, outlook on life. If you are one of those "If something can go wrong, it will" people, it's hard to change that notion—it's easier to create a financial reserve accordingly.

Your financial habits are the outward signs of an effective financial persona. Keeping track and occasionally checking your savings, investments, and net worth balances is a good habit. Keeping mental notes of money spent during the month and especially charges to credit cards is another. Holding off big purchases until funds are accumulated—or at least until budget impact is understood—is still another. Good financial habits are good management skills that include being aware, being in control, working with the people involved to achieve desired outcomes, making rational decisions, and adjusting to change.

### *The Persona Is Individual*

You can't delegate a financial persona, although many tasks can be delegated to other family members. Awareness, commitment, and control can't be delegated.

It won't work if one family member practices awareness and control, and the other spends freely. Everyone in the family unit must have and use a well-grounded financial persona, even though a single family mem-ber may take on the task of determining the budget, paying the bills, and monitoring wealth. Each family member must exercise the persona, and agreement among all on the details—goals, strategies, and objectives—is required so that the persona can work effectively in tandem.

### *It's a Full-Time Job*

Once you adopt your financial persona, you must adhere to it at all times. It just won't work if you leave it behind when you drive off to the mall. It should be present in "back of mind" for all financial decisions.

Your financial persona manifests itself as a set of financial habits. It can help you counteract the impulses and emotions of a moment and keep an eye on such important things as how much you've charged so far that month, whether you've paid the day-care bill yet, and how you would handle that $500 car repair, should your transmission break down tomorrow. An active financial persona takes stewardship of your finances, almost on an up-to-the-minute basis. Ultimately, this stewardship is necessary to keep your plan from disintegrating, as well as to keep your wealth-creation in progress.

### *Like Any Job, You Must Learn It*

As you set out to bring good personal finance into your life, don't get overwhelmed by the size and complexity of the task. As long as you devote attention to it, you will have no problems achieving a financially productive lifestyle. Start simple, and you will grow. Sooner or later, the things that took a lot of effort in the beginning—like budgeting—will become second nature. The amount of attention you should have to devote should decline as your financial plan and persona evolve. Eventually, you won't even need to write your budget down. It will simply become part of your financial persona operating in the back of your mind.

# 2 A Small Dose of Personal Finance Math

Certain aspects of personal finance require understanding of a few very specific and highly applicable mathematical principles. You don't need fluency in calculus or statistics to take control of your finances. Sure, you can run your own calculations, but there are also tools that can help you—the point is that you should be able to understand the principles behind the calculations. In this chapter, you'll learn about taxes, inflation, and the time value of money, as well as a few easy ways to apply these principles.

## Inflation: Depreciation of Currency

Inflation could be defined as the erosion in the purchase value of currency. Inflation renders each dollar (or whichever currency you use) less valuable—it purchases fewer goods and services than it did before. Does this affect your personal finances? It does, but not so much as you might think—if it is slow, steady, and predictable.

You don't need to worry a great deal about inflation unless you have significant dollar assets, are counting heavily on future investment returns, or are concerned about future interest rates. But you should always keep inflation in mind when thinking about your finanacial future and be prepared to adjust your figures accordingly.

Inflation means prices go up over time. If you have long-term goals, such as college and retirement, that sounds ominous—what will that trip to Paris cost twenty years from now, anyway? What makes it less of a concern is that, as a wage earner, your wages—the "price" paid for your labor—should also go up to keep pace. Will you lose buying power? Unless you work for a government, nonprofit, or other concern that is forced to freeze wages due to hardship or publicity, you shouldn't lose too much buying power. Where's the problem, then? It is where you are relying on economic wealth or income supplied other than by wages. Here is where inflation affects you the most:

- **Money assets:** If your assets are in the form of cash or are based on the dollar, you are exposed to declines in dollar value. If you had $10,000 in the bank, and next year's inflation rate turned out to be 5 percent, at the end of next year you would have about $9,500 in equivalent purchasing power.
- **Return rate:** If you are counting on an 8 percent growth in your asset base, and inflation is 3 percent, you must earn an 11 percent rate of return, in dollars, to achieve an 8 percent real growth. Otherwise, your wealth won't buy you as much in the future as you were counting on.

When projecting the growth of your assets, you must always adjust for inflation and keep in mind both a "before inflation" and an "after inflation" figure.

- **Interest rates:** Interest rates are driven in part by inflation and in part by expectations of inflation. That is, if inflation is at 10 percent, a person lending you money would expect to get a "real" return on their money, plus an adjustment for the inflation that occurred while their precious dollars depreciated in your hands. So even the best interest rates at that time might be 14 or 15 percent. Does that affect your personal finances? You bet. You need to keep track of inflation, because that may tell you which way interest rates are heading.

## Taxes—Here to Stay

You've heard it before. People think that if they get a raise, they'll just lose that difference to taxes. Or they think they can spend more money because they can write it off. Those thoughts are true—to an extent. You will get those tax deductions from a mortgage and you will pay more taxes if you get a raise, but it's not a one-to-one ratio. You don't get taxed a dollar on every dollar earned, nor do you save a dollar of taxes on every dollar spent.

The trick is to always be aware of the residual left over after taxes are paid. And that's where the formula (1 – t) comes in. This simple formula, where "t" equals the total marginal tax rate, allows you to figure out how much of your income will be left after income taxes. All you need to do is multiply the amount of money to be taxed by (1 – t) where "t" is the marginal (that is, highest applicable) tax rate.

Suppose the marginal tax rate (t) is 35 percent. What does that mean? Well, at that rate, for every new dollar you earn, you will lose 35 cents to taxes. Let's say you get a $1,000 raise. To figure taxes on that amount of money at this tax rate, use the formula like so: 1 – .35 = .65; multiply .65 by the amount of your raise, $1,000, and you find that after taxes, you are only getting $650. Likewise, for every dollar you spend on a deductible expense, you will reduce your taxes by 35 cents, so if you spend $1,000 a month on deductible home-mortgage interest, the real cost of that mortgage to you is $650 a month.

### *Federal and State Taxes*

How did we arrive at a total "t" of 35 percent? For a majority of readers, the federal marginal tax rate (as of 2002) is 27 percent; that is, every incremental taxable dollar is taxed to the tune of 27 cents. Many of you also have state and local income taxes, which would account for an additional 5 to 10 percent. You can figure your federal and state/local tax total like this. Let's say your state/local tax rate is 10 percent. To figure your total tax rate, subtract 10 percent of the federal tax rate from the rate itself: 27 – 2.7 = 24.3. Add the state/local rate, and we arrive at a full t = 34.3 percent (24.3 + 10 = 34.3).

## The Time Value of Money

Money has time value. A dollar in your possession today isn't worth the same as a dollar you may get tomorrow, next month, next year, or twenty years from now. Why? First, the dollar you have today allows you to do something or buy something *today*. Right now. And for most of us, not having to wait translates to value. Secondly, as just explored, inflation will reduce the purchasing power of the future dollar.

A person lending us money to use today is giving up his/her right to use it today, and wants compensation for that. What do we call that? Interest. *Interest* is a time-based fee or price paid for the use of money. As time goes on, interest payments accumulate with an investment. At the end of that period of time, the interest accumulated represents the value received for time committed to the investment. A sum invested today will retrieve the original investment *plus* the interest accumulated at the end of the time period. If you need a sum of money twenty years from now, you need only invest a smaller sum of money today, and let the interest received build up to the desired twenty-year total.

### *Value—Present and Future*

Suppose you have $1 today. You invest it at an annual rate of return (let's say, from interest) of 10 percent. After one year, you will have $1.10 (original investment plus 10 percent of that investment). At the beginning of year two, the entire $1.10 is invested, still at 10 percent. So at the end of year two, you will have $1.21 ($1.10 + 10 percent of $1.10). And so forth. If you're standing here at Day One looking forward, the original $1 is your *present value*, and the $1.21 is the *future value* at the end of two years.

The principle of *compounding* is one of the most important principles in both personal and business finance. Compounding was just illustrated: a sum of money $1 received a percentage return (10 percent) in the first year. The entire balance was left for another year, still at 10 percent, receiving the return not only on original principal but on last year's interest, too. Each year's golden eggs become part of the next year's goose, which in turn lays *still more* golden eggs. And after a number of years and with a good rate of return or "yield," that flock of geese can become quite large.

### Bringing the Future Back to the Present

In the previous example, a present value of $1 was invested and allowed to compound into a future value of $1.21 in two years at a rate of 10 percent. But what if all we need is $1, two years from now? What if $1 is our down-the-road objective?

Simply, we need to calculate what amount of money, if invested today, would compound to $1 two years from now. That figure will be obviously less than $1 (it'll be 82.6 cents, if you want to be exact).

Why would we need such a figure? Suppose we decide we need $500,000 to retire twenty years from now. What amount would we have to have today to reach that goal? It's the same principle—what number, if invested at 10 percent (or whatever rate you want) would become half a million twenty years from now? For those wanting an answer, it is $74,500. Yes, a mere $74,500 invested at 10 percent for twenty years would indeed become half a million, without a dime additional being added. Is this interesting? You bet. It illustrates both the time value of money and the incredible power of compounding. What follows is a deeper dive into the world of compounding and some quick tools to help you evaluate and harness its power.

Here is the basic formula for calculating the future value of money: $FV = PV \times (1 + i)^n$

- FV = future value
- PV = present value
- i = interest rate
- n = number of years

This equation should help you gain a better understanding of time value of money, and how the present and future values of money are related.

### *Calculating Future Value*

You can use **Figure 2-1** to figure out the future value of money at a particular interest rate and over a particular time period. The values presented here are for every dollar invested. So let's take an example and say that you would like to invest $10,000 for twenty years at a 6 percent interest rate.

FIGURE 2-1 **Calculating Future Value**

| Interest | Number of Years | | | | | | | |
|---|---|---|---|---|---|---|---|---|
| Rate % | 1 | 2 | 5 | 10 | 15 | 20 | 30 | 40 |
| 4.0% | $1.04 | $1.08 | $1.22 | $1.48 | $1.80 | $2.19 | $3.24 | $4.80 |
| 5.0% | $1.05 | $1.10 | $1.28 | $1.63 | $2.08 | $2.65 | $4.32 | $7.04 |
| 6.0% | $1.06 | $1.12 | $1.34 | $1.79 | $2.40 | $3.21 | $5.74 | $10.29 |
| 7.0% | $1.07 | $1.14 | $1.40 | $1.97 | $2.76 | $3.87 | $7.61 | $14.97 |
| 8.0% | $1.08 | $1.17 | $1.47 | $2.16 | $3.17 | $4.66 | $10.06 | $21.72 |
| 9.0% | $1.09 | $1.19 | $1.54 | $2.37 | $3.64 | $5.60 | $13.27 | $31.41 |
| 10.0% | $1.10 | $1.21 | $1.61 | $2.59 | $4.18 | $6.73 | $17.45 | $45.26 |
| 12.0% | $1.12 | $1.25 | $1.76 | $3.11 | $5.47 | $9.65 | $29.96 | $93.05 |
| 15.0% | $1.15 | $1.32 | $2.01 | $4.05 | $8.14 | $16.37 | $66.21 | $267.86 |
| 20.0% | $1.20 | $1.44 | $2.49 | $6.19 | $15.41 | $38.34 | $237.38 | $1,469.77 |
| 25.0% | $1.25 | $1.56 | $3.05 | $9.31 | $28.42 | $86.4 | $807.79 | $7,523.16 |

If you look up "6 percent" and "twenty years," you'll get a future-value factor of 3.21. This means that for every dollar you invest at 6 percent, you will get $3.21 at the end of twenty years. To get your answer, all you need to do is multiply the factor by the amount of money you plan to invest: If you multiply 3.21 by $10,000, you end up with $32,100 at the end of twenty years. It's that simple—no special calculators or exponents required.

### *Present Value of a Future Return*

Suppose you need a certain sum of money in twenty years; that is, you need a specific future value. How much do you need to deposit today? You can work backwards to the present to figure out the present value—the sum you would need to deposit today to achieve that future value. Use the table in **Figure 2-2** to determine what to invest.

For example, let's say you need $100,000 for a college education. Your son is now three years old, so you have about fifteen years to accumulate that sum of money. How much do you need to invest now if you can get a

FIGURE 2-2 **Calculating Present Value**

| Interest | Number of Years | | | | | | | |
|---|---|---|---|---|---|---|---|---|
| Rate % | 1 | 2 | 5 | 10 | 15 | 20 | 30 | 40 |
| 4.0% | $.0962 | $0.925 | $0.822 | 0.676 | $0.555 | $0.456 | $0.308 | $0.208 |
| 5.0% | $0.952 | $0.907 | 0.784 | 0.614 | $0.481 | $0.377 | $0.231 | $0.142 |
| 6.0% | $0.943 | $0.890 | 0.747 | 0.558 | $0.417 | $0.312 | $0.174 | $0.097 |
| 7.0% | $0.935 | $0.873 | 0.713 | 0.508 | $0.362 | $0.258 | $0.131 | $0.067 |
| 8.0% | $0.926 | $0.857 | 0.681 | 0.463 | $0.315 | $0.215 | $0.099 | $0.046 |
| 9.0% | $0.917 | $0.842 | 0.650 | 0.422 | $0.275 | $0.178 | $0.075 | $0.032 |
| 10.0% | $0.909 | $0.826 | 0.621 | 0.386 | $0.239 | $0.149 | $0.057 | $0.022 |
| 12.0% | $0.893 | $0.797 | 0.567 | 0.322 | $0.183 | $0.104 | $0.033 | $0.011 |
| 15.0% | $0.870 | $0.756 | 0.497 | 0.247 | $0.123 | $0.061 | $0.015 | $0.004 |
| 20.0% | $0.833 | $0.694 | 0.402 | 0.162 | $0.065 | $0.026 | $0.004 | $0.001 |
| 25.0% | $0.800 | $0.640 | 0.328 | 0.107 | $0.035 | $0.012 | $0.001 | $0.000 |

9 percent rate of return? According to Figure 2-2, your factor is 0.275, which means that you need to come up with $27,500 (0.275 × $100,000). As you can see, $27,500 wisely invested today will give you $100,000 to spend on your son's college tuition in just fifteen years.

### *The Rule of 72*

The rule of 72 is a computational shortcut that can help you to estimate time value of money. Divide 72 by the return rate, and you get the number of years it takes for your investment to double. Or divide 72 by the number of years you plan to invest, and you get the return rate it would require to double the sum in that number of years. Consider these examples:

- If the interest rate is 6 percent, your money will double in twelve years (72 ÷ 6 = 12).
- If you need your money to double in nine years, you need to earn an 8 percent return rate to make that happen (72 ÷ 9 = 8).

## Accumulation Annuities

Suppose you need $100,000 for college in fifteen years, but what if you don't yet have the $27,500 necessary to invest? Your best alternative is to set aside money over a period of time. This is called an *accumulation annuity.*

An accumulation annuity is a stream of equal payments over a defined period of time set aside to grow into a lump sum of money. As such, it is a basic model for a savings plan. Accumulation annuity calculations are used to figure out just how much you'll have to save each month or each year to reach a financial goal.

Of course, it means setting aside more than just $27,500, but you will still end up having to save less than the full $100,000. Suppose you save

$100 each month for five years. What would you have at the end of five years? You'd have the "original" $6,000, the money you have contributed over the past sixty months. But you would also have earned interest in ever-larger increments as each new $100 bill landed in that account, and interest on the interest. The sum representing the total of payments plus the interest received for the ever-growing balance is an accumulation annuity.

### Avoiding the Formula

Although there is a formula to help you calculate how much you would need to invest each month in order to arrive at a particular figure in a specific period of time, it's much easier to use the table in **Figure 2-3**.

To go back to the college-education example, let's say that you will need $100,000 in fifteen years and you are willing to choose a relatively aggressive investment plan that will give you an 8 percent return. To calculate how much you will need to contribute each month, you need to look up the factor for 15 years and 8 percent, which happens to be 27.2, and divide your desired sum ($100,000) by that factor. The result is $3,676.47 per year, or about $306 each month.

FIGURE 2-3 **Calculating Accumulation Annuities**

| Interest | Number of Years | | | | | | | |
|---|---|---|---|---|---|---|---|---|
| Rate % | 1 | 2 | 5 | 10 | 15 | 20 | 30 | 40 |
| 4.0% | 1.0 | 2.0 | 5.4 | 12.0 | 20.0 | 29.8 | 56.1 | 95.0 |
| 5.0% | 1.0 | 2.1 | 5.5 | 12.6 | 21.6 | 33.1 | 66.4 | 120.8 |
| 6.0% | 1.0 | 2.1 | 5.6 | 13.2 | 23.3 | 36.8 | 79.1 | 154.8 |
| 7.0% | 1.0 | 2.1 | 5.8 | 13.8 | 25.1 | 41.0 | 94.5 | 199.6 |
| 8.0% | 1.0 | 2.1 | 5.9 | 14.5 | 27.2 | 45.8 | 113.3 | 259.1 |
| 10.0% | 1.0 | 2.1 | 6.1 | 15.9 | 31.8 | 57.3 | 164.5 | 442.6 |
| 12.0% | 1.0 | 2.1 | 6.4 | 17.5 | 37.3 | 72.1 | 241.3 | 767.1 |
| 15.0% | 1.0 | 2.2 | 6.7 | 20.3 | 47.6 | 102.4 | 434.7 | 1779.1 |
| 20.0% | 1.0 | 2.2 | 7.4 | 26.0 | 72.0 | 186.7 | 1181.9 | 7343.9 |

Suppose you don't want to invest your money as aggressively. If you choose a more conservative investment strategy providing returns of 6 percent per year, your factor would be 23.3. To get $100,000 you would need to invest $4,291.84 per year or about $360 each month. With less risk you get less return, so you have to pull a little more of the sled.

With monthly compounding, your principal earns just a little more than annual compounding. That's because the interest is added to principal every month, instead of at the end of every year. So if you want to save $100,000 in fifteen years, you would need to invest $306 a month for interest compounded annually and $303 a month for interest compounded monthly. These differences get larger at higher interest rates, but the annual approximation is usually good enough.

You can also project future sums based on a current savings level. Suppose you're putting $500 away each month in a mutual fund earning 8 percent. That money is meant to be your retirement fund and you plan to retire thirty years from now. (Thirty years at 8 percent gives you a factor of 113.3.) Now, since you're working toward a particular lump sum, you need to multiply $6,000 ($500 per month × 12 months) by 113.3. The result is $679,800, a healthy sum for retirement.

## Distribution Annuities

A distribution annuity works like a pension except that it is set for a definite period. It is a sum of money that is distributed in equal incre-ments (or decrements, to be more precise). You can work forward to figure out how much you could withdraw each month from a sum you already have, or you can work backwards to figure out what you would need to establish as the lump sum in order to receive a desired monthly or annual income stream.

Understanding distribution annuities is useful if you want to pay yourself a supplemental pension when you retire. Suppose you decide that you want to pay yourself—to distribute—$10,000 a year for the next fifteen

FIGURE 2-4 **Calculating Distribution Annuities**

| Interest | Number of Years | | | | | | | |
|---|---|---|---|---|---|---|---|---|
| Rate % | 1 | 2 | 5 | 10 | 15 | 20 | 30 | 40 |
| 4.0% | 1.0 | 1.9 | 4.5 | 8.1 | 11.1 | 13.6 | 17.3 | 19.8 |
| 5.0% | 1.0 | 1.9 | 4.3 | 7.7 | 10.4 | 12.5 | 15.4 | 17.2 |
| 6.0% | 0.9 | 1.8 | 4.2 | 7.4 | 9.7 | 11.5 | 13.8 | 15.0 |
| 7.0% | 0.9 | 1.8 | 4.1 | 7.0 | 9.1 | 10.6 | 12.4 | 13.3 |
| 8.0% | 0.9 | 1.8 | 4.0 | 6.7 | 8.6 | 9.8 | 11.3 | 11.9 |
| 10.0% | 0.9 | 1.7 | 3.8 | 6.1 | 7.6 | 8.5 | 9.4 | 9.8 |
| 12.0% | 0.9 | 1.7 | 3.6 | 5.7 | 6.8 | 7.5 | 8.1 | 8.2 |
| 15.0% | 0.9 | 1.6 | 3.4 | 5.0 | 5.8 | 6.3 | 6.6 | 6.6 |
| 20.0% | 0.8 | 1.5 | 3.0 | 4.2 | 4.7 | 4.9 | 5.0 | 5.0 |

years. A $10,000 withdrawal will occur at the end of each year; in the meantime, whatever principal is left in your original investment will earn interest (in the following example, let's assume the interest is set at 6 percent). What sum of money would you need to start out with in order to achieve that payout?

To figure it out, simply find the factor for the time value of distribution annuities (from the table shown in **Figure 2-4**) at twenty years and 6 percent. Then multiply that figure (11.5) by the expected payout ($10,000) to get the sum that you will need to start out with: $115,000. Invest $115,000 at 6 percent, and you will be able to withdraw $10,000 each year for twenty years. Sounds pretty good, huh? Put in $117,000, and you get $200,000. That's the power of compounding.

## Now That You've Got What It Takes

You have now seen some of the basic math principles used in financial planning. They aren't too complicated, but they are immensely useful in helping you both to build your goals and to decide on the means to achieve them. You don't need to be able to quote the tables listed in this chapter verbatim, but you should be able to understand the concepts of inflation, compounding, and annuity as well as how they work.

The goals you set in your personal finances, and the means to achieve those goals, become much better defined when you "put the numbers" to them. Once the numbers are in place, you can save, budget, and invest with a clear purpose.

# 3 Managing Your Taxes

It isn't possible to examine every component of your taxes in detail. However, this chapter does provide an overview of key tax concepts, strategies to help you minimize your tax obligations, information on audits, and advice on how to get help with filing taxes and tax planning.

## Deconstructing AGI

Of all the tax-return elements you have learned about in the previous chapter, the two key elements are the adjusted gross income (the AGI) and deductions that you are able to make.

Why is AGI important? To the federal government, AGI is the truest indicator of your income status as a taxpayer. And while AGI isn't the basis for your final tax calculation, it is used to determine cutbacks, phaseouts, and other adjustments that ultimately determine your tax rates and total tax payment.

Let's review the AGI in greater detail. You get your AGI value by adding up the following income:

- **Earned income:** Wages, salary, tips, bonuses, and commissions.
- **Unearned income:** Consists of all the following, which may be calculated with the help of relevant schedules:
  - Dividends, interest: Schedule B
  - Net business income: Schedule C
  - Net capital gains income: Schedule D
  - Net real estate and royalty income: Schedule E
  - Net farm income: Schedule F

Then, you subtract the following AGI adjustments (as with most other tax-related matters, this is a sample, not a complete list of adjustments):

- IRA, pension, annuity, and other retirement plan distributions.
- Unemployment compensation.
- Social security benefits.
- Moving expenses (if the move is job-related and you move more than fifty miles away from previous residence).
- Self-employment expenses (one-half of self-employment tax, the self-employed version of FICA, and a percentage of self-employed health premiums).
- Alimony you pay.

Note that Social Security benefits may be taxable above a certain AGI level, and the calculation is frightening. If your AGI is above $25,000 (single) or $32,000 (joint) excluding Social Security, up to 85 percent of your Social Security may be taxable at your effective tax rate.

## Deconstructing Itemized Deductions

Deductions can be standard or itemized. If you have enough deductions, it makes sense to itemize. More specifically, "enough" is more than $4,700 (single) or $7,850 (married, filing jointly). If you have less, you are better off taking the standard deduction.

Itemized deductions should be listed in Schedule A. They include:

- **Medical expense deduction.** Medical and dental expenses, vision care, laser eye surgery, or health insurance premiums may all be counted up toward the deduction, but keep in mind that you can only use the amount spent *over* 7.5 percent of your AGI, which means that unless you have had unusually high medical expenses last year, you probably won't be able to rely on medical expenses for a deduction.
- **Deductible taxes.** State and local income taxes, property taxes, and certain others are deductible. Property taxes include real estate taxes and value-based (*"ad valorem"* is the official term) taxes on cars, intangible property, and the like. So a vehicle registration fee, by itself, isn't deductible, but a car tax, based on the value of the car, is. Gone are deductions for state sales taxes.
- **Interest paid.** You can deduct some forms of interest paid, for instance, mortgage interest up to $1 million on your primary and secondary residence. You can also deduct interest on a second or revolving equity line on real estate. Finally, you can deduct investment interest—"margin" interest paid for capital borrowed from your broker—against gains realized from those investments.
- **Charitable contributions can generally be deducted, with varying amounts of documentation required for gifts over $250.** For small cash donations, save your receipt. For small noncash donations, the IRS

leaves it pretty much up to you to value the merchandise. For higher value items—over $5,000—prepare to get a professional appraisal.

- **Casualty and theft losses can be deducted as well, but these involve complex rules and a high floor at 10 percent of AGI.** If you think you might qualify, some professional tax advice might be helpful.
- **There is a long list of unreimbursed job search, uniform, and educational expenses related to a job that may be deducted, and another list of expenses related to your personal finances—investment advice, safe deposit boxes, tax preparation, and so forth.** But the 2 percent AGI floor on the cumulative total puts this deduction out of reach for many.

## Tax Strategies

Taxes are a given in your personal financial life. They cannot, by and large, be avoided. However, you need to be aware of your tax situation, and you should work to reduce tax impact where possible. On the other hand, taxes are not a reason to make foolish financial decisions. This section will review a few good tax strategies to keep in mind as you make decisions in your personal finances.

### *Maximize Retirement Plan Contributions*

Qualified retirement plan contributions, usually done through IRAs and 401(k) plans (more info concerning those can be found in Chapter 28) make a lot of sense for most taxpayers. First, the money you put away into your retirement plan is not taxed and does not count toward your AGI, so you can keep yourself in a lower tax bracket and pay less taxes. Second, the capital invested in a retirement plan will grow, and the profits you make won't be taxed until you retire and withdraw that money. Finally, in many cases, your employer will match your contributions, effectively raising your total compensation without raising your tax base.

### *Pay in Pretax Dollars*

If you are employed, many employers offer "flexible spending" or "cafeteria" plans, in which you can set aside a certain portion of your pretax income (without having taxes taken out) up to a certain limit to pay for qualified dependent care as well as for medical and certain other expenses. There is some administrative work involved in making these plans work, but they can stretch your day care or medical dollar quite a bit. Pretax medical plans can be used for copayments or to buy more insurance coverage, to pay for an eye exam, or to purchase eyeglasses. The only problem with these plans is that you have to decide how much money you are willing to set aside for this pretax account. If you don't use up the entire amount, you lose the rest.

### *Timing of Income and Expenses*

There are situations where it makes sense to manage the timing of income and expenses. If you have an asset with a big capital gain and another with a big capital loss, and you wish to dispose of them, it makes sense to dispose of both in the same year. The loss will counterbalance the gain for tax purposes.

If you have a big gain and it is the last week of December, you may defer selling that asset until the following year, particularly if you expect to have less income in that year (or vice versa, if you expect to have more income). Carefully plan these timing decisions (with help, if need be), but don't get carried away.

### *Start a Business*

The IRS has strict rules about businesses. If you start a business, it must be intended to make profit and be profitable for a minimum number of years. That said, if you can create a business around an activity or service you perform, the rules for deducting expenses are usually more generous than for the typical individual taxpayer. Buy a ladder for your home, and there's no way you can write it off. But if you have a rental property, it becomes fair game—you can write it off as a valid expense against rental income. If you write books or articles, most printed matter that you buy becomes research expense.

You still must show proximate value for the business, and, again, it doesn't make sense to spend a dollar to save thirty-five cents. But if there's a business in the things you do already, you may be able to find some tax relief. To think this matter through, you may want to talk to a tax advisor.

### *Charitable Deductions*

Giving to those in need makes most of us feel good—and it also helps with taxes. Here is how it works. If you are in the t tax bracket, you will be able to write off that percentage on your tax returns. If you donate $100 to your favorite charity and your t is 35 percent, you are really spending only $65.

> These are only two samples of some of the key tax strategies you can employ. If you sit down for a consultation with a professional tax advisor, you can learn a whole system of tax management strategies, particularly if you own a business or have substantial investments.

Moreover, you can donate property—especially appreciated property, such as stocks—and get a bigger boost. You not only get to write off the appreciated value of the property, but you also avoid paying capital gains tax when you sell. If you invested $500, and your investment has grown to $1,000, you can donate the $1,000 and provide a $1,000 deduction against your current income (saving $350 in taxes at 35 percent). You would also save 20 percent (the capital gain rate) of $500, or $100, that you would have paid on the sale—so the donation would in reality cost you only $550.

## A Word about Audits

An audit is simply an examination of tax computations and the data that supports them. It's the IRS's way of monitoring taxpayers and helping to assure some degree of compliance with the law. There is no need to dread and fear an audit. Just because you are being audited does not mean you are guilty—and you shouldn't act that way!

Audits are typically done in greater percentages on groups of taxpayers who have more complex tax issues or who have a history (as a group) of underpayment. Typically, business owners (especially large businesses or businesses with persistent reported losses) are the most active recipients of audits. The IRS computes an analytical score based on your characteristics and some of the numbers that you report. If you have a high score and your number comes up, you may get an audit.

There are three levels of audit:

1. **Letter or correspondence audits.** If the IRS has a question about some aspect of your return, it may detail the question in a computer-generated message. These are usually simple to resolve by letter or phone.
2. **Office audits.** These audits cover issues too complex to be handled by mail. You will have to bring your records to the IRS office and talk to an auditor.
3. **Field audits.** Dreaded by most taxpayers, these audits involve a visit from the top IRS agents, who show up at your door to conduct a full investigation of your finances and taxes.

If you are being audited, you should prepare your position as well as possible and be prepared to explain your finances to the auditor. Remember that auditors are people with jobs to do. The easier you make their job, the more favorable the outcome will be. Be easy to work with, but stand behind your position.

## When It's Time to Get Help

If you are good with numbers and have lots of time, you're probably in a good position to do your own taxes and tax planning. There are many advantages to doing your own taxes: You may save a couple of hundred dollars on fees, and you will surely become familiar with the system if you learn as you go along.

However, many people just don't have the time or the skills to do their own taxes and tax planning. This is not a problem—there are a variety of tax resources available, ranging from storefront preparation services to CPAs and even tax attorneys. For most of you, it probably pays to at least sit down with a tax professional for a paid hour (the fee might range around $100–200) to review your situation and to see if you are missing anything obvious. For more complex situations involving business arrangements—especially corporations and partnerships—and complex real estate transactions (passive activity rules weren't even touched in this chapter), you'll probably want to engage a CPA or similar professional for tax advice, planning, and preparation.

# 4 Using a Financial Planner

You don't need a grand scheme to benefit from working with a financial planner. Most people just want help gaining control of their financial lives. You may not be able to afford a financial planner while you are still deep in debt. But if you are getting out of debt, have an emergency fund, and are beginning to save, a financial planner might help you achieve your goals.

## When You Might Want a Planner

Over the years our financial lives get increasingly complicated. We face second mortgages, 401(k) plans, traditional IRAs, Roth IRAs, education IRAs, bank competition, rising college expenses, decisions whether to buy or lease, more kinds of life insurance policies, tax laws, and so on. The rest of life gets increasingly complicated too: pressures at work, divorce, remarriage, kids, aging parents, the Internet, too much information, and too little free time.

These are some of the typical financial issues that cause people to seek the help of a financial planner:

- Coping financially with the death of a spouse or other family member.
- Determining whether they are saving enough for retirement.
- Helping with investment decisions and overall allocations.
- Handling an inheritance or a financial windfall.
- Saving enough to pay for education costs of children.
- Discussing how to have enough retirement income.
- Deciding how to leave assets to children.
- Buying or selling a business.
- Looking at whether they have the right kinds and amounts of insurance.
- Improving their income tax situation.
- Wanting a general review of their financial situation.

When you're far enough out of debt to afford a financial planner, the right person can become your partner in helping you reach your goals. Working together can be a rewarding experience, giving you a safe place to share your dreams and ambitions. The planner can offer suggestions, help you review the pros and cons of various ideas, and provide you with objective and informed opinions.

Financial planners typically charge from $75 to $250 an hour, an impossible sum at first even if you could find one willing to give you an hour's worth of advice. But as your financial situation improves, a financial planner can help you continue to become more financially secure.

However, not all financial planners are alike, and not all of them will be the best choice for you. You should plan to interview two to five planners before making a decision. And you may consider changing planners later in life as your circumstances change.

## Where to Start Looking

Begin your search by asking friends or family members who have used a financial planner about their experiences. They can probably offer good ideas about what to expect in terms of cost and services. Ask if their planner would be a good fit for you. You might also get suggestions from business associates or other financial professionals like your attorney, tax preparer, insurance agent, or banker.

Think about what would make a good fit. Do you want someone who chastises you for wrong decisions, criticizes your ideas, and impresses you with their knowledge but talks over your head? Or do you want someone who is able to listen objectively to your plans and help you meet your goals in a rational way that suits your financial attitudes, while at the same time educating you about alternative options or approaches? Only you can decide what style suits you best.

You should know that anyone can call herself or himself a financial planner. This term has no specific requirements and no government oversight. Calling yourself a financial planner does not mean you have any training, education, or experience. As a consumer, you need to look beyond the title to discover what this financial planner does and how.

### *Registered Financial Advisors*

People who give investment advice are generally regulated by a state agency or the Federal Securities and Exchange Commission. They are known as registered investment advisors or registered investment advisor representatives. To become a registered investment advisor, you are required to complete a form and pay a fee, but there are no training or experience requirements.

Registered investment advisors and their representatives are required to provide you with Part II of Form ADV. You should ask the planners you are considering if they are registered investment advisors. If they are, ask for both Parts I and II of their Form ADV. They may provide you with a brochure that contains the same information as Part II of Form ADV. Be sure you also ask for and receive a copy of Part I.

While Form ADV is a typical government form and hard to read, it contains important information about the firm and the individual you are considering. Look for disciplinary actions, conflicts of interest, how they are paid, and the background and credentials of the firm's employees. Be sure that what the planner tells you in an interview matches the information in the form.

What is Form ADV? This two-part government form contains important information about a registered investment advisor. Information can help you evaluate the advisor's credentials and whether that person or agency might be a good fit for you.

### *Other Planners*

Brokers who sell or trade investment products may not be registered investment advisors. If they are not registered investment advisors, they are paid only by commissions. They report to a broker-dealer who is regulated by the National Association of Securities Dealers (NASD). They are not required to provide you with a disclosure form similar to Form ADV, but you should still ask about credentials and designations.

People who sell insurance, as many financial planners do, are regulated by a state agency. Insurance agents are usually paid only by commission. They are not required to have disclosure documents.

Two professional associations offer ways to find financial planners in your area. The National Association of Personal Financial Advisors (888-333-6659, or *www.napfa.org*) can help you find a fee-only financial planner in your area. The Financial Planning Association *(www.fpa.org)* can help you find a planner near you who is probably a Certified Financial Planner.

Others who advise about taxes, estate planning, college planning, and many other financial issues have little or no licensing or regulatory oversight at the state or federal level. That doesn't mean these people do not have valid experience and training. It does mean you will have to ask more questions in your screening process.

## Finding the Right Financial Planner for You

Some financial planners may offer a phone interview where you can ask about their background and their approach to financial planning. Others may invite you to their office for a free-of-charge, no-obligation introductory meeting. There are many questions you should ask during those interviews. The rest of this chapter tells what to ask and what to listen for in the answers.

You may be surprised to discover that many financial planners do not seem to offer the services you are looking for. Many people calling themselves financial planners are really just looking to manage your investments for an annual fee. They have little interest in advice outside of the stock and bond markets. If you are truly looking for comprehensive financial planning, stay away from planners whose primary business is often called asset management or wealth management.

## The Kind of Help You Want

You don't just want the person to be a legitimate advisor, you want him or her to be a good fit for you. So ask anyone you're considering working with: What is your basic approach to financial planning? What kinds of services do you provide? Do you specialize in any particular areas?

Be sure the planners can articulate their approach to financial planning, and that their approach matches the level of service you are looking for. Use these questions to learn more about the planner and how they work. They let you find out if the planner shares your values. You want to be comfortable with the planner's approach to you and your issues.

It helps if you have thought about what you want a financial planner to do for you. Many people look for a financial planner when they want help with a specific issue. Others want either a second opinion on their overall financial situation or they want to delegate much of the oversight of their finances to a third party.

### *Help with Specific Issues*

If you just want help with a specific issue, you might look for a planner that specializes in that area. Some planners work with retirees, some with divorcing clients, others with parents whose children are getting ready for college. But each of these issues requires a look at other areas of your financial life. Your tax bracket, your risk tolerance, whether you are saving enough for other goals, and your debt level should affect the advice offered. If a financial planner isn't asking about other areas of your financial life, you should think about looking for another planner since he or she isn't willing to take the time to consider the bigger picture.

### *Second Opinion*

If you just want a second opinion on your overall financial situation, be sure you make that clear. And be open to the suggestions that are made to you. A financial planner who specializes in managing investments or one who primarily sells insurance products may not be the best choice for you. You need a comprehensive financial planner, rather than one who specializes.

Even though you are trying to save money, in many cases you probably are best served by a planner who charges you a fee, rather than one who is paid by commissions. You will really need to be good at saying no working with someone who is trying to sell you something.

### *Delegation*

If you are looking to delegate some of your financial tasks, you probably need to do more screening and research up front. You want to be sure you understand how the planner will operate, how your assets will be safeguarded, and that you approve of the level of risk and taxable income within your portfolio. Be sure you understand how the planner will be paid and that the amounts are reasonable.

## Other Questions to Ask

If the planner's basic approach seems to fit the help you're looking for, there are other questions to ask before you make it a working relationship. Some questions help you judge whether their experience and values are likely to help with your specific situation. Others relate to credentials and the motives underlying the planner's advice.

### *Types of Clients*

Ask the planner: What types of clients do you serve? Do I need a certain level of income? Should I have a certain amount of investment assets?

Be sure that you are a typical client for the planner you choose. You want your problems to be within their areas of expertise. Ask friends whose financial situation is like yours if they might be willing to recommend their own financial planner.

Some planners prefer to work with retirees or those very close to retirement. If you are a young married couple, this would not be the best match for you. Some planners only work with women, or doctors, or business owners, or widows. Others have more general practices. Decide if you need a generalist or a specialist and search accordingly.

Some planners only work with people earning $150,000 or more. Others require their clients to have over $500,000 of investment assets. Some will work with anyone. Be sure you ask these questions upfront so that you know if the planner you are considering will not be interested in you.

Financial planners who are interested in managing your assets generally have a minimum level of assets that they look for in their clients, typically $500,000 to $1,000,000. If you don't meet the minimum requirements, the fees will be quite expensive. It's probably not for you if you are reading this book and have just crawled out of debt, but who knows, may your assets will reach those heights in the future!

The National Association of Securities Dealers (NASD) Regulation Public Disclosure Program receives and processes information from brokers and member firms that sell securities. This information can help you decide if you want to do business with that broker. Visit *www.nasdr.com* or phone 800-289-9999 for specific information.

### Credentials

Ask: Are you a Certified Financial Planner (CFP)? What other kind of financial designations do you hold? What were the requirements to receive the designation?

This is a way to find out if the planner has a basic level of competence and also explore how much continuing education they get each year. Certified Financial Planners have generally completed a course of study in financial planning and passed an examination on financial planning topics. They must have a minimum of three years of financial planning-related experience and obtain thirty hours of continuing education every two years. They also ascribe to a code of ethics, which obliges them to act in the client's interest.

A Certified Public Accountant may have earned the title of Personal Financial Specialist (CPA/PFS). They also complete a course of study and pass an examination on financial planning topics. They must have a minimum of three years of financial planning-related experience and obtain seventy-two hours of continuing education every three years.

A Chartered Financial Consultant (ChFC) also completes a course of study and passes examinations on financial planning topics. They must have a minimum of two years of financial planning-related experience. And they must obtain thirty hours of continuing education every two years.

There are other designations that qualify people to work in the financial planning field. Ask about a financial planner's other designations to determine if there was a course of study or examinations. Ask whether the designation requires continuing education.

### *Education and Experience*

Ask the planner: What is your educational background? What kind of work experience do you have?

Many people come to financial planning from other careers—teaching, sales, law, accounting, and banking are typical backgrounds. Find out whether they went to college, what they majored in, and how they got into financial planning. There are no right answers to these questions. You are just trying to determine whether you are comfortable that their education levels and experience will be relevant to your situation.

### *Licenses*

Ask: Do you hold licenses to sell certain financial products, such as life insurance or investment products? Asking about licenses will allow you to continue to ask about commissions and other forms of compensation that the planner might earn on your behalf. It can help you know that the planner complies with applicable laws and helps you look for possible conflicts of interest.

If the planner holds licenses to sell financial products, they probably receive a commission or other compensation from the sale of those products. This sales-related compensation may dwarf any fee that is paid by the client. This can create a conflict of interest within the planner between the best recommendation to the client and sale that makes the most money for the planner.

For example, a typical commission on the sale of mutual fund investments is 5 percent. If you invest $10,000, the commission is $500. But if you invest $100,000 by rolling over your 401(k), the commission will be $5,000. And while there might be several appropriate investments where the commission rate is 5 percent, a particular mutual fund might be awarding trips to Hawaii to the salesperson who accumulates the most money for the mutual fund.

If you don't ask, you may not realize that the planner and his firm are earning $5,000 from your investment in addition to fee you paid initially. And you certainly won't be invited along on the trip to Hawaii. Rolling over your 401(k) into that particular mutual fund may be the best investment for you or it may not, but it certainly shouldn't be decided on the basis of someone getting a free vacation!

### Conflict of Interest

Ask the planner: Are there business or other relationships you have that might represent a conflict of interest? Does your spouse own an insurance agency? Is your sister an attorney?

Related party interests should be disclosed in Form ADV. If the planner claims to be fee-only but want you to buy insurance from an agency owned by a family member, this should be a warning sign. This is a conflict of interest on the planner's part since they have other financial motivations besides serving your best interests.

All planners will have some conflicts of interest. Even independent fee–only planners will have favorite insurance companies or mutual funds. The real question is whether planners know their own conflicts of interest and can tell you how they deal with them. Any conflict should always be resolved in the best interest of the client. Financial planners have a duty to their clients, always to put the best interest of the client over any benefit to the planner.

### Disciplinary Actions

Be sure to ask: Have you ever been subject to any regulatory or disciplinary actions? While you might think that financial planners who have been in trouble would no longer be in business, this is often not the case. You need to do some checking to guard against planners with spotty backgrounds.

Typically, after a period where any licenses are suspended, any fines are paid and any jail time is served, the wrongdoer is allowed to go back into the financial planning business. However, past actions do need to be disclosed. Carefully check Part I of the Form ADV, where fraud, bankruptcy, foreclosure, or theft are disclosed.

The CFP Board (888-237-6275) can confirm whether disciplinary actions have been taken against a CFP professional. Your state securities agency may tell you about action taken against investment representatives. The NASD (National Association of Securities Dealers) can tell you about actions taken against brokers under their umbrella.

Do take the time to ask for references. The planner may not give you the names of satisfied clients, since that would be a breach on confidentiality. But they might give you the names of other professionals who are familiar with their work, such as attorneys or tax preparers. Ask around to see if the planner's name evokes any negative reactions.

## Planning for Your Particular Needs

An important question to ask the planner is this: If I outline my situation, will you describe how you will address my particular needs? An experienced comprehensive financial planner should be able to suggest several ways to meet your particular needs, with advantages and disadvantages to each. Good advisors help you learn about these options so you can discover which one is right for you.

Actually, the best kind of financial planning can help you explore all of the possible places you might want to be the future. A planner can not only help you meet your current goals, they can point out where you could be in five or ten years. A financial planner starts with your raw numbers, then helps you look at the relationship between those numbers in the context of what you hope to accomplish.

As you have learned by getting your debts under control, one key relationship is how much you spend compared to what you have available to spend. Can the planner suggest tax saving ideas to further increase the amount you have to spend? Are there better investments or a different allocation that would be more appropriate for you? Do they have suggestions to help you continue to live within your budget?

Another key relationship is how many more years you will be accumulating assets compared to the number of years you expect to live off the income from those assets. A planner should be able to estimate how many more years you will need to work to accumulate an appropriate pool of assets to sustain your lifestyle when you stop working. If you want to be comfortably retired in five or fifteen years, a financial planner can tell you how much you need to save each year to do that, but only you can say whether that is a comfortable amount for you to save. If it's not comfortable, the planner should be able to help you with other ways to save more, work longer, or reduce your spending to meet your goals.

A planner or a computer program cannot tell you the "right" thing to do. Your financial goals and what price you're willing to pay to achieve them are ultimately your decision. Planners and computers can only tell you under what circumstances something might be possible.

It's important to be sure the planner's values line up with yours. If the planner is making recommendations that seem to go against your ideas, say so. The planner's response will tell you whether they're locked into a rigid method or they merely misjudged your level of risk tolerance and experience.

### The Planning Process

Ask: Can you tell me about the planning process? How many meetings will be involved? What will I receive from you? What about future services when I need to update my financial plan?

The process of financial planning begins with a planner listening to your goals and objectives. You should feel comfortable enough with this planner to outline your dreams, as well as the more routine parts of your financial life. And you should feel that the planner hears what you say and understands your motivations.

You may be embarrassed to tell the planner about your finances. Get over it; everyone wishes they had done some things differently in the past, even the financial planner. But just as you should tell your doctor about any new symptoms so you can be properly treated, you need to tell your financial planner where you are financially.

The planner will also need to know about your income and expenses, your assets, and your debts. Since you have been working with that information in your quest to get out of debt, it should be easy to gather. You may have two or more meetings with the planner to gather more information, outline your objectives, and get some preliminary information from the planner.

Financial planning may require the services of another professional in addition to the financial planner. For example, you may need the services of an attorney to prepare your will or a tax preparer to help you put it together for April 15.

The finished financial plan is usually a written document that outlines where you are now, the path you are on, and ways to improve your financial situation to take you closer to your goals. You can use it as a checklist to prioritize and implement the recommendations. For the plan to be effective, you need to revisit and revise your plan at least every two years, and more often when things change in your financial life—new job, new home, marriage, children, inheritance, promotion, college, retirement, or changes in your retirement plan.

### *Implementation*

Just writing a financial plan is no more useful than knowing your leg is broken. Without further action, things are not likely to get better. Ask the planner: How will the plan be implemented? Will you expect to implement the various recommendations or can I do that?

When the plan is finished, you should take some time to read it and ask about any areas you don't understand. Some of the language may be new to you. You may not have a framework to understand some of the recommendations, especially in relation to estate and income taxes. Don't accept or reject any of the recommendations until you are sure you understand them.

Be sure to ask if any follow up questions are included in the cost of the plan. Find out whether you will pay an additional fee for help with the implementation or if that is included in the original cost. You'll have to implement some parts of the plan on your own, such as changing your 401(k) or 403b contributions, continuing to pay off debt, opening a Section 529 account for college savings, changing joint accounts to ones owned separately by each spouse, and changing your income tax withholding.

Some of the recommendations in the financial plan will require another professional. You need an attorney to write a will or a trust. You might need to talk to your insurance agent about your current or new coverage. You might want to talk to your tax preparer about some of the tax changes.

Some financial planners might be able to sell insurance, sell investments, and prepare taxes. But it's not always clear they can do each of those things well. Think about whether using one person for everything creates a conflict of interest or simplifies your life. This might depend on the planner's background and how the financial planner gets paid.

Be wary if the financial planner insists on having you delegate all of the implementation to him or her. Some planners want to do your tax return or sell you insurance or manage your assets. While you may want the financial planner to implement some of the changes, keep your options open so you can make these decisions yourself.

## Payment and Fees

Be sure to ask: How will you be paid for your services? What is a typical fee? If you receive commissions, will you disclose the amount of those commissions to me in writing?

Financial planners get paid in a variety of ways. You often see them described as fee only, fee based, fee and commission, or they might say there is no cost to you. What do these terms mean?

Fee-only financial planners receive their fees from their clients. They do not sell insurance or investment products. They do not receive kickbacks or commissions from product sponsors or referral sources. Instead, they charge a fee on an hourly or a project basis for their services. You should ask the planner if they are fee-only all the time or if they switch between fee-only and fee-based engagements.

Fee-based or fee-and-commission financial planners also receive a fee by their clients. But they may also get a commission or free trips from selling you insurance or investment products. So they are paid both by the client and from the company that the client uses for investment or insurance products. Fees might range from $250 to $5,000 and commissions might range from 5 percent to 100 percent of the amount invested or the premium paid.

Planners who say they work at no cost to you do not actually work for free. Rather, they work for the commissions they receive by selling their customers insurance and investment products. They do not charge fees at all, but are more likely to insist that you use them to implement the recommendations.

A current trend in fees is to charge you based on your investment assets. Typically, the planner would charge 1 percent of your assets annually to provide you with investment management services and possibly also financial planning services. These planners typically require a minimum amount of investment assets so that the fee is a minimum amount. If you have $250,000 in assets, a 1 percent fee is $2,500. Sometimes fees may be as high as 2 to 3 percent of assets.

While it's reassuring to know fee-only planners have only your best interests at heart, they'll probably charge you a higher fee since they aren't also getting paid by somebody else. Per project fees might range from $600 to $10,000 depending on the complexity of the situation.

No payment structure is better than another. If you are investing only a small amount of money, you might find that paying a commission is cheaper than paying a fee. But you also have to decide whether a planner receiving commissions is working solely in your best interest, or if there is a conflict based on trying to serve both the client and the insurance or investment company.

## Are You Ready for Financial Planning?

To be ready to pay a professional to help you with your financial planning, you should understand that things in your life will change and be willing for that to happen. If you are part of a couple, you both need to buy into the idea that things need to change. You should be starting to save money on a regular basis and have your debts under control, giving the financial planner something to work with. You must be willing to take an active interest in your financial lives and learn more about taxes and investments.

You need to have some time to devote to the process. Financial planners can help you turn your dreams into reality, but you are the one who has to have the dream and the capacity to make it come true. You will need to spend some time working with the planner and then implementing the recommended changes.

If this sounds like you, you are certainly ready for serious financial planning. It might take a month or two to find the right financial planner and get started. But think how far you have come from the days you were deep in debt. Working with a planner can help you ensure those days never return.

# 5 Prioritizing Your Spending

This chapter helps you discover how much you spend every day and which of those expenses are important to you. You'll also find out how to stop spending altogether—a temporary situation, but a good technique to use when your spending is out of control. Chapters 5, 6, and 7 also help you figure out how to spend less, day in and day out.

## Understanding Why *Not* Spending Is the Key to Budgeting

You have two ways to free up money for your financial goals—making more or spending less. And neither one is better than the other, right? Wrong! If 18 percent of your income goes to state and federal taxes, then for every extra dollar you earn, you can use only eighty-two cents to pay off debt or save for the future. But if you can save a dollar of your expenses, you can apply all of it to your debt or put it into savings or investments.

When you open a checking or savings account, find out whether your employer offers direct deposit, a feature in which your check is deposited immediately into your bank account. Instead of a check, you receive a notice from your employer that the deposit has been made. You're more likely to save than spend if you use this feature.

## Totaling Your Daily Expenses

The method of totaling your expenses in **Worksheets 5-1** through **5-7** is pretty simple: you either report what you spent last week—day by day, expense by expense—or you start fresh this week and record every expenditure. If you choose to record your expenses this coming week, be sure you don't try to be "good," and spend less than you usually do.

You want to record every single expense that you pay out of pocket, even the tiniest ten-cent gumball you bought on your way out of the grocery store. (If you happen to pay your monthly or biweekly bills on one of these days, do not record those payments here—you'll do that in the following section.)

**WORKSHEET 5-1 Daily Expense Sheet: Monday**

| Item | Amount |
|---|---|
| | $ |
| | $ |
| | $ |
| | $ |
| | $ |
| | $ |
| | $ |
| | $ |
| | $ |
| | $ |
| | $ |
| | $ |
| | $ |
| | $ |

**WORKSHEET 5-2 Daily Expense Sheet: Tuesday**

| Item | Amount |
|---|---|
| | $ |
| | $ |
| | $ |
| | $ |
| | $ |
| | $ |
| | $ |
| | $ |
| | $ |
| | $ |
| | $ |
| | $ |
| | $ |

**WORKSHEET 5-3** Daily Expense Sheet: Wednesday

| Item | Amount |
|---|---|
| | $ |
| | $ |
| | $ |
| | $ |
| | $ |
| | $ |
| | $ |
| | $ |
| | $ |
| | $ |
| | $ |
| | $ |
| | $ |
| | $ |

**WORKSHEET 5-4** Daily Expense Sheet: Thursday

| Item | Amount |
|---|---|
| | $ |
| | $ |
| | $ |
| | $ |
| | $ |
| | $ |
| | $ |
| | $ |
| | $ |
| | $ |
| | $ |
| | $ |
| | $ |

**WORKSHEET 5-5** Daily Expense Sheet: Friday

| Item | Amount |
| --- | --- |
| | $ |
| | $ |
| | $ |
| | $ |
| | $ |
| | $ |
| | $ |
| | $ |
| | $ |
| | $ |
| | $ |
| | $ |
| | $ |
| | $ |
| | $ |

**WORKSHEET 5-6** Daily Expense Sheet: Saturday

| Item | Amount |
| --- | --- |
| | $ |
| | $ |
| | $ |
| | $ |
| | $ |
| | $ |
| | $ |
| | $ |
| | $ |
| | $ |
| | $ |
| | $ |

WORKSHEET 5-7 Daily Expense Sheet: Sunday

| Item | Amount |
|---|---|
| | $ |
| | $ |
| | $ |
| | $ |
| | $ |
| | $ |
| | $ |
| | $ |
| | $ |
| | $ |
| | $ |
| | $ |
| | $ |
| | $ |

## Categorizing and Prioritizing Your Daily Expenses

Now review your daily lists and categorize them in the most logical way you can: coffee, breakfasts, newspapers, lunches, video rental, clothing, toiletries, groceries, and so on. Use **Worksheet 5-8** to record your findings. Ignore the "Priority" column until you've listed all of your expenses by category.

WORKSHEET 5-8 Daily Expense Summary

| Category | Total Amount | Priority (1-5) |
|---|---|---|
| | $ | |
| | $ | |
| | $ | |
| | $ | |
| | $ | |

| Category | Total Amount | Priority (1-5) |
|---|---|---|
| | $ | |
| | $ | |
| | $ | |
| | $ | |
| | $ | |
| | $ | |
| | $ | |
| | $ | |
| | $ | |

Now go back and assign a priority to each category—5 being something you absolutely can't live without, and 1 meaning you'd barely notice if you no longer spent money on this one. Your priorities don't necessarily mean that you will continue to spend this money in the exact same way, but if you decide that your morning coffee is of the highest priority, you can either continue to buy it at the coffee shop every morning, buy it at the coffee shop three times a week and make it at home four days a week, or make it at home every day from now on.

## Assessing Your Monthly Expenses

Recording your monthly expenses in **Worksheets 5-9** through **5-20** works just like your daily ones, except that while daily expenses are often cash expenditures that you may not really notice, monthly expenses are more likely to be paid by check or money order for utilities, rent, and so on. For these monthly worksheets, you'll want to go back through your receipts, checkbook register, money order carbons, and so on, and also use your memory. If, instead, you record these as you go along, you'll have to wait an entire year before you can use the information—and that's valuable time that you could use to reach your financial goals instead of getting deeper into debt.

Be sure not to double up on daily and monthly expenses. If you've already recorded a certain expense on your daily expense sheets, do not record it here.

**WORKSHEET 5-9 Monthly Expense Sheet: January**

| Date | Item | Amount |
|---|---|---|
| | | $ |
| | | $ |
| | | $ |
| | | $ |
| | | $ |
| | | $ |
| | | $ |
| | | $ |
| | | $ |
| | | $ |
| | | $ |
| | | $ |
| | | $ |
| | | $ |
| | | $ |
| | | $ |
| | | $ |
| | | $ |
| | | $ |
| | | $ |
| | | $ |
| | | $ |
| | | $ |
| | | $ |
| | | $ |

**WORKSHEET 5-10 Monthly Expense Sheet: February**

| Date | Item | Amount |
| --- | --- | --- |
| | | $ |
| | | $ |
| | | $ |
| | | $ |
| | | $ |
| | | $ |
| | | $ |
| | | $ |
| | | $ |
| | | $ |
| | | $ |
| | | $ |
| | | $ |
| | | $ |
| | | $ |
| | | $ |
| | | $ |
| | | $ |
| | | $ |
| | | $ |
| | | $ |
| | | $ |
| | | $ |
| | | $ |
| | | $ |
| | | $ |
| | | $ |
| | | $ |
| | | $ |
| | | $ |

WORKSHEET 5-11 **Monthly Expense Sheet: March**

| Date | Item | Amount |
|---|---|---|
| | | $ |
| | | $ |
| | | $ |
| | | $ |
| | | $ |
| | | $ |
| | | $ |
| | | $ |
| | | $ |
| | | $ |
| | | $ |
| | | $ |
| | | $ |
| | | $ |
| | | $ |
| | | $ |
| | | $ |
| | | $ |
| | | $ |
| | | $ |
| | | $ |
| | | $ |
| | | $ |
| | | $ |
| | | $ |
| | | $ |
| | | $ |
| | | $ |
| | | $ |
| | | $ |

**WORKSHEET 5-12 Monthly Expense Sheet: April**

| Date | Item | Amount |
|---|---|---|
| | | $ |
| | | $ |
| | | $ |
| | | $ |
| | | $ |
| | | $ |
| | | $ |
| | | $ |
| | | $ |
| | | $ |
| | | $ |
| | | $ |
| | | $ |
| | | $ |
| | | $ |
| | | $ |
| | | $ |
| | | $ |
| | | $ |
| | | $ |
| | | $ |
| | | $ |
| | | $ |
| | | $ |
| | | $ |
| | | $ |
| | | $ |
| | | $ |
| | | $ |
| | | $ |

**WORKSHEET 5-13 Monthly Expense Sheet: May**

| Date | Item | Amount |
|---|---|---|
| | | $ |
| | | $ |
| | | $ |
| | | $ |
| | | $ |
| | | $ |
| | | $ |
| | | $ |
| | | $ |
| | | $ |
| | | $ |
| | | $ |
| | | $ |
| | | $ |
| | | $ |
| | | $ |
| | | $ |
| | | $ |
| | | $ |
| | | $ |
| | | $ |
| | | $ |
| | | $ |
| | | $ |
| | | $ |
| | | $ |
| | | $ |
| | | $ |
| | | $ |
| | | $ |

**WORKSHEET 5-14 Monthly Expense Sheet: June**

| Date | Item | Amount |
|---|---|---|
| | | $ |
| | | $ |
| | | $ |
| | | $ |
| | | $ |
| | | $ |
| | | $ |
| | | $ |
| | | $ |
| | | $ |
| | | $ |
| | | $ |
| | | $ |
| | | $ |
| | | $ |
| | | $ |
| | | $ |
| | | $ |
| | | $ |
| | | $ |
| | | $ |
| | | $ |
| | | $ |
| | | $ |
| | | $ |
| | | $ |
| | | $ |
| | | $ |
| | | $ |
| | | $ |

**WORKSHEET 5-15 Monthly Expense Sheet: July**

| Date | Item | Amount |
|---|---|---|
| | | $ |
| | | $ |
| | | $ |
| | | $ |
| | | $ |
| | | $ |
| | | $ |
| | | $ |
| | | $ |
| | | $ |
| | | $ |
| | | $ |
| | | $ |
| | | $ |
| | | $ |
| | | $ |
| | | $ |
| | | $ |
| | | $ |
| | | $ |
| | | $ |
| | | $ |
| | | $ |
| | | $ |
| | | $ |
| | | $ |
| | | $ |
| | | $ |
| | | $ |
| | | $ |

**WORKSHEET 5-16 Monthly Expense Sheet: August**

| Date | Item | Amount |
|---|---|---|
| | | $ |
| | | $ |
| | | $ |
| | | $ |
| | | $ |
| | | $ |
| | | $ |
| | | $ |
| | | $ |
| | | $ |
| | | $ |
| | | $ |
| | | $ |
| | | $ |
| | | $ |
| | | $ |
| | | $ |
| | | $ |
| | | $ |
| | | $ |
| | | $ |
| | | $ |
| | | $ |
| | | $ |
| | | $ |
| | | $ |
| | | $ |
| | | $ |
| | | $ |
| | | $ |

**WORKSHEET 5-17 Monthly Expense Sheet: September**

| Date | Item | Amount |
|---|---|---|
| | | $ |
| | | $ |
| | | $ |
| | | $ |
| | | $ |
| | | $ |
| | | $ |
| | | $ |
| | | $ |
| | | $ |
| | | $ |
| | | $ |
| | | $ |
| | | $ |
| | | $ |
| | | $ |
| | | $ |
| | | $ |
| | | $ |
| | | $ |
| | | $ |
| | | $ |
| | | $ |
| | | $ |
| | | $ |
| | | $ |
| | | $ |
| | | $ |
| | | $ |
| | | $ |

**WORKSHEET 5-18** Monthly Expense Sheet: October

| Date | Item | Amount |
|---|---|---|
| | | $ |
| | | $ |
| | | $ |
| | | $ |
| | | $ |
| | | $ |
| | | $ |
| | | $ |
| | | $ |
| | | $ |
| | | $ |
| | | $ |
| | | $ |
| | | $ |
| | | $ |
| | | $ |
| | | $ |
| | | $ |
| | | $ |
| | | $ |
| | | $ |
| | | $ |
| | | $ |
| | | $ |
| | | $ |
| | | $ |
| | | $ |
| | | $ |
| | | $ |
| | | $ |

**WORKSHEET 5-19 Monthly Expense Sheet: November**

| Date | Item | Amount |
|---|---|---|
| | | $ |
| | | $ |
| | | $ |
| | | $ |
| | | $ |
| | | $ |
| | | $ |
| | | $ |
| | | $ |
| | | $ |
| | | $ |
| | | $ |
| | | $ |
| | | $ |
| | | $ |
| | | $ |
| | | $ |
| | | $ |
| | | $ |
| | | $ |
| | | $ |
| | | $ |
| | | $ |
| | | $ |
| | | $ |
| | | $ |
| | | $ |
| | | $ |
| | | $ |
| | | $ |

WORKSHEET 5-20 **Monthly Expense Sheet: December**

| Date | Item | Amount |
|---|---|---|
| | | $ |
| | | $ |
| | | $ |
| | | $ |
| | | $ |
| | | $ |
| | | $ |
| | | $ |
| | | $ |
| | | $ |
| | | $ |
| | | $ |
| | | $ |
| | | $ |
| | | $ |
| | | $ |
| | | $ |
| | | $ |
| | | $ |
| | | $ |
| | | $ |
| | | $ |
| | | $ |
| | | $ |
| | | $ |
| | | $ |
| | | $ |
| | | $ |
| | | $ |
| | | $ |

## Categorizing and Prioritizing Your Monthly Expenses

In the same way that you worked with the daily worksheets (see "Categorizing and Prioritizing Your Daily Expenses" earlier in this chapter), group your monthly expenses into categories (utilities, rent, insurance) and add them to **Worksheet 5-8**. Then prioritize those categories (just as you did for your daily expenses).

## Prioritizing Which Items You *Want* to Spend Money On

You should now have a list of your expenses by category, with a priority attached to each one. If you have enough income to reach all of your financial goals and still spend money the way you currently do, you won't need this prioritized list. But more likely you can't come close to meeting your financial goals if you continue to spend. Use this list, then, to choose the areas that you absolutely do not want to cut back on (these are the items that have a priority rating of five). If you have too many items with a high priority to meet your financial goals, subprioritize those items so that you come up with just a few. Spend on these items with pleasure—it will make all the cutbacks easier to swallow.

Keep in mind that you are the only one who can determine your priorities. If you would rather drive an old car so that you can still afford to buy organic fruits and vegetables, do it. Your friends and neighbors may think you're nuts, but so what?

# 6 Paying Down Your Debt

Do you dread the arrival of your credit card statements each month? Do you cringe when your car payment is due? Then this chapter is for you. As you read on, you will learn how to begin reducing your debt and working toward eliminating all of your debt or at least getting it down to a manageable level.

## Take Inventory

Set aside a couple of quiet hours to get your debt organized. Gather statements for your credit cards, mortgage, car loans, home equity loan, personal loans, student loan, and any other payment plans that charge interest. Then gather outstanding doctor's bills, utility bills, legal or accounting fees, condo fees, and monthly rent. Look at the interest rate on each.

You should be able to find the current interest rate of any credit card on any month's bill. It is typically in a box on the collection of information that includes specific information about interest, how it is calculated, etc. For example, a recent Wal-Mart bill has a line at the bottom that shows the "periodic interest rate" (1.88333 percent monthly), the "annual percentage rate" (22.60 percent), the "portion of balance assessed this rate" (entire balance), how much of the balance is subject to the finance charge on this month's statement (in this case $128.92 of the $179.52 balance is subject to the rate), and the dollar amount of the actual interest charge ($2.43).

Arrange your loan statements so they are in a pile with the bill with the highest interest rate on top. Continue to organize your bills based on the interest rate, highest to lowest, until the one at the bottom of the pile has the lowest rate of interest. If two bills have the same rate of interest, put the one with the smaller balance above the one with the larger balance.

Interest rates change from time to time. The interest rate to use in your planning is the rate printed on your most recent statement. Don't go back to the original paperwork for when you were issued the credit card, since the rate will most likely have changed since then.

### *Making the Chart*

It will be helpful to make a chart or graph that shows the current balances on your loan statements. To make your chart, you need paper or a computer spreadsheet that has a column for each debt, plus another 5–10 blank columns. You'll use the blank columns to add new creditors as you are able to transfer your debt to lower interest rate loans.

Use the information from your statements to fill in the chart with each obligation, the total amount due, the annual interest rate, the minimum payment, the monthly interest rate, and the name, address, and telephone number of the lender.

At the top of the first column, write the name of the lender from the statement at the top of your pile. For example, you would write MBNA Visa or GMAC or Home Bank mortgage. Under that write the address and phone number of the lender. Now write the interest rate of the loan on the next line, and below that, the minimum payment due.

Skip down a few lines and write today's date in the left-hand margin. Now write the balance due on the loan as of today's date or as of the last statement date. Credit cards and mortgages often send monthly statements showing current balances. For car loans or student loans, you may have to call the lender to get a current balance. That's why it's useful to put the phone number on this worksheet.

Now move on to the next statement in your pile and fill in the next column of your worksheet. When you are done, you will have a summary of all of your debts in one place. And because you started by organizing your pile, you have prioritized them in order from the highest interest rate to the lowest.

### Charting Your Progress

In the simplest terms, to lower your debt you must pay more each month than you add in interest charges and new purchases. Therefore, you should not be buying anything with credit unless you know that the new payment amount is within your current budget. To reduce your debt the fastest, whenever you have extra money, you should apply it to the loan with the highest interest rate.

Post your chart on the inside of a closet or where you keep your bills. Each month, you update the current balance as you pay your bills. While progress will be slow initially, if you stick with your plan you will see the balances start to drop. Looking at this chart will serve to remind you that you are headed in the right direction. Hopefully, it will motivate you to stay on track as you slowly see the debts shrink.

What's the advantage of paying more than the minimum? Most loans charge interest on the outstanding balance each month. So the lower your balance is on the date the interest is calculated, the lower the interest charge will be. That's why it's to your advantage to pay more than the minimum whenever you have the money to do so.

## Interest Logic

Credit card debt is a revolving loan; you keep paying the money back and borrowing more whenever you charge something on your card. If you owe $1,000 on a credit card that charges an 18 percent annual rate of interest, you can determine what your interest charge will be. Since the interest is calculated monthly, you divide the 18 percent interest rate by the twelve months of the year and learn that you will be charged 1.5 percent on the $1,000 balance each month. Calculate 1.5 percent of $1,000 (or multiply $1,000 by 0.015) to learn that your interest for this month will be $15.

Most credit card companies charge a substantial fee for late payments. This late fee is charged directly to your card and shows up on your next statement. Doing this month after month will put you deeper and deeper in the hole.

If you pay only $15 this month, you will still owe $1,000 next month, plus another $15 of interest. If you pay $25 this month, the payment will be applied so that $15 pays the outstanding interest charge and $10 goes to reduce your total loan amount. Next month, if you haven't charged anything new, interest will be calculated on your $990 balance.

The interest charge next month will be 1.5 percent of $990 or $14.85. If you again pay $25, then $14.85 will pay the interest charge and $10.15 will be applied against principal. Over time, the interest charge will slowly decrease as the principal balance is paid off. Whatever extra you pay each month over the interest charge, the lender will apply toward the principal balance.

### Non-Revolving Loans

Loans designed to borrow all at once and pay back over a longer period work differently. When you take out a car loan or a student loan or a mortgage, the lender calculates a payment on the loan itself over the scheduled duration of the loan, calculates the interest charges over the life of the loan accounting for the interest decreasing as the loan is paid down each month, and then determines a fixed monthly payment amount that will pay that entire amount—the base loan (principal) plus the interest—in the time period allowed.

Paying ahead on a loan will save interest charges and let you pay off the loan earlier. If you made double payments the first three months of a four-year car loan, and then all of your remaining payments as scheduled, you would finish *more than* four months early—saving you more than one full car payment because you reduced the principal early in the loan.

If you miss three payments over the four-year car loan, you might discover that you owe four or five additional payments at the end. Because your missed payments kept the principal balance higher than the lender anticipated, you'll owe more interest than the original calculation assumed. Just making the three missed payments will not pay off the loan balance.

### Student Loans

You might hate your student loan because you've been paying on it for years. But the interest rate is probably half as much as on your credit cards.

If you have a $10,000 student loan at 9 percent for which you pay $180 a month, you will need to make payments for 6 years to pay it off. That means you will pay $12,960 in payments by the end of the loan—$10,000 in principal and $2,960 in interest.

But if you owe $10,000 on a credit card with an 18 percent interest rate and pay $180 a month, it will take 10 years to pay it off. That means you pay $21,600 in payments on the credit card, *even if you never charge another thing to it.* The higher interest rate means you pay $11,600 in interest over the ten years—almost four times as much interest as you will pay on the student loan!

So even though it is tempting to see your student loan disappear, if you have extra money you should pay the scheduled amount on your student loan and put any extra toward the credit card balance. By reducing the principal on the credit card sooner, you will lower the interest charged in the next cycle.

## Always Consider Interest Rates First

Don't pay off the small loans just to be rid of them. Eliminating several small balances only makes you feel better. That isn't a bad thing, of course, but financially it isn't the wisest thing to do. You should look at the interest rates first. If those small loans have low interest rates, then you will eliminate your overall debt faster by putting any excess funds toward the loan with the highest interest rate.

### *A Little Extra Adds Up*

Initially, you might see that you have only $10 a month in extra funds once you've accounted for all required minimum payments. Put that toward the debt in the far left column of your debt worksheet. In a year, you will have done two things. You will have paid down the highest interest loan by an extra $120 and you will have made progress on all of your other loans by making the minimum payments.

Compound interest is interest paid on interest earned or owed. Savings accounts grow faster if you don't withdraw the interest because it will earn interest. If you have a loan for which you don't pay the total interest due each payment, you will be paying interest on the interest due—and that adds up fast!

In fact, you may have paid off one or two of your small loans that have lower interest rates. Apply that amount to the remaining loan with the highest interest. For example, when you pay off two small loans by making their minimum payments of $10 and $25 each month, you should increase your payment on the highest interest rate loan by the same amount. Counting the $10 you put in from excess cash and the $10 and $25 you add when the small loans are paid up, you are actually paying an extra $45 a month, reducing your high interest rate debt even faster!

### *A Sample Debt Payoff Strategy*

Let's say you have $600 a month to put toward loan payments. Your car loan is at 9.5 percent interest and the monthly payment is $350. You have an ABC credit card with a rate of 18 percent and a minimum payment of $200. Your student loan is at 8 percent interest with a monthly minimum payment of $25.

The best strategy is to pay the minimum payment of $25 on your student loan at 8 percent, $350 on your car at 9.5 percent, and the remaining $225 on your ABC credit card at 18 percent. Any extra money is always put toward paying down the ABC credit card. When the ABC credit card is finally paid off, the entire $225 that you've been putting into that is added to the $350 car payment so that you are now paying $575 towards the car and still just the $25 minimum on your student loan. When the car is paid off and you've worked on your student loan until it is finally paid off, start putting the entire $600 a month into savings for a new car, retirement, or other long-term goals.

## Lower the Interest Rate

In addition to paying high interest rate loans faster, you can also try to reduce your debt faster by lowering the interest rate on each existing loan you have. This can be done in several ways.

### *Move Balances Around*

One way is to switch high interest rate credit card balances to credit cards with lower interest rates. Since nearly all American adults (even those with terrible credit histories) receives credit card solicitations in the mail regularly that offer "low-interest balance transfers," this is often an easy move.

However, it is important to compare the potential new credit card with the existing credit card. The new card might have an introductory interest rate of 4.9 percent or 2.9 percent or even 0 percent for some time period. But that is not the whole story. Many common pitfalls can trap you into paying more than you planned. Here are some things to consider:

- Does the new card charge an annual fee?
- Does the new card charge a fee to transfer the balance?
- What is the interest rate on the balance transfer after the introductory period?
- Will the card bump up its rates in case of skipped or late payments?
- Does the low introductory rate apply to new purchases on the new card or only to the amount transferred from another loan?

Transferring a credit card balance to a new card and letting your old card expire does not close out the account of the old credit card. To close the account, ask the old credit card company in writing to close your account *at your request,* so it is reported that way on your credit report and doesn't scare off potential lenders.

### *Interest Rate Shopping*

Another way to lower your interest rates is to call your current lenders and tell them that you are shopping for lower interest rates on your debts. Ask if they are willing to lower the interest rate on your current debt. This works best if you have a good credit record and a history of paying on time. In any case, be clear that you intend to move this account to any lender who offers a lower rate. You might be surprised to discover that your current lender will lower the rate for you based on that phone call.

The credit card company that charges you low interest on your balance transfer will apply your payments as it sees fit, between the low interest balance transfer and any higher interest purchases. Generally the credit card company chooses to pay off the low interest rate balance transfers faster, leaving you to accumulate higher interest charges on the new purchases.

If you apply for a lower interest rate credit card, call each lender on your debt table and ask if the old lender will match the new rate on the new credit card. You might be surprised to find that they will, just to keep earning something on your account. When any of your lenders adjust their rates, don't forget to change the order they appear on your table accordingly.

## When You Can't Make the Minimum Payments

Up to this point, we have assumed that you can pay your monthly bills. We've suggested you might even have a little extra to put towards your high interest debt. But what do you do if you don't have the money to make the minimum payment on each of your debts each month?

Immediate action: you must make every effort to stop increasing your debt this minute. Buying on credit or using a cash advance from one credit card to make the minimum payment on another credit card is just postponing the crisis. The bottom line is that you must devote more of your resources to paying off your debt. And the only two ways to do that are to spend less and/or increase your income.

As you figure out how to get out of the hole you've gotten into, the first issue to address is whether you have the income to make the payment every month by budgeting more carefully or whether your income is truly too low for your debt load. If you have enough coming in but spend too much of it too soon, paying a different lender late every month will catch up with you over time. You need to create a budget, leave your credit cards at home, go on a three to six month spending diet, and get current with all of your lenders.

If your income is truly too low for you to pay for food, shelter, clothing, transportation, and health care while paying off your debts, you need to make major life changes. A new course of action might be to take a second job, sell your house, cash in your investments, declare bankruptcy, or negotiate with your lenders. Even though you're in dire straits, taking action now may allow you to keep your home and your retirement savings as you climb out of debt.

Do not take withdrawals from your retirement plans or IRAs to pay off debts. If you are under 59 1/2, then you can expect to pay at least 40 percent in taxes and penalties on these withdrawals. And borrowing against your 401(k) is risky: if you leave your job it's considered a withdrawal unless you can pay the loan back immediately.

## Case Study

Theresa and Wayne had accumulated enough debts through one casual expenditure and another that they could barely pay them each month. One week when Theresa was paying their bills, she realized that they didn't quite have enough money for one of the bills. Their savings were at an all-time low even though they hadn't taken a vacation in two years. She suggested to

Wayne that they make time the next night to review their immediate financial situation.

They agreed they'd each volunteer three ways to cut their spending, starting now. Theresa offered to make coffee each morning and carry a full thermos to work so she wouldn't stop at the coffee shop on the way. Wayne suggested he would stop at the grocery store on his way home three nights a week for easy-to-fix food so they wouldn't resort to restaurants or carry-out so often. Theresa also said she would begin withdrawing $50 for spending money each week on Monday from the ATM and making it last all week rather than stopping every time she was low on cash. And they both decided that instead of their usual weekend movie outing, they could have just as much fun renting videos and making popcorn at home.

These minor sacrifices saved them a couple of hundred dollars a month to put toward their debt instead of running out of money between paychecks. By using the extra money to pay down their high-interest credit cards first, they got the cards down to a level where they could pay the full balance each month, avoiding interest charges altogether. And Theresa and Wayne went about it in a way that avoided arguments about money by both volunteering their own ways to cut, rather than suggesting cuts for each other. After a few months they could fit in a movie out once in a while without breaking the bank!

Whether your level of debt requires big lifestyle changes or small ones like Theresa and Wayne, enjoy the beauty of momentum. Make your chart and follow the debt-reduction method described in this chapter. Initially your debt balances may seem stuck in place but at least you'll be paying the bills. Look again in six or twelve months you will see progress. With determination, discipline, and patience, you'll pull yourself out of the mire of debt.

# 7 Freezing Your Spending for the Short Term

If your spending is getting the best of you and creating more and more debt for your family, try freezing your spending for the next several months. Freezing your spending isn't easy, but it can stop your accelerating debt dead in its tracks.

## What Freezing Really Means

*Freezing* means going cold turkey on your spending: you temporarily stop buying. This isn't permanent—you won't stop buying forever. But for the short term, you cut out all but the most essential spending; your cuts will include personal appliances, home appliances, clothing, shoes, CDs, decorative items, linens, computer accessories, and so on. You freeze your spending for a predetermined amount of time—usually six to twelve months—and just stop shopping. Of course you can still buy groceries and the required supplies for your home, but you don't buy anything else.

Some people believe that they must spend in order to keep the American economy going. While consumer spending does impact how much money many businesses make, your six or nine months of thriftiness is not going to spin the economy into an uncontrolled recession. Besides, you'll be back someday.

## Reducing Temptation During a Freeze

People who temporarily freeze their spending usually find that the best way to stay the course is to steer clear of opportunities to spend money:

- Don't read the ads that come in the Sunday paper.
- Don't stop at outlet malls when you travel.
- Recycle all the catalogs you have in your possession.
- Call all the catalogs you receive and have them both remove your name from their mailing lists and stop selling your name to other companies.
- Don't go to the shopping mall food court for a quick meal.
- Don't visit Internet sites for catalogs and stores.
- Don't meet friends for an afternoon at the mall or any other store.
- Don't go window-shopping at an appliance, music, or computer store.
- Discontinue any music or book clubs, even if you have to buy your remaining required purchases to do so.

- When shopping for toilet paper, don't inadvertently wander into the towel or clothing section of the store.
- Send gift certificates instead of actual purchases as gifts, so that you don't have to browse a store, catalog, or Web site.

The following sections help you freeze your spending a little less painfully.

## Establishing What's Really a Need

Understanding the difference between a *need* and a *want* is really the crux of sorting out your financial difficulties. In an effort to make ourselves feel better about being consumers first and foremost, we continually elevate wants to the level of needs. But we humans actually have few needs—at least in the realm of products that you can buy:

- Shelter
- Clothing
- Food and water

Thousands of years ago this list meant a mud, straw, or wooden hut, along with some animals skins and just enough calories to survive. Today we have escalated these basic human needs, and they have become so intertwined with wants that we're not sure how to separate them. Yes, you need shelter, but you do not need a four-bedroom, spacious home with a separate, formal living room, a fireplace in the great room, a three-car garage, a kitchen with cherry wood cabinets, and a bonus room over the garage. That's a want.

The same is true for clothing. Humans need a way to stay warm and dry, but they do not need ten suits or eight pairs of jeans or fourteen pairs of shoes. Those are wants. And while everyone needs food and water to survive, that food does not have to come from a five-star restaurant—or even from a pretty good deli. And you only need enough calories to survive, not enough to add three to five pounds each year, as the average American does.

The desire to own and consume is very strong in Americans, and it enables us to justify nearly any purchase in the name of *needs*. Don't buy in to it. Instead, use **Worksheet 7-1** to list every need you have—you might want to use a pencil, though, and keep a good eraser handy. Be very specific in your list: don't just list "house"; instead, write a description of the house you need and the amount it will cost.

WORKSHEET 7-1 **Needs Versus Wants**

| Need (Description) | Cost | Consequences of Not Buying |
|---|---|---|
| | $ | |
| | $ | |
| | $ | |
| | $ | |
| | $ | |
| | $ | |
| | $ | |
| | $ | |
| | $ | |
| | $ | |
| | $ | |
| | $ | |
| | $ | |
| | $ | |
| | $ | |
| | $ | |
| | $ | |

### *Identifying the Consequences of Not Meeting a Need*

After you've listed all your needs, identify what would happen to you if you didn't get each one, asking yourself the following questions:

- Would you or others around you die?
- Would you or others suffer physical pain or extreme physical discomfort?
- Would your health or the health of others suffer in the long term?
- Do you know for sure that you would lose your job without this item?

If none of these would happen, it isn't a need—it's a want—and you have no business buying it during a spending freeze. Remember this the next time your mind tries to talk your wallet into giving in.

### Establishing—And Sticking To—A Shopping List for Your Needs

Before you leave the house and head out to any opportunity to spend money, write out a shopping list of your needs (which are likely to include only groceries and toiletries). Be sure, first off, that they're needs. Don't pad the list just because you're in the mood to buy. Keep in mind that you are probably feeling deprived, so you may try to satisfy your spending itch by splurging like crazy on groceries and toiletries.

Before you leave for the store, write down everything you need to get, and also scribble in an estimate of how much each item will cost. Then total the bill. If it's less than you planned to spend, stop writing out your list and immediately go to the store. If the total is more than you planned to spend, begin crossing items off your list before you go, until you get down to the budgeted amount.

Don't justify veering from the list because something is "such a good deal." Instead, remember that the best possible deal is to spend $0, so even if an item is half price, you can't buy it unless it's on your list.

Then—and here's the important part—buy only the items on the list. Don't do the classic spender's trick of adding items to the list—and then crossing them off—while you're standing in the checkout lane. Instead, stick absolutely to your list. If you see something you're sure you need but it isn't on your list, put it on next week's list when you get home. Today, though, you can buy only what's on your list.

Be vigilant about this process, and you'll never overspend on groceries and toiletries again.

## Putting Away Your Credit Cards

No, seriously, put them away for at least *six* months. Put them in a safe place that's hard to get to, such as a safe-deposit box at the bank (which will probably cost around $20 per year, an amount that's worth spending if it keeps you from getting further into debt). The farther away the credit cards are from you, the better.

For six months, pay for all of your day-to-day purchases with cash and pay your bills with a check. When you're shopping for purchases that are allowed—such as groceries and toiletries—write out a list before you go, estimate how much you'll need, and take no more than $10 over that amount. When you're not supposed to be making any purchase, limit the amount of cash you carry around to $5 and a few quarters. That will allow you to pay for parking if you need to, but not lunch . . . or a DVD player!

## Tucking Away Your Debit Card

Although a debit card is technically like cash or a check, in reality it feels much more like a credit card. Because you don't hand over cash, you may feel as though you're not really paying for this purchase—much like when you use a credit card. And if those funds are earmarked for other needs (like paying off your debt or saving for a vacation), you'll end up without enough money to meet your needs by the end of the month.

If you take $80 in cash to the grocery store, you'll be very careful not to exceed that amount with convenience foods. But if you take a debit card, you're not likely to be nearly as careful. Put the debit card in the same place you put the credit cards—your best bet is in a safe-deposit box.

## Creating a Wish List

A wish list is an outlet for your hot little fingers and creative mind while you're in a spending freeze. The basic idea is that you write down everything you'd ever like to buy—everything! The list may range from a new TV, to whitening strips for your teeth, to a sailboat. Anything you're not allowed to buy during a spending freeze is fair game. Nothing on the list has to be sensible or practical or a wise financial decision.

Sometimes when you're not spending, you feel disconnected from our consumer-oriented society, and a wish list makes you feel like your old self again. When you feel the itch to spend, go online or look at a friend's catalogs and write down the item number, description, page number, and so on of any item that looks interesting. Act as if you're really going to buy the item. But don't. Just add the item to your list and let it sit there for awhile. The act of writing the item down will feel, strangely enough, very similar to how you feel when you actually buy something. It sounds completely crazy, but it works! (See Chapter 20 for additional tips on how to survive a spending freeze.)

### *Paring Down the Wish List*

Just listing the items can be cathartic when you want to buy, buy, buy. But listing the items on **Worksheet 7-2** can also help you cross some items off the list. When you write down an item's name and cost, also check off one of the three needs categories: need it today, need it this month, or need it someday. If none applies, don't check anything off. Tomorrow, revisit any item that you indicated you needed today. Is the need still strong? Do you still need it on this new day? In a month, review any items that you needed this month, and also look at the items that you'd like someday. Do you still feel strongly about them? Cross off any item you no longer feel you need and/or check off new categories for some items.

> Just as you're likely to find that writing the item down on a list satisfies your need to accumulate stuff, the passage of time usually makes you realize that you really don't need it at all.

**WORKSHEET 7-2 Your Wish List**

| Item Name | Cost | Need Today? | Need This Month? | Would Like Someday? |
|---|---|---|---|---|
| | $ | | | |
| | $ | | | |
| | $ | | | |
| | $ | | | |
| | $ | | | |
| | $ | | | |
| | $ | | | |
| | $ | | | |
| | $ | | | |
| | $ | | | |
| | $ | | | |
| | $ | | | |
| | $ | | | |
| | $ | | | |
| | $ | | | |
| | $ | | | |
| | $ | | | |
| | $ | | | |
| | $ | | | |
| | $ | | | |
| | $ | | | |
| | $ | | | |
| | $ | | | |
| | $ | | | |
| | $ | | | |
| | $ | | | |
| | $ | | | |
| | $ | | | |
| | $ | | | |
| | $ | | | |
| | $ | | | |

### *Reviewing a Sample Wish List*

Your wish list may look like **Table 7-3:**

**TABLE 7-3 Sample Wish List**

| Item Name | Cost | Need Today? | Need This Month? | Would Like Someday? |
|---|---|---|---|---|
| Handheld blender | $20 | ☒ | | |
| Honda CRV | $18,000 | | | ☒ |
| Garden arbor | $225 | | | ☒ |
| Luggage | $300 | | | ☒ |
| Two pairs of jeans | $60 | | ☒ | |
| DVD player | $175 | | | ☒ |
| Cabin | $160,000 | | | ☒ |

Now suppose thirty days have gone by, and the list looks **Table 7-4:**

**TABLE 7-4 Sample Wish List, Round Two**

| Item Name | Cost | Need Today? | Need This Month? | Would Like Someday? |
|---|---|---|---|---|
| Handheld blender | $20 | | ☒ | |
| Honda CRV | $18,000 | | | ☒ |
| One pair of jeans | $30 | | ☒ | |
| DVD player | $175 | | | ☒ |
| Cabin | $160,000 | | | ☒ |

Thirty days later, the list may look like **Table 7-5:**

TABLE 7-5 **Sample Wish List, Round Three**

| Item Name | Cost | Need Today? | Need This Month? | Would Like Someday? |
|---|---|---|---|---|
| Handheld blender | $20 | | | ☒ |
| One pair of jeans | $30 | | ☒ | |
| DVD player | $175 | | | ☒ |

At this point, you've narrowed your list to items you would clearly like to own and can begin to save for when your spending freeze is over. You also have a ready-made list if anyone asks you what you really want for your birthday.

# 8 Restructuring a Heavy Debt Burden

If your debts are crushing you, you may need to take action to restructure them through a number of means: credit counseling, debt consolidation, or selling some of your assets. This chapter helps you understand the basics of debt restructuring.

## Understanding How Debt Is Restructured

Does this sound like you? You have too much debt to handle—maybe you've charged more than you can afford on several credit cards and store charge cards, you have school loans plus a car and house payment and the usual payments for utilities and food. You're having trouble making monthly payments, perhaps you are already a few months behind, and you're starting to be (or have been for some time) hassled by debt collectors. If so, debt restructuring is exactly what you need! The idea is that you change the way your debt is structured—by lowering interest rates, lengthening repayment schedules, combining several payments into one smaller payment, or getting some of the debts forgiven—and at the same time, you stop getting further into debt. You may have to give something up (for example, if you're given the privilege of combining several payments into one at a lower interest rate, you may have to give up using all your credit cards and store charges until your current debts are all paid off), but you'll probably come out way ahead in the long run.

If you've been using a check-cashing service to get cash for your paycheck (or a cash loan against your *next* paycheck), stop immediately! They charge a ridiculous amount of money for their services. Instead, open a bank account (look for a totally free one), which you can start with anywhere from $5 to $50.

There are a number of ways to restructure your current debts. You might see a credit counselor to discuss your options (this is often a good place to begin because it's usually free), consolidate most of your debts into one payment, sell some of your assets, use the equity in your house to pay off your debts (see Chapter 9), or declare bankruptcy (see page 98).

## Getting Credit Counseling

Credit counseling is usually a free, nonprofit service that offers an alternative to bankruptcy (discussed in Chapter 14). Each agency assigns you a counselor who reviews your debts, assets, income, and so on, to help you identify your best financial options other than bankruptcy. Sometimes the credit counselors are bona fide financial gurus, but more often they're simply well-trained, well-meaning volunteers who offer an excellent service. All credit counseling agencies offer their services in complete confidentiality and may offer services over the phone and Internet, as well as in face-to-face consultations.

Keep in mind, however, that not all credit counseling agencies are nonprofit, and some are almost like scams. You can find out more in the "Consolidating Your Debt" section in this chapter.

### *Making Sure the Counseling Is Free*

Your initial counseling session(s) should be completely free. If they aren't, get out as fast as you can! Many wonderful nonprofit credit counseling agencies exist, so don't waste your money on an agency that charges you for counseling. While you may have to pay a small fee to consolidate your debt (see "Consolidating Your Debt" later in this chapter), the counseling session itself—in which your finances are sorted out and advice is offered—should be free.

### *Getting Comfortable with Your Counselor*

Be sure you trust your counselor and feel confident in his or her abilities. If you don't, find out whether you can have another counselor assigned to you. Keep in mind, however, that your agency is a nonprofit organization with limited resources. You should have a darned good reason for wanting to be assigned a new counselor before you ask for this special treatment.

### *Taking Advantage of Free Financial Educational Opportunities*

Credit counseling agencies often offer free short seminars or informational brochures on how to get out of debt, manage money, save for a down payment on a house, save for retirement, and so on. They do this as a service to the community, like any nonprofit agency may do.

If you're not ready to speak to a counselor but want more information, consider attending one of these seminars. There you'll meet one or more of the counselors who work for the agency, and you may become more comfortable with the idea of confiding in this perfect stranger! Credit counselors are listed in the Yellow Pages and on the Internet.

## Consolidating Your Debt

Instead of writing a check for the minimum amount to three credit card companies, two store charge cards, and your student loan, in addition to paying your other bills, all of that unsecured debt (debt that doesn't have a sellable item, like a house or a car, attached to it) can be turned into one payment—usually at a much lower interest rate—that you can more easily manage each month. This is what debt consolidation is all about.

Debt consolidation is not a loan, nor is it a forgiveness of your debts: you do pay off all your debts in due time. But debt consolidation often offers a lower interest rate than you're currently being charged, and if your debts are with collection agencies who expect immediate payment, you may be able to take more time to pay those debts. The best part? The harassing phone calls and letters will stop immediately. Usually you sign an agreement in which you allow your credit counselor to contact your creditors, let your counselor submit a budget on your behalf, agree to make your new payment on time (or have your payments automatically withdrawn from your checking or savings account), and agree not to get into further debt. If your creditors agree (and they usually do), you are usually in a position to be free of these debts in three to six years, provided your budget allows for this. And your credit counselor will put you on a tight budget until your debt is paid off.

Keep in mind that debts that are secured, like your house or car, are not usually renegotiated by a credit counseling agency (but this is not always the case).

### *Using an Accredited Agency*

Most, but not all, debt consolidation is performed by credit counseling agencies. Before you sign on with any agency, check with the Council on Accreditation of Services for Families and Children, the National Foundation for Credit Counseling, and the Better Business Bureau.

Remember that not all credit counselors are the same! Credit card companies have always appreciated credit counseling services that help people figure out how to pay back their debts, even if it takes them a long time. This is because when cardholders file for the alternative—bankruptcy—the credit card companies often get no payment at all. So to help these nonprofits, credit card companies sometimes donate a percentage of the card balance to the credit counseling service. Some entrepreneurs, hungry for the fee that credit card companies give for credit counseling, have started for-profit businesses that advertise as credit counselors. But these companies often push the consumer (that's you!) to pay the credit card companies first—or worse, will work only with debts owed to creditors that pay them—which may not be in your best interest.

### *Examining the Fee—If Any—For Debt Consolidation*

Most nonprofits charge a nominal fee for debt consolidation. Expect this, but do not pay more than $25 per month for this service. The money goes to a good cause—paying the agency's considerable expenses—and because of your lower interest rates, you'll still save a bundle of money.

### *Reviewing the Terms of Your Agreement*

Be sure you read the terms of your agreement carefully. You'll usually be expected to make your monthly payment on time—with no exceptions—and you'll also agree not to get into any more debt. This is a bit of tough love because, ultimately, you can't break your cycle of debt if your credit counseling agency bails you out and then you get right back into debt again. Because they're going to all the trouble of intervening on your behalf, you have to agree to change your lifestyle. It's a tall order, but it's the only way most credit counseling agencies will work.

### *Consolidating Your Debts on Your Own*

Another way to consolidate your debts is to use one of your credit cards to pay off all your other debts. Many credit cards even provide checks or special forms that help simplify this process.

Under most circumstances, however, consolidating this way—on your own and without the guidance and support of a counselor—isn't a good idea. Because you won't have signed an agreement not to rack up any more debt, you may be tempted to use your now-paid-off credit cards to spend more money, making your situation worse.

In addition, even if one of your credit cards is offering a low interest rate to transfer the balances from your other cards to theirs, the rate is usually good only for a limited amount of time (like six months) and may skyrocket after that. Many credit cards also charge a transaction fee to pay off the balances of other cards. A credit counselor can usually arrange for an even lower interest rate for your debts—and it won't expire.

## Selling Some Assets

Besides debt consolidation, there is another way to raise money to pay off your debts: sell some of your assets. If your house, apartment, storage unit, or parent's house is stocked with items belonging to you that you no longer use and that may have some resale value, consider selling them and using the money to pay down your debts.

Don't confuse pawnshops with tag sales, where you drag out all your stuff and try to make a few bucks. Let's be clear: The people who run pawnshops are nearly always loan sharks, often charging as much as a 25 percent annual interest rate. Steer clear!

### *Selling Valuable Items*

Items that you may be able to sell—and that may be valuable—include furniture, jewelry, an automobile or motorcycle, exercise equipment, recreational toys (pool table, bike, off-road vehicle, Ping-Pong table, Foosball table, portable basketball backboard), paintings, signed books, computer equipment, guns, memorabilia (baseball cards, signed sports balls), coin or stamp collections, and outdoor equipment (grill, riding mower, tractor).

Whatever items you plan to sell, if you expect a high price for them, make sure they're in excellent condition. If they're not nearly new, consider holding a tag sale (see the following section).

Don't sell any items that don't belong to you! That may be considered theft, landing you in hot water. Also, don't sell anything that has a loan against it unless you plan to pay off the loan that same day. Contact your lender about how to sell an item that they hold a lien against.

You can sell valuable items in a variety of ways:

**Advertise in your local newspaper or a pay-only-if-you-sell publication.** Although an ad in your local paper can be a bit pricey, you won't have to mess with shipping the item to an out-of-town buyer. And classified ads in some papers are quite inexpensive. The pay-when-you-sell publications, either online or in print form, allow you to advertise for free until you sell the item, at which time you pay a percentage of the selling price—sometimes as much as 15 percent. This option is a good idea if you're not sure your item will sell.

Don't sell anything you would rebuy later. The point isn't to become your own pawnshop—selling when you need money and buying when you have it—but to pare down possessions that you no longer want or need, and raise some money in the process.

**Visit a reputable dealer in antiques, paintings, guns, jewelry, books, coins, or stamps.** If you think your item has some value, see a dealer who resells the type of item you wish to sell. Don't visit a pawnshop or any other shady business. Go to the best, highest-class dealer you can find and present your item for sale. If you aren't satisfied with the price, go elsewhere. That particular dealer may simply have too many of what you're trying to sell; another dealer may not.

**Auction off the item, either online or with a service in your community.** Your items will have to be fairly valuable to others to warrant a live auction (call your local auction company to arrange an appraisal), but even inexpensive items can be auctioned via online services like eBay (*www.eBay.com*).

If you choose an option that will require you to send an item to another city or state (and this is usually the case with online auction services), make sure you find out how much FedEx or UPS will charge you to send your item, insured, via one- or two-day service. Add that cost to your base price. Also, *do not* send your item without first receiving payment: either send it C.O.D. (cash on demand, in which the delivery service receives cash from the buyer and turns it over to you) or require payment from the buyer before sending the item.

### *Holding a Tag Sale*

If you own a lot of items, but none is of much value, consider holding tag sale (also called a yard sale or garage sale). Although your items will sell for much less than you paid for them, you may be able to make hundreds of dollars selling items you consider to be junk. Don't forget, however, that lugging all your items out to the garage or yard, marking them with prices, and being anchored to your sale for a day or two are time-consuming and challenging!

Don't set your prices too high! Even though you paid $48 for your blender, it probably won't sell for more than $5, even if it's in great condition.

Be sure to mark the price on every single item and include a range of prices, from twenty-five cents for old kitchen towels to $40 for a dresser that's in good condition. This will keep your buyers happy.

To attract customers, set out an attention-grabber—an item that's highly unusual or brightly colored—near the end of your driveway. And make your sale seem full by pulling some of your larger items out of the garage into the driveway. If you don't think you have enough stuff to attract attention, consider combining a sale with neighbors, friends, or family.

Be sure to advertise your sale in your local newspaper. For a fee (generally $8 to $20), your sale will be advertised a few days in advance, and you may even receive some signs to place near your house, at intersections, or on busier streets, showing shoppers how to find you. Your ad should include directions, hours, a list of items, and whether you'll hold your sale in the event of rain.

Expect early birds to arrive from sixty to ninety minutes before your posted time. If you're not ready to open, ignore them and reiterate that you'll be opening at the time listed in the paper. Most of these early shoppers are antique or resale shop dealers who want the pick of your tag sale litter. If you let them in early, regular folks who saw your ad and thought it'd be fun to go garage-saling may be furious with you!

Good garage sale operators get change (a roll of quarters plus small bills) the day before the sale—but if you do this, keep the money box in your hands at all times. A common scam is for one person to distract you while another steals the money box. Also, if you're not good at addition, keep a calculator nearby.

### *Cashing in Savings Bonds or Stocks*

If you own bonds or stocks that aren't earmarked for your (or your child's) education or for your retirement *and* they are currently valuable, consider cashing them in to pay down your debt. Before deciding, visit your local bank or stockbroker to determine the value of these assets, as well as any penalties and other costs or commissions associated with selling them.

## Using Your House to Pay Off Your Debts

Using your home's equity to get out from under crushing debt is so popular today that this book devotes an entire chapter to it. The next chapter will give techniques for tapping your home's equity, which is the value of your home minus the mortgage owed on it.

## Declaring Bankruptcy

Bankruptcy generally isn't a good idea because, although it probably seems much easier than credit counseling or selling some of your belongings, it can haunt you for a good portion of your life. Think of it this way: Would you ever loan money to a friend who once borrowed it but never paid it back? Neither will lenders, including those that loan money for cars and homes and those that offer unsecured loans like credit cards and store charge cards. You may even have trouble getting the utilities for your house or apartment hooked up if you've declared bankruptcy. (This means you'll have to prepay these services until you establish a good payment record.) In addition, many stores and other companies won't accept checks from you if you've recently declared bankruptcy.

# 9 Refinancing Your Home and Tapping Your Equity

Your house may be a source of riches or a money pit, depending on how well you take advantage of the refinancing options available to you. In addition, if you choose to tap the equity that has built up in your home, you may be able to pay off your existing debt. This chapter shows you how.

## Finding Money in Your Home

When you think of finding money in your home, you probably think of those pennies and dimes that find their way under the cushions of your couch. Or perhaps you think of the hideous painting your uncle left you that's sure to be worth millions at an auction.

But the real trick to finding money in your house is to understand how to reduce your monthly mortgage payment (which is probably your largest financial obligation each month) and/or tap your equity. This chapter explains the process from top to bottom. If you don't own a home, you may not find this chapter very useful—but you may want to move on over to Chapter 16 to find out what's involved in buying a new-to-you house.

## Refinancing Your House

If interest rates are lower than they were when you bought your existing house *and* if you plan to stay in your house for at least two more years, consider refinancing. When you refinance, you stay in your current house but get a new loan at a lower interest rate than you got on your first mortgage. Ideally, you want to keep the same number of years in your new mortgage as you have left on your old one.

While you want to shop around for the best refinancing interest rates, also shop around for closing costs—the costs associated with sealing the deal on your refinancing. Your current lender may have a slightly higher interest rate than other lenders, but may not charge you for a new inspection, new credit report, and so on. Keep in mind, too, that you can often roll these costs into your mortgage.

When you refinance, many lenders will offer you cash to pay off your credit card debt, to take a vacation, or to spend on whatever you feel like buying, using the equity in your home (the amount your house is worth minus the amount you owe). If your debts are crushing you, you may decide to use the equity to pay them off and start with a clean slate (see the following section). But if you would use that money for anything other than getting rid of large amounts of high-interest debt, don't succumb to this sneaky trick on the part of lenders. They just want your loan to be bigger so they can make more money. But you want your loan to be smaller—both in terms of monthly payments and the number of years before you pay it off—so don't ever take this option unless you're absolutely sure you will use the cash effectively.

Remember that refinancing your car or house doesn't mean you shirk your financial responsibility on these loans. Instead, by locking in a lower interest rate than you originally borrowed at, you can either reduce your monthly payments or keep the same monthly payments and reduce the length of your loan.

Many people ask how much lower than your current interest rate your new mortgage interest rate has to be to make refinancing attractive. Some say the rule is two percentage points. Others say that even half a percentage point can make a difference for some mortgages. To find out how much difference one percentage point can make, visit *www.smartmoney.com* and follow the links to Personal Finance, Tools & Worksheets, Mortgage Calculator. (If you don't have a computer, take a trip to your local library to use their Internet service.) There you'll find just about the coolest mortgage calculator ever invented. Type in your mortgage information, and you can see the impact of changing not only the interest rate, but also any extra payments you might want to make each month (under the prepayments section), lump-sum payments (like putting a bonus from work toward your mortgage), changing the length of the mortgage, and so on.

## Understanding Equity

Equity is the portion of your house that you own, mortgage-free. You can calculate your equity as follows:

1. **Determine the current value of your home.** This amount may be higher—in some cases, *much* higher—than the amount you paid for it.

The value may also be lower than what you paid if the house was overvalued when you bought it or if the real estate market in your area has slumped. A mortgage company requires an appraisal, done by a professional, to determine this value, but you can guess, based on what homes in your neighborhood have been selling for.

2. **Determine the current payoff on your mortgage.** If you don't receive a monthly statement or receipt that tells you the payoff amount, call your mortgage company and ask for it.
3. **Subtract the payoff from the current value.** This is the equity in your home.

Instead of calculating the current value of your home, some lenders use the value when you bought the home. If that was more than a couple of years ago, the current value may be much higher.

## Refinancing Your Home and Taking Out Equity

Refinancing your home and turning some of the equity in your home into cash is a logical way to ease your current debt load. Refinancing is simply financing your mortgage again in an attempt to decrease your monthly payments, the interest rate of your mortgage, the length of your loan, or all three.

Suppose your house is worth $170,000 and you owe $120,000; your equity is $50,000. If you refinance without touching the equity, your new loan will be for $120,000, which will make your payments lower than when you bought the house. And if interest rates are lower than when you first obtained your mortgage, your payments will be lower still. You can then decide whether you want to decrease the length of your loan (say, from thirty years to fifteen) while keeping the same monthly payment as before, or whether you want to keep the length of the loan the same and have a lower debt obligation every month.

You can, however, also use some of the equity in your house to pay off other debts. Refinancing and removing equity at the same time amounts to getting a new loan for a higher amount than you currently owe on your home. Instead of refinancing your home for $120,000, you can receive cash for some portion of your equity—perhaps $15,000—and refinance for $135,000 ($120,000 owed on your mortgage plus $15,000 cash).

Not all of the equity in your home will be available for you to cash in. Some lenders require you to keep 20 to 25 percent of your home's value as an ongoing down payment. Other lenders don't allow you to use the current value of your home, and instead use the original purchase price to determine your equity.

### *Do You Have Enough Equity?*

If you bought your house with a 3 percent down payment on a thirty-year loan four years ago, and your house hasn't increased much in value, you may not have enough equity to tap. Thirty-year loans (and—horror of horrors—those that are even longer) are notorious for building equity very slowly. In fact, if you finance $100,000 on a thirty-year loan at 7 percent with $5,000 down, you'll have paid just $4,400 of your mortgage after four years; $13,600 after ten years.

On an identical loan for fifteen years, though, you'll have chewed up almost $17,000 of your mortgage after four years, nearly $53,000 after ten years. Before applying for a refinance with cash back, make sure you have enough equity.

Keep in mind, however, that when interest rates are lower than they were for your original loan, you should still consider refinancing without cashing out any of your equity, either to lower you monthly payments and relieve some of your monthly debt or to reduce your mortgage to fifteen years, allowing you more options for saving for retirement or your child's college education.

### *Do You Have a Solid Retirement Plan?*

This may seem like an odd question in a chapter about tapping your home's equity. If your retirement years are well provided for, either by your company's retirement plan or by investments you've made, lowering the equity in your house by refinancing and getting cash back is a fine idea. But if your retirement savings is shaky or nonexistent, keep the equity in your house and refinance for the fewest number of years possible.

> You can sell your large home and move to a smaller one when you retire, paying cash for the smaller home and putting the difference into your retirement fund. See Chapter 23 for more on saving for your retirement.

If you refinance your home for fifteen years when you're forty years old, you'll own your home free and clear when you're fifty-five. You'll realize two benefits: you can spend the ten years from fifty-five to sixty-five putting the amount of your previous house payment into retirement savings *and* you won't have house payments when you retire, which means you'll need less retirement income.

## Qualifying for Refinancing

Whether you refinance with or without taking out some of the equity in your home, you want to make sure the refinancing meets the conditions in the following sections.

### *You Must Have Good Credit*

Your credit rating is a reflection of how responsibly you've used credit and paid your bills over the years. If you're interested in refinancing your home but have poor—or even moderate—credit, you may want to wait a year or two while improving your credit rating. A poor credit rating is usually the result of the following, and it can be improved in the following ways:

**High debt-to-income ratio.** Your new house payment should take up no more than 28 percent of your monthly income; your total financial obligations (mortgage payment, insurance, car payments, credit card payments, utilities, and so on) should total no more than thirty-six percent of your monthly income. To improve your debt-to-income ratio, you'll need to pay off and/or reduce some of your financial obligations—or increase your income. See Chapters 5 through 7 for ways to reduce your expenses; check out Chapter 10 for ways to increase your income.

**Late payments.** If you have a history of paying any of your bills—and especially your mortgage payments—after they're due, you're likely to be denied a new mortgage. To deal with this problem, spend a least a year paying every single one of your bills early or on time, and then apply for a refinanced mortgage. In your application, include a letter stating your new commitment to cleaning up your poor payment history and explaining your diligence over the previous year.

**Too much credit.** If you apply for every charge card or store credit card every time you receive an application, you may struggle in your refinancing plans. Having too much credit, even if you don't use it, worries lenders because if you should choose to fill those charge cards, you might have trouble making your mortgage payments. To compensate for this potential setback, immediately cancel all but two of your credit cards and store charge cards and don't apply for any new credit.

To obtain a copy of your own credit report, contact Experian (1-800-301-7195, *www.experian.com*), Equifax (1-800-525-6285, *www.equifax.com*), or Trans Union (1-800-680-7289, *www.transunion.com*). For a fee of no more than $8.00, these companies send you a copy of your credit report so that you can set about improving it, if necessary. (If you are ever denied credit, you can get a free copy of your credit report within sixty days of the application.)

Remember that credit reports can be wrong. It doesn't happen that often, but to be sure, request a copy of your credit report every year or so and correct any mistakes that you see (in writing).

### *Interest Rates and Closing Costs Should Be Low*

Before considering any refinancing, make sure the interest rate is low enough to make the charges (which are usually lumped into what's called closing costs) associated with refinancing worthwhile. **Worksheet 9-1** helps you determine how much money refinancing will save you (or cost you!)—you'll need to use a loan calculator like the one at *www.smartmoney.com* (click on Personal Finance, Tools & Worksheets, Mortgage Calculator).

**WORKSHEET 9-1 Financing and Closing Costs**

| | | |
|---|---|---|
| Current mortgage amount (total owed) | | $________ |
| Closing costs (if added into loan amount) | + | $________ |
| Total new mortgage amount | = | $________ |
| Mortgage rate | | $________ |
| Approximate new monthly payment (from calculator) | = | $________ |
| Monthly escrow | + | $________ |
| Total new monthly payment | = | $________ |
| Current monthly payment | - | $________ |
| Monthly difference* | = | $________ |
| | | |
| Closing costs (if upfront payment is needed) | | $________ |

*If this is a positive number, you'll pay more for your new mortgage.

Escrow is an account that mortgage companies usually create for you when you have a low-down-payment mortgage: one-twelfth of your annual homeowner's insurance and property taxes is added to your mortgage payment. The mortgage company then pays your insurance and taxes from the escrow account when those payments are due. Putting your tax and insurance money into an escrow account may seem convenient, but it costs you a bundle of money in the interest that you *could be* earning on that money throughout the year. If you're currently paying escrow and have paid down 20 to 25 percent of your purchase price, ask your mortgage company to terminate your escrow account and send you a check for the balance (which you should put into savings!). You can then deposit your insurance and tax payments into a savings account, out of which you pay those annual or semiannual costs yourself.

## Understanding Home Equity Lines of Credit

Applying for a home equity line of credit is similar to—but much simpler than—refinancing your home. Instead of refinancing, which can include expensive closing costs, you simply apply for a line of credit against the equity in your home (see the preceding section for the lowdown on equity and how much is enough). A line of credit is like a loan, but instead of getting cash or a check from the lender, you get a checkbook to spend your equity on anything you want. If you write checks from that account (to yourself or anyone else), the line of credit is considered activated, and you must pay at least the minimum loan payment, an amount that repays the check(s) you've written in ten years. The more checks you write, the higher your payment will be. Using the account also lowers your equity in your home until you pay the loan back.

The following sections help you determine the advantages and disadvantages associated with home equity lines of credit. In addition, Table 10-2 helps you decide whether a home equity line of credit is right for you.

### *Advantage: You Can Pay Off Debts with a Lower-Rate Loan*

Although home equity lines of credit carry an interest rate that's usually about two percentage points higher than your primary mortgage interest rate, if you use the line to pay off high-interest credit card debt, you'll save a bundle.

Most lenders change their home equity line of credit interest rates daily or weekly. You might write a check when the interest rate is 8 percent and end up paying it off for several years at 10 or 12 percent. For this reason, plan to repay your line of credit as soon as possible after tapping it.

### *Advantage: Interest on Most Home Equity Lines of Credit Is Tax Deductible*

The interest on your line of credit is usually tax deductible if you itemize—just like the interest on your mortgage payment is tax deductible. If you're paying less in taxes, you are, in a sense, lowering your interest rate even more. See Chapter 16 for more on the tax advantages of owning your home.

### *Advantage: Applying Is a Cinch When You Buy or Refinance Your Home*

If you're applying for a new mortgage or are refinancing, you can often apply for a home equity line of credit at the same time. This eliminates duplicating the loan application paperwork and may also save you some fees associated with applying for a loan (like paying for your credit report).

### *Advantage: You Can Plan Ahead*

If you know that your income is going to drop in the future—if you're planning to work part time after having a baby, for example, or if you're going to quit your job and start your own business—you can apply for a home equity line of credit long before this drop in income happens. Even though you won't be as good a credit risk after you reduce your income, you'll still have the home equity line of credit locked in and can use it if you need to.

### *Disadvantage: Annual Fees Can Be High*

Some lenders charge annual fees of $20 to $150 for home equity lines of credit. Be sure to figure that amount into your calculations if you're planning to pay off a high-interest-rate debt with your home equity line of credit.

Some lenders offer periodic "sales" on annual fees for home equity lines of credit. If annual fees are too high for you, ask whether the fees are ever discounted, perhaps during a slow month for applications or when you open a checking or savings account with the lender.

### *Disadvantage: You May Have to Make Two Mortgage Payments*

If you're using a home equity line of credit to pay off existing high-interest debt (like credit cards), your monthly payment for the home equity line of credit will most likely be lower than for the high-interest debt, due to the lower interest rate and the relatively long life of the loan (usually ten years).

But if you're going to use the money to make improvements to your home or for any other new financial obligation, you'll have two monthly house payments instead of one, although the home equity line of credit payment is likely to be much lower than the payment for your primary mortgage. If you want to make only one payment, you'll have to refinance and take equity out of your home (see "Refinancing Your Home and Taking Out Equity" in this chapter).

### *Disadvantage: You Must Have Enough Equity Available in Your Home*

In order to get a home equity line of credit, you must have equity available in your home. After all, you're borrowing against the equity, and if you don't have much, you don't have anything to borrow against. Your home equity line of credit, then, will only be as large as your available equity, minus whatever down payment amount the lender expects you to maintain with them (and that can be as much as 25 percent—check with your lender).

### *Disadvantage: You Lower the Equity in Your Home*

If you're planning to use your home as part of your retirement plan (for example, paying it off in full, selling it, moving to a smaller home or condo, and using the profits to finance part of your retirement expenses), using a home equity line of credit will reduce your ability to do that. The more you tap into your equity, the less you'll receive in cash when you sell your house.

### *Disadvantage: You Must Own Your Own Home*

You must own (or have a mortgage on) your own home in order to quality for a home equity line of credit. Even if you've been living in your grandmother's home for twenty years and have made all the payments on it, if the house isn't in your name, you can't get a home equity line of credit. See an attorney if this is your situation.

WORKSHEET 9-2 **Is a Home Equity Loan Right for You?**

## If you can answer yes to seven or more of the following questions, a home equity line of credit may be right for you!

| | YES | NO |
|---|---|---|
| You own your home (with or without a mortgage). | ❒ | ❒ |
| You have enough equity* in your house to tap for a home equity line of credit. | ❒ | ❒ |
| **Equity equals the current value of your home minus the payoff on the mortgage.)* | | |
| The interest rate on the home equity line of credit is lower than the debt you'll pay off with the home equity line of credit. | ❒ | ❒ |
| Your total monthly payments will be lower than your current monthly payments after you tap your home equity line of credit. | ❒ | ❒ |
| You can afford both the home equity line of credit payment and your primary mortgage payment, along with your other debt. | ❒ | ❒ |
| The annual home equity line of credit fees are $40 per year or less. | ❒ | ❒ |
| You itemize deductions on your taxes (that is, you fill out Schedule A). | ❒ | ❒ |
| Your retirement account is well financed, so you don't need to pay off your house before you retire. | ❒ | ❒ |

# 10 Adding Income

If you've reduced your expenses as much as you can and still have trouble finding the money to reach your financial goals, consider temporarily or permanently adding to your income and putting that money toward your debts or into savings.

## Recognizing What Additional Work Can Mean for You

Extra work can be both a blessing and a curse. Extra income can help you pay off nagging debts that you just can't seem to get anywhere with any other way. Working a second job can also help you build new skills that could lead to a different full-time job or a new business of your own. And nearly anyone can put up with a crazy schedule for a few weeks or even a couple of months, especially if you know exactly when the long hours will end and can count down the days—and add up your extra income.

But managing a heavy workload isn't easy. You have to juggle your responsibilities at home, your relationships with the people who are important to you, and your need for rest and relaxation with your new requirements on the job.

The following sections help you define the pluses and minuses of additional work, and give you some tips for smoothing the rough road ahead.

Before trading in your time for money, be sure you can't cut back on your expenses enough to gain the extra money you need. Chapters 5 though 7 give you tips and tricks for reducing your monthly financial obligations. Consider adding income only as a last resort.

### *New Skills That May Lead to Different Work*

One approach to choosing your second job is to look for one that builds your skills in a way that will help further your career. Suppose, for example, that you don't have any computer skills at all. You see an advertisement for a job that requires fifteen hours of work each week at your local library reshelving books. But you also know that the library's checkout system is completely computerized, so at your interview, you ask whether you would be able to spend a few hours a week learning the system and, at some point, helping patrons use the system, too. Within just a few months, you may develop enough computer skills to be able to update your resume and apply for a completely different day job—one that requires a basic knowledge of computers—with your current employer or with a new one.

### A Foundation for Starting Your Own Company

If you're hoping to go into business for yourself and want extra income to pay off debts before you start the company or as a cushion against uncertain income, you can start your business on a very part time basis—perhaps on evenings and weekends—and build both a client base and a reputation before you go into the business full time.

Suppose, for example, you're thinking of starting a landscaping company. Using the additional evening daylight hours in the summer months, you could begin your landscaping business during evenings and weekends. Let your coworkers, friends, and neighbors know about your new business, and let word spread about your great product or service. As your business picks up, you can begin to cut down your hours at your other job or quit that job altogether.

If your new business will compete with the company you work for, take extra care. Don't advertise at work and be sure never to use your company's equipment or ideas for your own business. And never work for yourself when you're on company time.

Besides landscaping, some business ideas that might lend themselves to evenings and weekends include catering, photography, graphic design, Web site design, furniture refinishing and repair, selling antiques, home remodeling and repair, closet and room organizing, dog training, tutoring, selling cosmetics, and so on. This is by no means an exhaustive list—see the "Starting a Small Business" section at the end of this chapter for more information on getting started running your own company.

### *Far Less Available Time*

The hours you spend working more will have to come from somewhere. Unless you have hours and hours of unfilled free time right now, your additional work is probably going to keep you from spending time with your family, running errands, exercising, futzing with your house or car, visiting friends and extended family, taking a vacation, working on your hobby, reading, playing with your pets, and so on. This isn't trivial—remember the saying that "all work and no play makes Jack a dull boy"? Working too much can dull your senses, making life seem as though it revolves around work, when, in fact, a healthy life revolves around the people and events that make you happy.

If you're planning to add extra income for a short time—say, until your $6,500 credit card debt is paid off—you can plan ahead with friends and family, agreeing, perhaps, that they'll help you by running some of your errands or walking the dogs while you're working to pay off this debt. And you may also be able to agree that as soon as the debt is paid off, you'll quit earning the extra income and immediately spend more time with them, maybe even by taking a well-deserved vacation. (Just don't get back into debt with your vacation spending! Instead, save for it in advance—you'll enjoy it more and break your cycle of debt.) Although the thought of extending your extra income indefinitely into the future may seem like a wise financial choice, keep in mind that life isn't all about work—if you do nothing but work and make money, you'll be likely to either lose the valuable parts of your life (time with family and friends, walking in the woods, indulging in your favorite hobby or book) or burn out on your existing jobs and begin to dread them.

Always include your family in your plans to work additional hours. Not only will they miss spending time with you (at least, you hope they will!), but they'll probably also be asked to pick up some of your chores around the house, so they deserve to be included from the start.

If you're planning to add extra income for a longer time—perhaps taking on a higher-paying job that requires far more working hours—try to find ways to gain back some of your free time: move closer to work (to reduce your commute), hire someone to help with errands and chores (lawn mower, cleaning person, dog walker), exercise or meet with friends before work or during your lunch hour, listen to books on tape while you drive (if you enjoy reading), take fun (nonworking) vacations, and so on. Then when you are home, be fully in the moment, not working, thinking about work, or preparing for the next day of work.

### Added Stress

Working too much taxes you physically and emotionally, and that can make you fatigued, subject to illness and injury, and irritable, none of which makes you a very good companion, parent, or friend. In addition, if your work is highly mental in nature, you may suffer mental stress that can rob you of your ability to converse intelligently and work on detailed hobbies or other projects during your down time.

If you're adding work temporarily—for a few weeks or months—you can probably survive this additional stress without damaging your health or relationships. But if you plan to continue to work a lot, find ways to reduce stress and continue to connect with those around you.

### Higher Taxes

Ben Franklin said that "a penny saved is a penny earned." Technically, though, he should have said that a penny saved is about 1.20 cents earned, because taxes can eat up that much (or more) or your earnings. If, on your current income, you can find a way to cut ten dollars from your expenses, you'll have ten more dollars to put toward paying off debt, into savings, into your retirement account, and so on. But if you work more, you'll have to earn between $12.50 and $13.25 (depending on your tax rate) to pay off $10 from your debt or add it to your savings account.

Because of taxes, it's always more efficient to make the same income—or even to make less income—and cut your expenses than it is to add more income. Using the tax calculator at *www.freedom.gov* (and then following the links to Tax Relief Info, then Tax Calculator), fill out **Worksheet 10-1** to see just how taxes take a bite out of your extra income.

WORKSHEET 10-1 **Does Extra Income Equal Extra Taxes?**

| Income | Total Taxes Due |
|---|---|
| Current | $ |
| + $500 | $ |
| + $1,000 | $ |
| + $2,000 | $ |
| + $3,000 | $ |
| + $5,000 | $ |
| + $10,000 | $ |
| + $15,000 | $ |
| + $20,000 | $ |

## Changing Jobs

One of the simplest ways to increase your income is to look for a new full-time job. In fact, many job counselors advise their clients to look for new work every few years simply as a way to boost their income (and increase their contacts within the industry). If you receive a 3- to 5-percent raise every year at your current job, you'll have to work about two to three and a half years before your income goes up by 10 percent. But you may be able to get a 10 percent raise next month by getting a job at another company.

If you do change jobs, however, be sure the new job—with its higher income—doesn't end up costing you more. It could, if the new job is ten miles farther away, requires expensive clothing that must be dry cleaned, doesn't offer free parking, requires that you carry a cell phone or laptop computer at your cost, and so on. Before accepting a job offer, ask detailed questions about your new responsibilities and the costs that may be involved. If your new job is with your existing company, don't shy away from asking these same questions. Different departments within large corporations often require different dress codes and standard equipment.

One way to boost your income by staying at your existing job is to change shifts. Often the third shift (which usually runs from somewhere between 10:00 p.m. and midnight to anywhere from 6:00 to 8:00 a.m.) pays much more per hour—even as much as fifty cents or a dollar more.

## Getting a Second Job

Getting a second job can help boost your income—and can be fun at the same time. To make it as enjoyable as possible, try to find work that suits your personality and interests. If, for example, you have a great love of photography or athletics, but for your day job you work on the line at a local manufacturing plant, consider getting a second job at a camera shop or at an athletics store or gym. If you tend to be outgoing, try to find work that allows you to interact with people. If you're shy, consider working behind the scenes at a company that interests you, instead of having to work with people. By matching your personality and interests to your second job, the extra work may not seem as difficult to endure.

Don't let your employee discount get you further into debt. If, for example, you work at a camera shop and find yourself buying thousands of dollars worth of equipment that you wouldn't normally have purchased, your second job could add up to little more than a new way to get into debt.

One of the best times to find a second job in retail is during the holidays. Companies hire seasonal employees from the week of Thanksgiving through the New Year. At that point you're usually out of a second job, but if you've worked out well for the company and express interest in continuing to work for them, you may be called back for the next holiday season and at various time throughout the year.

## Working Overtime

Unless you are a salaried employee who is expected to work as many hours as necessary to complete your work, you may have opportunities to work overtime at your current job and receive additional income.

One of the best perks of working overtime is that you're usually eligible to receive more pay per hour for hours over forty per week—sometimes as much as time and a half or double time. That can add up to a lot of additional income in just a short amount of time.

Whatever you do, don't count on overtime income for your everyday expenses! Companies are notorious for eliminating all overtime work whenever the economy contracts a little bit. You may be told that you'll be earning extra income for six months, only to find the work eliminated six weeks into your stint.

Be aware of the overtime commitments that your company may require, however. Some companies expect you to commit to working overtime for a set period, even six months or a year, before they'll allow you to sign on. And the time required may be open-ended, so that you're getting home at 6:30 one day and 8:00 the next. Before accepting this opportunity for additional income, be sure you're clear on exactly what's involved.

## Freelancing for Your Own Company

Although freelancing is similar to working overtime because you're doing work outside of your normal working hours for the company you already work for, it's a little different. In general, freelancing involves taking on a project that no one within the company has the time (or the expertise) to complete; it can involve projects from typing a handwritten manuscript or sewing a banner to creating a graphics-heavy company brochure or catering a company event. You work on the project in your spare time, usually on your own equipment at home.

Freelancing can bring several benefits:

- Freelancing allows you to use your unique skills and talents to earn extra money.
- Freelancing on a particular project doesn't lock you into working extra hours for an indefinite period of time.
- Freelancing can improve your reputation with your current employer, especially if you're able to come through on a difficult or time-sensitive project.
- Freelancing can spin off into a full-time gig if you're able to find a few clients in addition to your current employer.

## Starting a Small Business

Starting a small, home-based business is one of the hottest trends in the United States today, but it doesn't have to be a full-time investment if you don't want it to be. If you're trying to find a way to earn extra cash but want some control over how and when you work, starting a small business from your home might be just what you're looking for. The following sections help you answer some important questions about starting a part-time business. **Worksheet 10-2** can help you determine whether earning extra money by starting a small business is right for you.

WORKSHEET 10-2 **Business Expenses**

| Expense | One-Time Costs | Monthly Costs |
|---|---|---|
| | $ | $ |
| | $ | $ |
| | $ | $ |
| | $ | $ |
| | $ | $ |
| | $ | $ |
| | $ | $ |
| | $ | $ |
| | $ | $ |
| | $ | $ |
| | $ | $ |
| | $ | $ |
| | $ | $ |
| | $ | $ |
| TOTAL | $ | $ |

### *Finding the Best Small Business for You*

The best small business for you is the one that you're enthusiastic and passionate about. This means that your business idea has to mesh with your skills, unique qualities, and personality. If, for example, you're thinking about starting a catering business but don't really enjoy cooking, you probably won't succeed. If, on the other hand, you've always loved cosmetics and like dealing with people one-on-one, you might want to try your hand as a Mary Kay consultant or Avon representative.

If you're planning to start your business part time to earn extra money, be sure you choose one that doesn't require a large commitment of time or a large investment of cash. Although you may turn your business into full-time work sometime in the future, you on't want to jeopardize your current job by taking on more than you can handle.

Matching your work to your personality, qualities, and skills is the topic of hundreds of books. If you're unsure which business idea will work best for you, take a trip to your local bookstore or library and find one that offers self-tests and ideas about home-based businesses.

### Determining Whether You're Passionate about Your Business Idea

Finding out whether you're passionate about a business idea is pretty simple—just decide whether you agree or disagree with this statement:

Now that I've come up with a potential business, the thought of *not* pursuing it seems impossible.

If you agree, you're plenty passionate. But if you disagree; that is, if you think your business concept is just okay or seems like too much work, don't bother pursuing it—you won't have the energy required to make it succeed.

### Estimating Your Potential Income and Expenses

Estimating your potential income and expenses is always difficult. To keep the number realistic, come up with three scenarios for both income and expenses: best case, average case, and worst case. If, for example, you think you can get three catering jobs per month, use that as your best case, but also figure out how much you'll make with just two catering jobs (average case) or one (worst case). Do the same with your income. If you're planning to offer graphic design services from your home and will rely heavily on a desktop computer and color laser printer, figure in the cost of paper, toner cartridges, and software updates in your best-case scenario. But also figure in repair expenses on that equipment in your worst-case scenario.

Keep in mind that many small business owners underestimate how much expenses really cost. If you're running a business part time, you may not need to install a second phone line (which can cost $25 to $50 per month) or buy elaborate equipment, but on the other hand, you may find that you need to buy office equipment (fax machine, cell phone, computer, printer), business equipment (riding mower, cooking utensils, home improvement tools), inventory for your business, advertising space or brochures and business cards, a booth at a local antiques mall, and so on. Use Worksheet 11-2 to estimate your business expenses.

Whatever equipment will be essential to your business's success, include it in your worst-case scenario.

### *Keeping Your Overhead Low*

After you think of all the possible equipment you'll need to make your business a success, determine which items would just be nice, which are absolutely necessary, and which you can buy secondhand. Too many first-time business owners spend hundreds or thousands of dollars outfitting their offices, only to find that those expenses don't increase business traffic one bit!

Suppose you decide that you don't need a fancy desk for your office—a small wooden one will do just fine. You read the classifieds and look through sale flyers from office equipment stores and find one that's just $75. That's a few hundred less than a new desk would cost, so it's a good deal, right? Not if you're planning to run a business that doesn't require a desk! If you can do your paperwork at the kitchen table, don't bother buying a desk until you find that you really need one. The same goes for other office furniture, a computer, fax machine, cell phone, Rolodex, bookshelf, and so on. To make your business earn as much money as possible, question every single expenditure, asking yourself this question: Will this expense make my business more profitable? If not, don't buy it.

### *Understanding Business Taxes*

Too many small businesses have folded because their owners failed to estimate their taxes properly. The federal government (and, possibly, your state government, too) requires you to pay approximately one quarter of the taxes your business will owe for the year's income at four separate times throughout the year: April 15, June 15, September 15, and January 15. This is known as the "pay as you go" system.

In order to make these tax payments, you'll need to estimate how much you'll owe in taxes at the end of the year, divide that amount by four, and send a check for that amount by each due date. If you fail to do so, you may have to pay a penalty when you submit your next tax return. Estimating these taxes can be a bit tricky, however. The best way to determine how much you'll owe is to do the following:

1. Estimate your income and business expenses for the year.
2. Locate a copy of last year's income tax forms (or last year's tax software program) for both federal and state taxes.
3. Fill out Schedule C of the federal form 1040 by using your estimated income and business expense data.
4. Using last year's income (from your and your spouse's jobs) and last year's federal and state income tax forms, and adding in your business estimates, find out how much more you would have owed last year if your business had been up and running then.
5. Subtract the amount you actually owed from the amount you would have owed if your business had been in operation. This is how much more you estimate your taxes will be this year.
6. Divide that number by four and send that amount on each quarterly due date.

Continuing to use last year's tax return forms, keep recalculating this number as you go through the year. If your expenses are higher or your income is lower than you thought, you'll pay less in taxes. If your expenses are lower or your income is higher than you anticipated, you'll pay more. Although tax forms change from year to year, using last year's forms will give you a pretty close estimate.

### *Deciding Whether You're Ready*

**Worksheet 10-3** can help you decide whether running a small business is the right idea for you.

WORKSHEET 10-3 **Is a Small Business Right for You?**

## If you can answer yes to all of the following questions, starting a small business will probably be right for you!

| | YES | NO |
|---|---|---|
| | | |
| You're passionate about your business idea. | ❐ | ❐ |
| You have the expertise and skills required to do this job well. | ❐ | ❐ |
| You have a reputation as someone who can be trusted to do a good job. | ❐ | ❐ |
| You've estimated your expenses and income and feel that the business will | | |
| bring in the extra income you need. | ❐ | ❐ |
| Your business idea doesn't require a lot of up-front cash. | ❐ | ❐ |
| You're willing to spend a great deal of time getting your business off the ground. | ❐ | ❐ |
| | | |
| You can continue to excel at your full-time job while running your part-time business. | ❐ | ❐ |
| You don't mind completing a few hours of paperwork once a month or so. | ❐ | ❐ |
| You're disciplined enough to work during evenings and weekends, | | |
| even when no one is looking over your shoulder or pressuring you to do it. | ❐ | ❐ |
| Your family is enthusiastic about your business and wants to help. | ❐ | ❐ |

# 11 Surviving Unemployment

Losing your job may be the toughest financial blow you'll ever have to take, yet people do survive unemployment; they often emerge on firmer financial footing (because they've quickly learned to budget and cut back) and with greater confidence in their abilities. This chapter shows you how to move from desperation to success.

## Sorting Out Severance Packages and Unemployment Insurance

Your first step should be to assess how much money you may still have coming in—usually from two sources: severance pay (a lump-sump check from your employer) and unemployment insurance.

Many companies don't offer severance packages, so it's certainly not guaranteed. If the company is laying off employees because it is having financial difficulties, you probably won't be offered any severance pay, but you may be offered a severance package that might include job-placement assistance, continued use of an office so that you still appear to be employed, and freelance opportunities to finish projects that you've been working on. This assistance is not common, however.

If you are offered severance pay, the amount will most likely be based on how long you've worked for the company: a month's pay for every two years worked, for example. If you're offered this pay—six months' worth of income, say—immediately put it away in a safe, interest-bearing account so that it will last you six months (or, perhaps, even longer). If you're not offered any severance, or if the severance pay is so paltry that it runs out before you've even had your resume printed, you're not alone. Sadly, few companies offer this assistance—those that do are usually companies that have recently merged (and, therefore, have a lot of cash) and have laid off a small part of their staff.

You're far more likely to receive unemployment benefits, however. The moment you hear you've been laid off, call your state's unemployment insurance agency (you'll find the number in the blue pages or government section of any phone book). While you may have to visit the unemployment office, some states now allow you to file a claim by phone or online.

The amount of your unemployment insurance and the length of time you'll receive it is based on how long you've been employed, the state you live in, and the general economic condition in your area. (In times of severe economic downturn, unemployment benefits are often extended for many more weeks than in relatively healthy economic periods.) Your state's unemployment office will know how many weeks you're eligible for and whether you have any chance of having those benefits extended.

If you were fired from your job because of misconduct, unemployment insurance and COBRA-defined coverage will probably not be available to you. These benefits are meant to assist employees who lose their jobs through no fault of their own.

As soon as you find another job, your unemployment benefits will stop. Some states, however, have begun a self-employment assistance plan that encourages you to start your own business. You receive the same benefits as you would if you were looking for work, but instead of sending out resumes and going on interviews, you're spending your time getting your business started. Ask your state whether a self-employment assistance program is available to you.

## Locking in Your COBRA-Defined Medical Coverage

The Consolidated Omnibus Budget Reconciliation Act (COBRA) of 1986 was designed to help employees who leave their jobs and are, as a result, without medical insurance coverage. If your former employer had twenty or more employees, COBRA allows you to continue medical insurance coverage for up to eighteen months after leaving your company. The fine print? Well, it's a doozy. You have to pay the *entire* cost of your insurance—the portion you paid before (it was probably deducted from your salary) and the portion your employer paid on your behalf, which may have run several hundred dollars per month. (Your former employer is also allowed to charge you a 2 percent administration fee.) The coverage you receive—including deductibles and limits on coverage—should be identical to the coverage you had as an employee.

When you're laid off, you should receive information about continuing your medical coverage under COBRA. If you don't receive it, ask for it! You usually have sixty days to elect to continue your coverage (and when you sign up, the coverage is retroactive to your last day on the job) and pay the first payment. If you fail to make the payments, which are usually due monthly, the coverage will be terminated.

It's no small irony that when you can least afford to pay the entire portion of your medical insurance costs, you have to, in order to continue your coverage. However, if you're tempted to just go without insurance, don't! Doing so may turn a bad financial situation into a catastrophic one.

Before deciding whether to accept COBRA coverage, call around or search on the Internet for short-term health care coverage. If you're willing to go with a high-deductible plan (up to $2,000), you may be able to pay hundreds less per month for insurance and still have coverage if a catastrophe occurs. Many conditions, including pre-existing ones and pregnancy, aren't covered, and most of these policies can't be renewed after they expire (usually in six to nine months). COBRA's biggest benefit could be that even though it expires eighteen months after you sign on, if you still haven't found work, you're eligible for insurance policies that aren't allowed to exclude pre-existing conditions.

## Seeing to Your Other Insurance Needs

If you're able to lock in COBRA insurance for the next eighteen months, you have one major insurance need taken care of, even if it is frighteningly expensive. But you want to think about your other insurance coverage as well, especially insurance that may have been covered by your employer and insurance that you may be tempted to let lapse while you're unemployed.

### *Employer-Sponsored Insurance*

Your employer may have paid for life, disability, dental, and vision insurance, in addition to medical coverage. Of these, life insurance is the one that's most important to secure while you're unemployed.

Some people think of life insurance as a way to leave great wealth to their children or spouse upon their death, but for most people, life insurance is simply a way to help your family pay for funeral costs and get through a year or so without your income. Many people, therefore, buy enough coverage to pay funeral expenses, pay off the mortgage, and pay for one or two months of income or unemployment benefits. Funeral expenses vary by area—call your local funeral home for an estimate, but if you live in a small town, reassure the person you're speaking to that you're simply try to estimate your life insurance needs, now that you have to pay for it yourself. You don't want to leave the impression that you're think of ending it all.

You can find out your mortgage balance by calling your mortgage lender and asking for the payoff amount. Use **Worksheet 11-1** to see how large your life insurance policy should be.

**WORKSHEET 11-1 Amount of Life Insurance Needed**

| | |
|---|---|
| Funeral expenses: | $ |
| Mortgage payoff: | $ |
| Monthly income or unemployment benefits: | $ |
| Other amount needed: | $ |
| Other amount needed: | $ |
| Other amount needed: | $ |
| Other amount needed: | $ |
| Other amount needed: | $ |
| Other amount needed: | $ |
| Other amount needed: | $ |

### *Insurance You've Been Paying For*

Your employer has probably had nothing to do with your homeowner's or apartment insurance and car insurance (except for the obvious connection that you've been using your paychecks from that company to pay the premiums). When you're unemployed, you want to keep those insurance policies intact, although this is a good time to shop around for a better price and, if necessary, higher deductibles.

You may also have had a retirement plan at your company. For now, don't feel that you need to do anything with this plan *unless* you think your company might be in danger of declaring bankruptcy. Otherwise, let it sit until you've had a chance to figure out your next move.

Most states won't allow you to let your auto insurance lapse (they'll take away your license plates), and most lenders won't allow you to let your homeowner's insurance lapse (they'll cancel the mortgage and force you to sell your house). Although this may seem intrusive on their part, consider what would happen if you had a fire in your house and didn't carry insurance. The mortgage company wouldn't have a house to sell in order to recoup their loan, so they would make you pay that loan in full immediately. Don't let unemployment go from bad to worse by not maintaining some insurance coverage for your house and car.

## Beginning to Look for a Job as Soon as Possible

If your company offers job-hunting assistance, use it, even if it's not the greatest service or assistance available. If nothing else, beginning your job hunt the day after you are laid off doesn't give you much time to worry or get too angry. Both emotions are, of course, perfectly normal reactions to losing your job, but both can also paralyze you. Take the time you need, but if you find yourself unable to get out of bed or unwilling to get off the couch (you now know the names of every character on *Days of Our Lives*), you may be letting your emotions keep you from getting that next interview.

Looking for a job—especially if you use an office or other location (away from your home) that's been set up for you—gets you out of the house, dressed professionally, and ready to look for your next course in life. In fact, that's often the best approach when job hunting: treat your job search as though it's your full-time job. Use any facilities your company has provided for you, which may include office space with a telephone, copy machine, computer and printer, resume consultation service, and so on.

If you don't have a top-notch resume and don't have access to any free services that offer resume assistance, take a trip to your local library to review its books on resumes and cover letters, especially those that can be submitted electronically.

If, on the other hand, you aren't offered any job-searching assistance from your company, you can use the same ideas to find your next job. If you need to get out of the house while searching the Internet or newspapers, visit your local library or the Kinko's copy center in your area. (Keep in mind, however, that Kinko's charges by the minute for Internet access. They do allow you to make high-quality, inexpensive copies, however, and have thick resume paper available.) When you do go out, dress professionally and set goals for the day, such as "I'll find and follow up on three leads today."

Never pass up the opportunity to network! Although you may prefer that people not know you've lost your job, the people you run into at the coffee house, your daughter's track meet, or a social gathering with your spouse may be able to help you find your next job.

When searching online, search first for job listing services that are specific to your industry. For more general searches, go to America's Job Bank (*www.ajb.dni.us/key.html*), Monster.com (*www.monster.com*) or HotJobs (*www.hotjobs.com*). And don't forget the classifieds in your local paper.

## Starting a Consulting Firm or Small Business

Many laid-off or downsized employees use their misfortune to springboard into a career they've always wanted, as a consultant or small business owner. There are, however, some important points to consider.

### *Wait to Pursue Big-Business Dreams*

If your plans for a business are large in scope—say, you want to open a retail store, start a factory in your town, or open a large consulting firm in a glitzy downtown office—while you're unemployed may not be the best time to establish your business. For a large business that's going to have a lot of overhead (rent, inventory, equipment, and so on), you're going to need money, either from a lender or from investors. Unless you received a large severance package or have plenty of money in savings that you could give up as collateral (a guarantee for the lender), you're probably not going to qualify for an influx of cash from a lender or investor while your future is so uncertain. That doesn't mean your big-business plans are impossible, but you'll have a better chance of success if you keep your plans small (see the following section).

### *Keep Your Plans Small*

Concentrate your self-employment plans on the lowest-overhead business that appeals to you. Plan, for now, to be the only employee (or work with a few other self-employed professionals who have their own businesses), so that you can eliminate complicated withholding taxes and paperwork and can work out of any spare space in your home. Keep your overhead to a minimum, buying only the items that you absolutely need to run the business. (You can purchase more for your business later, as it grows and prospers.)

Chapter 10 gives you tips on starting a business. The emphasis there is on starting a small business as a means of earning extra income (in addition to your regular job), but much of the information applies to your situation, too.

A local office of the Small Business Administration (SBA) offers free seminars, books, and other products to help you get your business off the ground. In addition, the Service Corps of Retired Executives (SCORE) offers free consultations with experienced (and now retired) execs.

## Holding Down a Couple of Part-Time Jobs

If you're unable to find a full-time job to replace the one you had, one way to get your financial picture back in focus is to look for a couple of part-time jobs and combine the hours to work full time (or longer). The following sections give you a few tips for successfully managing two part-time jobs.

Keep in mind that working long hours can take a toll on you and your family (see Chapter 11).

### *Make Each Employer Aware of the Other*

If your hours aren't fixed at either job, make sure that each employer knows you have another job—and let each employer know what hours you're available to work. You'll have a better chance of making this situation work.

### *Establish Boundaries*

Scheduling two part-time jobs can be extremely difficult unless you establish some boundaries for the hours you work on each job. For example, Job A might be weekday mornings only—anytime from 6:00 A.M. to 1:00 P.M., Monday through Friday. Job B might include weekend hours, from early in the morning 'til late at night.

You'll still have some conflicts—like when your weekend boss has you working until midnight on Sunday and your weekday boss wants you in at six on Monday. But by establishing some boundaries for each job, you'll have less overlap.

### *Try to Get a Set Weekly Schedule*

When you look for part-time work, give priority to jobs that give you the exact same hours each week. That way, you'll be able to work your other part-time job around the first without any overlaps.

## Considering Another Geographic Location

If you're struggling to find work in your immediate area, you can always expand your prospects by branching out into another geographic area. This sounds simple, right? Unfortunately, it isn't. Finding out about out-of-town positions is easier than it has ever been, thanks to the Internet. Actually landing the job, however, can be much more difficult. In general, employers in other geographic locations find that out-of-towners are expensive to hire and often flee back to their home area the first chance they get.

The Web site for HotJobs *(www.hotjobs.com)* is easy to use and lists thousands of jobs by the dates they were posted, so you always know how hot the lead is. If you're interested in taking on work nearly anywhere in the United States, make a point of checking this site every morning.

To make yourself a more attractive candidate in the eyes of an out-of-town employer, consider the tips in the following sections.

### *Clarify that You're Not Looking for Relocation Assistance*

The main fear of out-of-town employers is that you're going to expect relocation assistance if they offer you a job. That assistance can include the costs of house hunting in advance of the move, the move itself, help selling your house (including, but not limited to, actually buying your house from you if it doesn't sell), help finding employment for your spouse, paid trips back to tie up loose ends, and so on.

These costs can be incredibly expensive even for large companies, so put their mind at ease by indicating in your cover letter that you're planning to pay for your own move and will not require any relocation assistance.

### *Say You'll Pay for Interview Expenses*

If you were happily employed and had the leisure of weighing out-of-town job options, you might expect to be flown out for an interview. But given that you want to find work immediately, mention in your cover letter that you plan to pay for your own interview expenses (driving or flying out, staying in a hotel, paying for meals, and so on).

One way to get out-of-town employers to respond quickly is to let them know that you'll be in the area on a certain date—say, four or six weeks out—and that you'd like to set up an interview at that time. This gives the company a chance to see you in person, but it also forces them to interview you on a timely basis.

### *Indicate that You're Moving Regardless*

Even if you aren't planning to move without a job, make your cover letter sound as if you're definitely relocating to the area and are looking for employment in advance. This, combined with your readiness to pay for your own interview and relocation expenses, may make you as attractive as an in-town candidate.

Be sure to mention all of the non-work-related reasons that you're moving to the area. (Hint: Make up some of these reasons if you don't have any!)

# 12 Understanding Credit

Is credit a mystery to you? It shouldn't be. Instead of being intimidated by your credit and how the world of credit works, you should think of credit as your friend. In this section, you will get to know your friend a little bit better. You can find out where it came from, what it does, and where it is going. You will also understand what credit reports and credit scores are.

## Your Financial Reputation

Your credit is simply your financial reputation. It gives lenders, and others, a tool to help decide whether or not they will do business with you. If you want to use their services, they want to manage their risk. The last thing a lender wants to do is give out money, only to have the borrower default on the debt. When this happens, the lender loses money. Of course, lenders are not charities—they are in business to earn money from interest payments, not to lose it.

The system of using credit in the United States serves a variety of purposes. First, this is a big country with a lot of people. It is difficult for any business to know everything about everybody. When the world was a much smaller place, a lender might make a lending decision based on an individual's reputation. In small communities, this would be easy. However, these days most loans come from large national, or international, organizations. They don't know your personal reputation, so they have to check your credit. In this way, credit serves as a way for lenders to share information so that they can make good decisions.

The fact that everybody can share information about you is extremely significant. Knowing that your creditors will spread the word about you gives you an incentive to pay your debts as agreed. If you knew you could borrow money and get away with defaulting on the debt, you might be tempted to do so quite often. After all, free money is enticing. Alas, there is no such thing. You might get away with it once or twice, but you will build up a bad reputation. Creditors depend on the fact that you want to have a good reputation so that you can borrow from others in the future.

## Where Credit Information Comes From

Where does your credit come from? Are you born with it? No—if you don't use credit, you don't have credit; your credit is a result of your behavior in the world. Some of the most important information comes from your dealings with creditors. Of course, it is your credit, so the most relevant information comes from your use of credit.

### *Information Sources*

The information that makes up your credit comes from numerous sources. Other sections of this book describe the sources in greater detail. For now, suffice it to say that there are a lot of organizations talking about you:

- Lenders
- Prospective lenders that you never worked with
- Government and court systems
- Collection agencies
- Credit-reporting companies

Depending on how you define your credit, information can come from a number of additional sources. Insurance companies report information on their customers to specialized databases. Landlords who rent properties share and use information about tenants. Finally, banks and retailers may share information about your check-writing habits.

### *Credit Scores*

When you think about credit, you may think of the concept of a credit score. What exactly is a credit score? The credit score is a number that attempts to rank you on some level of creditworthiness. The credit score might tell potential lenders how likely you are to make late payments.

> Your credit score does not determine whether or not you get a loan. The credit score is simply a number that ranks you with the rest of the population. Your lender may have a policy on granting loans based on credit scores, but the scoring programs do not know that. They just generate a score.

Imagine how difficult it must be to predict whether or not a customer is likely to pay late. Imagine yourself as a loan officer in a bank sitting across the desk from a potential borrower. What criteria do you use to judge this person's creditworthiness? You may pull credit reports from the major credit-reporting companies—if you have ever seen these reports, you know that they are full of information and can be several pages long. Then, you might read through their reports to get an understanding of how your potential borrower has behaved in the past. Finally, assume that you have three more potential borrowers waiting to see you, and you have not had lunch yet.

This scenario helps to highlight why credit scores may be useful. People have to make lending decisions with several goals in mind. They may want to grant the loan so that their organization earns interest income. They may also be motivated to grant loans in an effort to help serve the community, for example, making mortgage loans available to low-income households. On the other hand, the person making the lending decision has to try to minimize losses. The organization won't be able to help anybody if it loses all of its money.

### Automate It

To make lending decisions easier, lenders often use credit scores. A computer program does a lot of the work, leaving just a few items for the person responsible for making a decision to fill in. In some cases, the computer program does all of the work, and human eyes never see the potential borrower's credit information. The credit-scoring model looks for good things and bad things in the borrower's history. It looks for late payments, bankruptcies, and maxed-out credit cards, among other things. These are the same items that a human would look for. Of course, the computer can do it in a split-second.

A 2005 study released by the Consumer Federation of America and Providian put a number on how much you can save with a better credit score. For consumers with an average credit score, a thirty-point increase would result in $76 of annual savings on finance charges. Of course, more significant positive changes in your score would yield more significant savings.

In addition to speeding up the process, credit scoring can level the playing field. Lenders might have biases that influence their decisions when considering an applicant's creditworthiness. From a fairness standpoint, creditworthiness should be the only factor considered. However, people responsible for making lending decisions might be swayed in one direction or the other for irrelevant reasons: if the applicant is good or bad looking; if the applicant has a health issue with negative stigma attached; or if the applicant seems friendly or unfriendly. In some cases, lenders may discriminate because of an applicant's sex, race, or creed. Credit-scoring models can eliminate these biases from the equation, because they look strictly at the credit history data. If the applicant has a good credit history, the score is high regardless of any personal traits.

### *Who to Lend To*

Credit scoring makes it possible to make a large number of small loans. Lenders get flooded with applications for credit. How do they determine which ones to process? If they are strapped for resources (time and personnel), they might decide to limit themselves to the loans that are more profitable. In this case, they might focus on the larger loans only because smaller loans require the same amount of processing but pay less interest. Credit scoring makes it efficient to look at loans of all sizes, which makes it easier for consumers to get loans.

### *Where Scores Come From*

Where exactly do these credit scores come from? There are a variety of companies that create credit scores. These companies are described in greater detail later in this book. For now, you should understand that the credit score may or may not come from your lender. In many cases, it does not. External companies create the computer programs used to generate scores.

The computer programs are just empty programs that take in information and process it. They're designed to work with different systems. For example, the FICO credit score is designed to work with the data held at the major credit-reporting companies (TransUnion, Equifax, and Experian). The credit-reporting companies load the software, and then load the credit history for the individual who they are going to score. The software spits out a score, and it is forwarded to whoever asked for the report.

### *Mass Confusion*

The world is full of confusion about credit scores. In part, this is because credit scores were unavailable to consumers for many years. In addition, the entire world of credit and credit histories can be intimidating. Unfortunately, ignorance is not bliss when it comes to your credit. The majority of consumers, 69 percent of them, have not checked their credit within the last year.

In 2005, a study released by the Consumer Federation of America, Providian, and myFICO.com explained the state of affairs. They found that about half of the American population does not understand the basic concept of a credit score. Indeed, only 51 percent of respondents in the study knew that a credit score represents credit risk. The other 49 percent thought a credit score described credit availability, credit IQ, or levels of debt. In addition, 45 percent of respondents thought that getting a substantial pay increase would result in a higher credit score. While it is possible that there might be an indirect link between your pay level in your credit score, many highly paid people borrow too much (the more you earn the more you spend) and can end up with a very low credit score.

## Not All Scores Are the Same

Many people are under the impression that they only have one credit score. In fact, if you have one credit score, then you likely have many more credit-based scores. For the most part, when a lender refers to your credit score they are talking about your FICO credit score. This is a score based on the Fair Isaac Corporation's credit-scoring model. At the present time, it is the most commonly used score.

When you take on the goal of improving your credit, it is essential that you get a little bit more specific. You need to know which credit score you need to improve. That will depend on your current goal, whether it's buying a house, getting insurance, or landing a job.

### *Variations on the Theme*

While the FICO score is the current gold standard, you most likely have several FICO scores. Each of the three major credit-reporting companies can calculate a FICO score for you, but they also sell their own proprietary scores which are not based on the FICO model, so be careful what you buy. Because the major credit-reporting companies all have different data on you, your FICO credit score will most likely be different at each company. Most experts suggest that you use the middle credit score (not the highest or lowest one) as a gauge of your creditworthiness. Your lenders, on the other hand, might use a different method. They might give you the benefit of the doubt and use your highest score, or they might just buy a single score from one of the credit-reporting companies that they have a relationship with. If you are not sure which score they will use, just ask.

A lot of organizations will offer to sell you a credit score. Before you fork over your hard-earned money, find out what you're getting. Scores from different sources can look deceptively similar, but you need to use the same score that your lender is using if you want to know where you stand.

### *Other Scores*

There are other scores in addition to your multiple FICO credit scores, and any company that you do business with may have its own internal model. The most common internal model might be an application-based model. These models judge your creditworthiness using information you provide on your credit application. For example, your lender may ask how long you have lived at your current address, how much money you make, or how long you have worked at your current job. Of course, lenders won't make a lending decision based solely on your answers to the application. Instead, they use that information as a supplement to the information found in your credit history.

### *VantageScore*

VantageScore is a relatively new scoring model developed by the three major credit-reporting companies: Equifax, TransUnion, and Experian. They suggest that the FICO credit-scoring system is too confusing for consumers. FICO scores range from 300 to 850. A pretty good score is 750, but you might not know that by looking at it. VantageScore uses a scoring system much like your high school teachers', with scores running from 500 to 990. If you remember the good old school days, a 99 percent was an A, anything from 80 percent to 90 percent was a B, and so on. The credit-reporting companies are hoping that this simplicity will help them win market share.

### *Behavior Scores*

The scores described so far are used for a specific purpose, like deciding whether or not to grant you a loan, and at what terms. However, your credit information is used for a variety of other purposes. These stores might use the same credit-file data as your classic FICO credit score, but they analyze the data in a different way. In addition, they might incorporate information from other sources. The goal of these scores is to understand other parts of your behavior.

### *Profitability Scores*

One of these scoring models is designed to determine how receptive you might be to new offers from your credit card company. If you are more likely to accept a given offer, the company is more willing to splurge and mail you an advertisement. Somehow, the way you use products and accounts can reveal how likely you would be to say yes.

Other scoring models help your creditors predict how profitable you will be as a customer. They get an idea of how much revenue you will generate, and they can predict how likely you are to switch brands. Presumably, they make attractive offers to customers who are less likely to switch, and they might create incentives (or penalties) to retain customers who are likely to switch.

### *Bankruptcy Scores*

Creditors can even score you on the likelihood that you will declare bankruptcy. Not surprisingly, your credit history is a main ingredient to the score. A bankruptcy score is slightly different than your FICO credit score. The FICO score attempts to rank you based on the likelihood that you'll be ninety days late on any bill with any creditor. The bankruptcy score goes even further: it tries to determine whether or not you will declare bankruptcy and default on all of your debts.

### *Expanding the Reach*

The FICO scoring model can only generate a credit score for you if you have a sufficient credit history. If you have not used credit accounts enough (perhaps because you are young or a new arrival to the country), there will not be enough data in your credit history to generate a score. In the past, individuals without a score had a hard time getting credit. However, Fair Isaac has remedied this situation in recent years. They created a score they call the Expansion credit score. This score judges your creditworthiness based on information from alternative sources. They examine your past for evidence of bounced checks, delinquencies with service providers, and other behaviors that might describe your creditworthiness.

The best thing you can do for yourself is be a responsible consumer. Pay your bills on time, and don't bounce checks. If you get in over your head, your credit scores will follow. A lot of different organizations check into your credit, so just do a good job and make it easy on yourself.

If your credit history is not sufficient to generate a FICO credit score, then you may be able to get credit because of the Expansion credit score. Once you get your foot in the door with lenders, you are building up your credit history. Over time, there will be enough information about you in the major credit-reporting company databases. As a result, they will be able to generate a FICO credit score on you eventually.

### *Insurance Scores*

Insurers look at your FICO credit score to determine whether or not you are an attractive customer. In addition, there are specially designed insurance scores that help them further evaluate you. Based on your ranking, insurers may decide that they do not want you as a customer, or they might offer you coverage at higher-than-normal rates. The reverse is also true: if you score well, insurers may offer you a discount.

## What's Not Part of Your Credit

The body of information called your credit is quite extensive. It contains data on all of the following:

- Every credit card you've ever used
- Every loan you've applied for
- Every loan you've actually used
- Any public records relevant to your credit
- Your residence and employment history
- And more

While some of these items may not appear in a given credit report, they are still part of your credit. However, your credit does not tell the complete story about you. There are a variety of things that are not part of your credit.

### Irrelevant to Credit

A number of characteristics that might describe you are irrelevant to your credit because they have nothing to do with your creditworthiness. For example, certain characteristics are excluded by laws designed to limit discrimination. Of course, some of the common ones are race, color, religion, national origin, and sex. In addition, lenders may not discriminate against you based on the likelihood that you will have children or get married.

Despite these regulations, some of this information may be used by a potential lender. Although a credit-scoring model will ignore these characteristics, a human who looks at your credit report may be able to make some educated guesses. They may be able to guess your race or national origin based on your last name. Likewise, an applicant named Robert is most likely a male, while one named Susan is probably a female.

In the 1700s, borrowers could end up in prison if they did not pay their debts. Debtor's prisons punished defaulted borrowers, a stark contrast to today's practices. Ultimately, lawmakers found that debtor's prisons did not create enough of a deterrent to keep people from defaulting.

### Your Personality

Your personality is also irrelevant to your credit. You may be the nicest person in the world, but you won't get a loan unless you have good credit. Creditors will base their lending decisions on their knowledge of your previous actions. In some cases, you have the opportunity to sit face to face with a lender and explain that you have no intention of defaulting on your debt. For the most part, that's not an option. You have to work within the system and build good credit.

### *Your Burdens*

Whether you love it or hate it, your credit just reports how you have paid your debts in the past. You might have missed some payments, or defaulted entirely, for a variety of reasons. Perhaps it was because you took on more debt than you should have. On the other hand, a freak accident or sickness could have overwhelmed you with medical bills. Whatever the case, your credit does not care. Credit scores don't explain why you missed payments or declared bankruptcy. They just slice and dice your account history and spit out a number.

### *Your Paycheck*

Some people think that your salary is an important factor in your credit. It certainly is important for some scoring models, and those that ask for your salary on the credit application are obviously going to use that information. However, salary may be less important than you think. It is not a part of the FICO credit score. Therefore, you can have a high credit score even with a modest income. All you have to do is use credit wisely.

> If you feel that you have been discriminated against, or you have any other credit-related complaints, start with the Federal Trade Commission (FTC). Their Web site (*www.ftc.gov/credit*) has a wealth of information on your rights. From there, you can find out exactly who to contact.

The opposite is also true: you can have a terrible credit score even with a million-dollar income. Creditors don't care how much money you have, or how much you make, they just want you to pay according to the terms of your agreement with them. If you can't do that, they get nervous and would prefer not to deal with you.

### *Net Worth*

Creditors don't care whether you are rich or poor. Again, they just care how you manage your credit. You can have bad credit even if you have a lot of money in the bank and another million or two in the stock market. Granted, you could pay off your debts without batting an eye. However, your creditors do not want to spend extra time, money, and energy collecting debts from you.

## A Brief History of Credit History

How did we get to this point? Credit is a part of our everyday lives, and good or bad credit can make you or break you. Because of credit, you can buy a home for your family without hundreds of thousands of dollars in the bank. You can spread out the payments on a large item like a new automobile. If you need a loan, your prospective lender can make a decision extremely quickly.

### *Old-Fashioned Credit*

People have been borrowing since ancient times. How did somebody with resources know who to lend to? They made a decision based on that person's character. The grocer might allow a regular customer to pay later based on past experience. Since the customer always paid for her purchases, she would likely pay again in the future.

In cities and towns, a variety of merchants might offer credit. They would allow customers to walk out without paying for food, clothing, furniture, and more. As populations grew, it became harder to know every customer personally. Therefore, merchants began to share information on their customers. They formed associations that are the roots of today's gigantic credit-reporting companies. Chambers of commerce were also responsible for forming early credit-reporting associations. For the most part, these associations were within a limited geographical area, like a single city.

The National Association of Retail Credit Agencies, the first national credit-reporting association, changed its name to the Associated Credit Bureaus, Inc. Currently, it is known as the Consumer Data Industry Association (located on the web at *www.cdiaonline.org*), and membership consists of about 500 American credit-reporting companies.

As the population and the economy grew, it became necessary for associations to gain a wider geographic reach. A consumer might move to a town, but have a credit history in another town. To meet this need, a trade association was formed in 1906. The National Association of Retail Credit Agencies allowed associations to pool their knowledge and increase the number of consumers that they could report on.

### *Evolution of Credit*

Through the years, smaller associations have merged or been bought by larger organizations. Bigger and bigger companies emerge with a single focus on consumer credit reporting. They developed sophisticated computer systems, and they amassed more and more information on consumers. Today, the market is dominated by three of the largest consumer reporting companies: Equifax, TransUnion, and Experian.

When consumer credit-reporting companies first started to operate in the United States, they mostly helped merchants. People did not use credit cards or finance companies in their everyday lives. Instead, the merchant would extend credit. For example, a clothing store might allow customers to pay for their purchases over time. If a customer failed to pay, the clothing store owner would lose money. These days, things are different. If you buy clothes with a credit card and then go bankrupt, the credit card company loses money, not the clothing store.

In the early 1900s, most debt was held directly with a retailer. Today, most debt is on the balance sheet of a finance company. Retailers benefit because they do not have to take the risk that somebody will not repay. They're in business to sell products, not manage loans. Finance companies also benefit because they earn interest. Part of the reason for this shift is the fact that finance companies were prohibited from charging interest rates high enough to make a profit on small loans. Because usury laws have changed, banks and finance companies can now make a profit on these loans.

## Consumer Rights

Around the 1960s, consumers and regulators began to see just how important credit could be. It was a way for people to buy a home in pursuit of the American dream. However, there was almost no transparency in the credit-reporting industry. The credit-reporting companies were mysterious organizations behind impenetrable walls. They had friends in high places, and they worked to protect their interests.

Consumers were powerless against the credit-reporting companies. Nobody knew who was checking up on them, and individuals were concerned about their privacy. Furthermore, a lender might deny credit to somebody based on information held in the credit bureaus. The lender did not have to explain why, so consumers were left in the dark. Often, there were errors in a consumer's credit history. Unfortunately, those errors persisted, because nobody could check their credit for errors.

### *Gaining Ground*

Once consumers were granted the right to check their credit, they gained some ground. However, they were still largely powerless. Credit-reporting companies recklessly made errors and allowed them to persist. They made a point of digging up dirt on consumers, and were reluctant to fix errors. The history of credit reporting is marred with some truly sad stories about individuals who unfairly suffered from problems with their credit reports.

Regulators and consumer advocates agree: education is your most powerful tool. By knowing what your credit is and how it works, you make great strides toward protecting yourself. You need to know who is involved, what they do, and why they do it. Then, it is your responsibility to be vigilant and proactive.

Consumer protection continues to evolve. Over time, consumers have begun the process of understanding and managing their credit. Regulators have held the credit-reporting companies more accountable for errors and abuses. Consumers slowly earned more and more rights: the right to request a credit score; the right to a free annual credit report from any consumer- reporting company; and the right to have errors fixed in a timely fashion. Regulations continue to evolve as the times change. Identity theft and its effects on your credit is just one of the latest hot topics in credit-reporting regulation.

### *Collections*

Debt collection is an area related to consumer credit rights. When a lender cannot collect a debt from a customer, they have to take extra steps to try and get the money back. Sometimes they outsource collection activities to a dedicated debt-collection agency, and sometimes they do it in-house. Whatever the case, collectors have certain rules they must follow. In the past, some of the worst agencies made life miserable for delinquent borrowers. Regulators have to walk a fine line between conflicting goals. They want to protect the consumer, while allowing lenders to collect the money that is owed them.

## A Look into the Crystal Ball

As Yogi Berra explained, it's hard to make predictions, especially about the future. Nevertheless, you can try to look ahead to see what might lie beyond the horizon. What does the future hold for your credit? How will credit be used? And what should you do about it?

### *Global Credit*

Credit scoring and reporting is well entrenched in several developed countries. However, other countries have not come as far. This makes it difficult for individuals who travel between countries. They might have to build credit under a new system, even though they have been a responsible borrower under another system for many years. Standard global scoring models can help with this. According to the Fair Isaac Corporation, the world is asking for it.

Credit scoring will also be refined so that it is used in more and more places. As businesses and regulators look at how to use these systems fairly, you'll see more and more scores. Hospitals and utilities might be pioneers in this area. Who knows? You might see suburban neighborhoods that limit who can live there based on models similar to your credit score.

### *Laying the Groundwork*

The credit reporting and credit-scoring industries have shown how data can be used. Whether you love it or hate it, organizations that buy credit scores believe in them. Banks and insurers may not understand exactly how the models work, but nevertheless, they're happy with the results they get from using credit scores. More and more nonfinancial organizations may jump on the bandwagon. They will likely tap into the knowledge and processes that lenders have been using, and modify them for their own purposes.

Law-enforcement agencies have already begun to do this. The California Penal system has contacted the Fair Isaac Corporation to build models in the past. The proposed models would help predict whether or not released inmates were likely to commit another crime. ChoicePoint, a large consumer-data repository, works with small and large government agencies to fight crime and terrorism.

# 13 Anatomy of a Credit Report

Your credit report contains the main ingredients in the feast called your credit. It is a repository where various lenders send information so that they can share experiences. These ingredients get measured, mixed, and baked, and the final product is your credit score. While there are other factors that are important to your credit, your credit report has the most important information. This section makes it easy to understand exactly what your reports contain.

## Who Are You?

Your credit report has a section that contains personal information about you. Don't worry, it's not *that* personal. It is simply identifying information, so that creditors can report on you and find out more about you later. This section contains details such as:

- Your name
- Your date of birth
- Your Social Security Number
- Your current and previous employers
- Your current and previous residence addresses

There might be a few other pieces of information in there, such as phone numbers and information about your spouse.

You might be surprised at what you learn about yourself as you read through this section. Perhaps there are Social Security Numbers that you didn't know existed, or misspellings of your name. You should try and get everything corrected, but you might not have much luck. Even an erroneous Social Security Number often sticks. The reason? The credit-reporting companies do not want to fix something that they think is not broken. If they start using the correct SSN, they will lose all of that good information from your old SSN. Therefore, you should first try to get it fixed with whatever creditor is reporting with the wrong number.

All of the information in this section came from somewhere. Most of it came from information you gave your lenders when you applied for a loan. When they ask "Who do you work for?" you tell them who your employer is. Next thing you know, it shows up on your credit reports. The same thing goes for your residence history.

The first section might also contain a Consumer Statement. This is a statement that you add to your credit reports, typically to explain the less-flattering items within your report. You might mention that you had a bankruptcy because of a medical emergency, and you can hope that lenders will take this information into account. Truth be told, these statements probably do not add much value. First, automated credit-scoring models do not consider the statement because they can't understand the words, they just crunch numbers. Second, if you are going to have a human lender read your credit reports anyway, you will probably have the chance to explain any blemishes to that person, because you'll be sitting across the desk from them.

Your personal information in this section is what gets used when data is merged from a variety of sources. In other words, your Social Security Number might be the common link among various creditors, and between credit-reporting companies. Since different organizations have different borrowing information, it's important that they are able to merge everything correctly.

## Executive Summary

The next section in your credit report is likely a summary of all of your accounts. This is a kind of scorecard that compiles all of the different items in your report so that you and your potential lenders can review them with a quick glance. This section is particularly helpful when you are trying to determine the differences between the major credit-reporting companies. If you view your credit report online, you can usually click on portions of the summary to drill down to the data underneath. The summary will typically show you the following items:

- **Total Accounts.** A count of all accounts that have ever shown up on that credit report. The accounts may currently be open or closed.
- **Type of Account.** The categories you might see are Mortgage, Revolving, Installment, Auto Loan, or Other.
- **Open and Closed Accounts.** A count of how many accounts are open or closed. While the Total Accounts section does not distinguish whether or not you've closed the accounts, this section breaks it down. Keep in mind, the accounts must be reported as closed by the creditor.
- **Accounts in Good Standing.** This section shows how many of the total accounts, both open and closed, are in good standing. To be

in good standing, you must have paid, or be paying, everything as agreed.

- **Delinquencies.** Also known as Past Due, this section shows a count of how many accounts you are currently behind on.
- **Derogatory Items.** Sometimes referred to as Negative Account History. These are accounts that are reporting negative information about you and damaging your credit score. These might be accounts that you were previously delinquent on, or these could be accounts that were charged off or settled.
- **Total Balances.** The total balances section shows how much debt you currently have. In addition, this section might be broken down by account type: mortgage, revolving, and so on.
- **Total Payments.** If the information is available, this section contains the total of all of your monthly payments.
- **Good Standing.** A count of all of your accounts that are in good standing: your total accounts minus delinquent and derogatory accounts.
- **Public Records.** The lower the better. It is simply a count of how many public records are in your file. Public records are explained in greater detail below.
- **Inquiries.** The Inquiries section shows a count of inquiries in the last twelve or twenty-four months. Again, you want a low number here. Only hard inquiries, inquiries made when you apply for a new loan, are counted here.

## Account History

Your account history is the meat and potatoes of your credit report. This is the detail section that is used for much of the summary information described above. It shows you, and your potential lenders, more of the raw information that your creditors report about you.

This section can be really easy or really difficult to read, depending on where you get your credit report. The credit-reporting companies have taken steps to improve readability, but there is still a ways to go. Some credit reports have the account history nicely formatted, with bold account names, and colorful payment history sections. Others are pretty much just text.

As with your summary information, the account details might be broken up into sections. You might find individual accounts grouped by type: mortgage, revolving, auto loan, and so on. However, not all credit reports do this. The ones that have gone to the effort to format things nicely are more likely to categorize for you as well. If your accounts are not broken into sections, you'll just see them listed one after another.

A trade line is an account that appears on your credit report. You probably just call them accounts or loans, but your lenders may refer to them as trade lines. This is just another way of talking about a loan's attributes, like your balance, status, credit limit, and so on.

Your account history section shows you a few important details about all of your accounts. They tell other lenders and credit-scoring computer programs all about the loan in question. You should see the following bits of information:

- **Account Name.** Also known as Creditor Name, this field tells you where the account is located. It might say the name of the bank or credit card company that issued you a loan. If an entry has an error, this is the organization that you need to contact.
- **Account Number.** You might have several accounts with the same lender, so it is important to know which account is being reported in case of errors or disputes.
- **Account Type.** You already know this from the summary section. It tells you whether or not this is a mortgage, auto, revolving, or other type of loan.
- **Date Opened.** How long ago did you open the account? As you may know, it's good to have some old ones lying around. Check here to make sure your account age is accurate.

- **Balance.** How much the credit reporting company thinks you owe. This information comes from the lender, but it is not updated in real time. Therefore, recent payments and purchases may not be reflected.
- **Account Status.** Also known as Pay Status, this field notes whether or not you are paying as agreed. If not, it may have additional details about your delinquency. See that these are updated if you have recently made amends with a creditor.
- **Remark.** Sometimes a Comment field, this is where you will often see a remark that your account was "closed by consumer" if you have requested that they close the account.
- **Date Updated.** This is the last time the creditor reported information about you to the credit-reporting company. This can help you figure out why any recent activity is missing.
- **Responsibility.** This section states what your responsibility is to the account. You might be the only user on the account, or you could share it with others.
- **Terms.** Here you see the terms of your agreement. If it's an installment loan, how many payments, and how frequent are the payments? If it is a revolving loan, this section may be blank. Sometimes you'll see a minimum payment here.
- **Past Due.** This displays the dollar amount that you are behind on. Ideally you want to see a "0" here.
- **Credit Limit.** The maximum amount you are allowed to borrow for that account. This is most important on revolving accounts. This number is used to determine how much of your available credit you are using. In addition, high credit limits on your report can show that some lenders trust you.
- **High Balance.** This is like a high-water mark for revolving loans—it notes the highest balance you've ever had on the account. For installment loans like mortgages and student loans, this number is the original loan amount.
- **Scheduled Payment.** This shows your minimum payment due.
- **Actual Payment.** The last payment that you actually sent in before your account details were sent to the credit-reporting company.

Your account history makes up the bulk of information that the credit-scoring models use to determine your credit score. You need to make sure all of this is accurate in order to ensure a reasonable score.

## Public Records

Your credit report shows any public records related to your finances. In general, you want this part of your credit report to be empty. You can expect that almost anything that happens in a courtroom will appear in the public records section. However, nonfinancial matters will not show up. The types of public records most likely to appear on a credit report are:

- Bankruptcies
- Tax liens
- Civil judgments against you
- Foreclosures
- Wage garnishments

As you can probably tell, if these items show up on your credit report, it will hurt your credit. These items will stay for seven years, and then drop off. However, if you owe a tax debt, it will never go away—you have to pay it and then wait seven years for it to disappear. Tax liens can come from the federal government, as well as state and local agencies.

A Chapter 7 bankruptcy will stay in your reports for ten years. Chapter 13 bankruptcy, like most other negative items, will drop off your reports after seven years.

## Inquiring Minds

Your credit reports show a history of all inquiries made into your credit. This section shows who has been asking about you, and you may be surprised to see how many people care about you. Inquiries will remain on your credit report for up to two years.

### *Hard Inquiries*

Hard inquiries are the most important as far as your credit scores go. Hard inquiries are inquiries that happen anytime you apply for new credit. The potential lender checks you out by pulling your credit, and a history of this activity stays in your credit files. Why would this be important? If you run all over town asking for credit, it could be a sign of trouble. Lenders want to know if you are opening up a bunch of new accounts at once. In fact, each hard inquiry costs your FICO credit score a few points (less than five).

Hard inquiries will be shown on your credit reports with the following details:

- Name of the inquiring company
- Contact information for the company
- Date of inquiry

If you use a merged, or 3-in-1, credit report, you will also see which credit-reporting company reported the inquiry.

> See if you can figure out exactly when your lenders report to the credit-reporting companies. If they report at the end of the month, send payments in before that date. That way, your balances look lower, and you can boost your credit score. Even if you pay in full each month, your credit reports might always show a balance.

### *Soft Inquiries*

Soft inquiries are inquiries that do not affect your credit score. In fact, you might be the only person that can view these inquiries. Your prospective lenders do not see them, and they are not included in the inquiry count in your credit report's summary.

After you open a credit account with a lender, they periodically check in on you to see how you are doing. No, they don't call you up to ask how you are. Instead, they pull your credit. They want to see if you are taking on too much debt, or if anything else of interest has happened. Note that these inquiries are the ones that can get you in trouble with a variety of lenders. If you have universal default clauses on your credit cards, these inquiries will let them know if you've defaulted or paid late anywhere else.

Watch your inquiries for signs of identity theft. If you see a bunch of new inquiries and you cannot figure out where they came from, you should make sure it's not an identity thief. Inquiries will be the smoke before the fire, and you can limit the damage by alerting the credit-reporting companies early.

### Promotional Inquiries

You will also see a slew of soft inquiries that are promotional inquiries. These inquirers do not get to see your entire credit report, but they learn something about you. When you get a preapproved offer, chances are it is a result of a promotional inquiry—you met their criteria for the marketing campaign. Note that you can opt out of those offers by telling the credit-reporting companies to stop selling your information. Alternatively, you can call 888-5-OPTOUT to opt out for two years.

### Who Gave You the Right?

Your credit report contains sensitive information. A credit inquiry can give somebody a wealth of information about your finances, and it might not be any of their business. In addition, hard inquiries can ding your score up, and having too many will make your loans more expensive or unobtainable.

For the reasons listed above, there are limitations on who may request your credit report. An inquirer must have permissible purpose when requesting your credit. If they don't have permissible purpose, they can't get the report without your permission. Credit-reporting companies may provide your credit reports in these situations:

- As required by a valid court order
- With your written permission
- For a credit transaction
- For employment decisions
- For underwriting insurance
- In the application process for some licenses
- Ongoing checkups of existing customers
- Some procedures related to child-support awards

As you review your credit reports, see who is asking about you. If they do not appear to have a permissible purpose, they may be violating some serious laws. You can stop them from requesting your credit reports.

## What's Not in a Credit Report

Credit reports have a lot of information in them. If they tried to add any more, it probably would not even fit. Fortunately, there are plenty of things that are not, and cannot, be in your credit reports. Since the definition of credit report is somewhat fuzzy, this section only refers to credit reports issued by the three major credit reporting companies: Equifax, Experian, and TransUnion.

### *Hot Potatoes*

There are several bits of information that cannot appear in your credit report. These are items that could potentially cause a lender to discriminate against you. Of course, you wouldn't want to work with lenders who discriminate anyway, but there are regulations that help to reduce discrimination.

Some of the items that are kept out of your credit report are the usual "hot potatoes" that can get lenders in trouble. These include:

- Your ethnicity
- Your religious beliefs and affiliations
- Your political beliefs and affiliations
- Your sex

### *Out with the Old*

Credit reports are important because they let everybody know if you have been a responsible borrower in the past. If you have made mistakes in the past, it's reasonable to expect that you might make mistakes again. However, everybody makes mistakes, and ideally you learn from your mistakes. Therefore, old items need to be deleted from your credit reports so that you can get a fresh start now and again. After seven years, almost all negative items fall off your credit reports. These include:

- Charge offs and settlements
- Collections
- Chapter 13 bankruptcy (Chapter 7 stays for 10 years)
- Late payments

Once these items fall off your credit reports, it is easier to get loans and improve the terms on loans that you already have. You might not see dramatic changes, because the most recent items on your credit reports carry the most weight. However, you will see improvement.

As with most rules, there are always exceptions. The FCRA allows information older than seven years to appear in some situations. Presumably, these are situations where somebody is taking a great amount of risk on you, and they should be allowed to know more about you. These situations include:

- Credit transactions for amounts greater than $150,000
- Underwriting life insurance for more than $150,000
- Employment for a job paying more than $75,000 annually

### *Other Business*

The major consumer credit-reporting companies only create reports that deal with consumer credit. Other factors may be relevant to your credit-worthiness; however they are not necessarily shown in your credit reports. If a lender, landlord, or insurer is going to use additional information, they have to get it somewhere else. They might ask you for the information on your application, or they might use a variety of other consumer reporting organizations to get the information they need.

Does everything fall off a credit report after seven to ten years? No. If you have tax liens, they are not going anywhere until you actually pay the taxes you owe. Back taxes due to the IRS, for example, will not go away until seven years *after* you have paid the money due.

### *Rubber Checks*

Consumer credit does not include your check-writing behavior. While writing rubber checks is probably a bad sign for lenders, it is technically not a credit account. However, don't get any wild ideas: there are consumer-reporting companies that track check-writing behavior.

ChexSystems, as well as a number of smaller companies, keeps files on consumers who have a history of mishandling their accounts. Note that ChexSystems operates differently from the major consumer credit-reporting companies. The credit-reporting companies track any information they receive, both good and bad. If you always pay as agreed, there is a record of it. On the other hand, ChexSystems only keeps a file on you if you have been reported for writing bad checks. In other words, it's good to have a credit file, but it's bad to have a ChexSystems file. Institutions that use ChexSystems report bad-check writers, and check on new account applicants to see if they've had trouble in the past.

For people with no credit history at all, your check-writing behavior is very important. The FICO Expansion Score, a newer score for the previously "unscorable," uses a variety of information other than your credit reports to determine your creditworthiness. One of the things they look at is how you have used checking accounts.

### Medical Information

You will not find information about your medical history in a credit report issued by the major credit-reporting companies. As discussed elsewhere, that data is kept by the Medical Information Bureau, among others. However, confusion arises because medical bills can appear on your reports. Because accidents and sicknesses tend to be quite expensive, patients and their families often can't pay the whole bill at once. These bills sometimes show up as collection items.

In the past, one could make a pretty good guess at what happened based on your credit report. For example, there might have been an entry for The Broke-Your-Ankle Recovery Clinic or the Chronic Depression Treatment Center. In an effort to reduce discrimination, recent regulations require that these entries do not identify the type of organization where you originally received care. When a potential lender sees your credit report, the entry is identified only as a medical entry. However, when you look at your report, the entry is more detailed. This allows you to contact the information provider if you need to dispute the entry.

### Not Applicable

You could list thousands of things that are just not relevant to your credit report. Your favorite color, night owl vs. early riser, and so on. While these examples might be obvious, there is no shortage of confusion about which consumer records and public records pop up in a credit report. In general, the only records that appear are those which would reasonably be related to your handling of personal financial matters.

Because a business loan is not a personal financial matter, business loans are not included in your credit report. However, keep in mind that if you signed on as taking personal responsibility for the loan, it will appear on your credit.

For many new businesses, a business loan is simply a personal loan, but the bank calls them business loans to make you feel important. One way to tell if it is a personal loan: did they ask for your Social Security Number? If yes, you are probably personally on the hook for any unpaid debts.

In addition, your criminal and driving records are not on your standard credit reports. If this makes you breathe easier, don't forget that other organizations do collect and sell that data. For lending decisions, you might not be affected by a few run-ins with the law. However, if you are seeking employment or licensing in a sensitive area, your prospective employer will surely purchase a background check and ask about any blemishes.

## Consumer Resources

The bottom of your credit report has resources and information that help you manage your credit reports. Most of this information should not be news to you; it is placed at the bottom of credit reports for people who do not know how to improve their credit. Even though after reading this book you will have a head start, you should still read over the disclosures so that you are fully informed about your legal rights.

You will find a summary of your rights under the FCRA, complete with contact information if you need help from the regulators. If you enjoy the legalese, you might want to read the entire Fair Credit Reporting Act (or at least skim through it). The Act shows you what the regulators are trying to accomplish, and why.

In addition to the summary of the FCRA, you will find details on how to dispute or correct information contained within your credit report. You should see complete contact information, and instructions on how to submit corrections. Finally, your credit report might have additional state law resources and information.

# 14 Watching Your Credit

It's essential that you keep an eye on your credit. Nobody knows your credit better than you do, so if there are errors, you'll know it. Is somebody stealing your identity? You'll know that, too. You'll be able to gauge whether your credit is looking good, getting better, or getting worse. With this knowledge, you can manage your credit and make it better. This section focuses on the variety of ways you can monitor your credit and enlist others to do it with you.

## Your Free Credit Reports

The Fair Credit Reporting Act (FCRA) is a good deal. Under the FCRA, all U.S. consumers are entitled to a free credit report each year. This allows you to get a free credit report from each of the three major credit reporting companies annually. Before paying for a credit report, take advantage of this benefit.

When you go through the process of viewing your reports, you get a credit-file disclosure. This disclosure has all of the information that the credit-reporting company might send to a potential lender, employer, or other party that asks for your report. It also has information meant for your eyes only, such as soft inquiries and more detailed information about any medical accounts. These additional details help you keep tabs on who is doing what with your credit.

### *Instant Access to Your Reports*

The quickest and easiest way to get your free credit reports is online. The three major credit reporting companies—Equifax, TransUnion, and Experian—joined forces to create a Web site for this purpose, *www.annualcreditreport.com*. When you visit the site, you can view your report immediately, provided that you prove your identity. To do this, you'll need to provide the following:

- Full name, including middle initial and suffix (Jr., Sr., etc.)
- Current address (and any recent previous addresses)
- Social Security Number
- Date of birth

You'll then have a choice of which credit report you want to view, Equifax, TransUnion, or Experian. In addition to the personal information above, you'll have to provide additional details to each credit-reporting company for final verification. You'll be asked a question that only you should know the answer to. For example, you might be asked for an account number, payment amount, loan provider, or loan balance.

When you successfully prove your identity, you'll be able to see your credit file online. In addition to your reports, the credit-reporting agencies will offer to sell you a credit score and other services at this time.

### Other Ways to Order Reports

As part of the FCRA's free credit-report program, you can order your credit-file disclosures in a variety of ways. If you can't or don't want to view your reports online, you can order them via phone or mail. To order your credit reports over the phone, call 877-322-8228. You'll go through a verification process similar to the one described above. Your reports will be mailed to you within fifteen days.

Watch out for imposters and online scammers! You might think you're at a reputable Web site, but in fact you're giving out information that will be used for identity theft (you may have misspelled the Web site's address or followed a deceptive link). Always double check before you submit your personal details.

If you'd like to request your reports via the mail, you have to send in a request. You can download a request form at *www.annualcreditreport.com*. If you can't use the Internet, simply write a request with the information in the bulleted list on page 58, and instruct them to send you a report from one, two, or all three of the credit-reporting companies. Mail your request to: Annual Credit Report Request Service, P.O. Box 105281, Atlanta, GA 30348-5281.

### Don't Get Them All at Once

You don't have to order all of your free credit reports at once. The program keeps track of which credit-reporting company you have ordered from each year. If you want to get all three at the same time that's fine, and it's a good way to compare the differences among reports. You'll probably find that one company has more complete or accurate information. A one-time snapshot helps you see the different information credit-reporting companies have on you.

If you want to stagger the dates, you can get periodic reports throughout the year. For example, you might get a credit report from a different reporting company every four months. This would help you monitor your credit over time. You won't have to wait a full year to discover if somebody is reporting that you make late payments. Also, you can see if there are any new unauthorized accounts in your name, which might indicate identity theft.

## Other Ways to Get Free Information

The free credit reports that you can get are a great resource. You should take advantage of the program as a first step toward watching your credit. However, there are other ways to get free access to credit scores and the information in your credit reports.

### *Free Credit Report Triggers*

The laws described above entitle you to view your credit reports annually no matter what. In addition to those rights, federal laws entitle you to free credit reports in specific situations. If you are denied credit, insurance, or employment based on information in the reports, you should receive a notice explaining what happened. Simply ask the credit-reporting company named in the notice for a free report within sixty days.

When somebody pulls your credit, they are required to inform you if they've used the information against you. Any adverse action like a denial of credit, employment, or insurance triggers the disclosure. They must also give you contact information for the credit-reporting company that they used to make the decision.

There are a few other triggers as well. If you're unemployed and you intend to apply for a job within the next sixty days, you can ask for a free credit report. People on public-assistance programs can ask for free reports. Finally, placing fraud alerts in your credit files entitles you to a free credit report to check for signs of fraud.

### *Inquiring Minds Can Tell You*

Since your lenders keep tabs on your credit, they can help you do so, too. Lenders periodically check your reports to make sure that you have not become a greater risk to them over time. They may offer you some of this information as a value-added service. For example, some credit card companies will show you your FICO score, as well as a charted history of your FICO score values, free of charge. By keeping an eye on that number, you'll know if anything major is happening to your credit.

Every time you get your credit checked, for a mortgage, loan, employment, or phone service for example, you can ask the inquirer what your credit reports say. They may or may not have details, but they can probably at least tell you whether it's excellent or not. Make a habit of asking anytime you authorize somebody to check your credit. In some cases, you might be able to request a copy of the reports when you authorize the credit check.

## Purchasing Credit Information

There are a variety of ways to get free information from others. However, you have to qualify, and you might not qualify. Annual credit reports from each credit-reporting company are extremely helpful, but a lot can happen at one of these companies in a year. Therefore, you might consider purchasing credit information so that you're even more informed.

### *3-in-1 Reports*

Some people pay for credit reports because they like 3-in-1 reports. These reports consolidate the information from all three major credit-reporting companies. This saves you the trouble of getting the three reports yourself and then matching up all of your accounts.

Because 3-in-1 reports are fairly inexpensive, if you're really curious about your credit they might be worth it. One reason to pay for them is that you get a better idea of what lenders see when they look at your credit. Lenders often use 3-in-1 reports because not every account shows up at every credit-reporting company. Data from the different sources is merged to put everything onto one sheet. You might be surprised at how the merging works, or doesn't work.

### *FICO Scores*

Along with your different credit reports, you can purchase your FICO score from each of the major credit-reporting companies. Because each company has different information, they'll end up spitting out a different FICO score. You never know if a lender is only going to use one or two FICO scores in the lending decision, so you'll want to make sure they're all good. You can easily have a difference of fifty points among credit-reporting companies. By knowing the score, you can see if anything is really hurting or helping one of your FICO scores.

### *Paying for Protection*

There's a right time and a wrong time to pay for your credit information. If you've got an ordinary life and you're careful about your personal information, you might not need to pay a cent. However, plenty of situations arise when you'll need to watch your credit like a hawk.

These days, your Social Security Number is everywhere. It is considered to be one of the most sensitive pieces of data, but is not treated that way by most organizations. You might find your Social Security Number on your paycheck, as your student ID (in college), on contracts that you sign, on a variety of employment documents, and, of course, on credit applications. Think of all of the people who can get access to your Social Security Number. If there are a few too many of them, you might benefit from paying for help.

If you've had problems with identity theft or fraud, one or two credit report reviews each year is not enough. You'll want to consider a credit-monitoring service, and manually review your credit reports periodically. If you haven't had any problems with fraud but you're really worried about it, go ahead and pay for a service—the peace of mind is worth it.

### *Pay for Peace of Mind*

Another time to pay for credit information is when you're considering a large purchase. Mortgage loans in particular tend to be large loans, so it's worth it to make sure your credit is as clean as possible. A slightly higher rate on a mortgage can cost you thousands over the years, so a few dollars to review your credit information is money well spent. Make sure you get your credit information well in advance of the day you apply for the mortgage—it can take a few months to find, fix, and follow-up on errors.

As you shop for an information provider, make sure you are buying your FICO credit score. Because of the FICO's dominance and history in the marketplace, lenders typically use that score. For a purchase as important as your home, you want to look at the same score your lenders will look at. There are a variety of places that offer to sell FICO credit scores, including the consumer site of the Fair Isaac Corporation, *www.myfico.com.*

## Credit-Monitoring Services

To keep tabs on your credit, it's best to enlist the help of others. Checking your free credit reports and purchasing additional reports throughout the year is great, but you can take an even more proactive approach. Credit-monitoring services can keep you up-to-date with the most important information.

### *What They Do*

Credit monitoring services "push" information to you so you don't have to "pull" your credit. They periodically check your credit reports and inform you of any changes. You might receive an e-mail every time an inquiry is made or a new account is opened in your name. In addition, they typically offer unlimited viewing of one or more of your credit reports and credit scores. Sometimes you can view your FICO score, sometimes it's just a proprietary credit score. Note that your scores and reports may not be updated daily; rather, they might only update weekly or monthly.

### *Finding a Credit-Monitoring Service*

Credit-monitoring services are not hard to find. In fact, it's really hard to check your credit report or credit score without getting an offer to use a service. If you need to go looking, you can start with the major credit-reporting companies—Equifax, Experian, and TransUnion. Next, you might visit myFICO.com (run by the Fair Isaac Corporation) for services offered there. Finally, see if your bank or credit card company can get you a deal.

## Credit-Monitoring Service Benefits

Before you fork over the money to use a credit-monitoring service, make sure you're using all of the free resources available to you. The most extensive services are quite expensive, and you might not need them unless you're really worried or you're having a hard time getting your credit reports fixed. If you are going to use a service, make sure you get everything you need.

When shopping for a credit-monitoring service, make sure you get what you need. This section highlights some of the features you will find most useful.

Credit-monitoring services are best for people who need and want a lot of information. Victims of identity theft and people who want constant access to their credit information and scores will benefit most. If you won't take the time to order and review your free credit reports, you might also benefit from using a service.

### Frequent Monitoring and Notification

You want a service that checks early and often. Find out how often they access your credit files to check for changes. Likewise, find out how often they notify you of any changes. Ideally, you want them to do it daily.

### Who do They Monitor?

Some monitoring services only monitor one credit-reporting company. Others monitor all three of the big ones, and they track other databases that you might be interested in. You'll benefit from more information, not less.

### Error-Resolution Services

Some services help you fix errors and recover from identity theft. They typically say they'll do most of the work once you alert them to a problem. This will cost more, but you might want it. Make sure you read the fine print and understand what you do, and don't, get from this.

### Identity-Theft Insurance

Some services offer to reimburse you for your time and expenses related to recovering from identity theft. The ID theft must occur while you're using the service. Again, this costs money and you will want to view the insurance contract so you know what to expect.

## Pitfalls of Credit Monitoring

You can get a lot of valuable information from a credit-monitoring service. In addition, you save time and automate a process that you might not enjoy. Nevertheless, there are a few pitfalls associated with using these services.

### *Not Enough Information*

In the past, most credit-monitoring services were offered by the main three credit reporting companies. These services only included information held in your credit files at that company. If you've ever checked your three credit reports at the same time, you know that information and errors can differ among credit reports. Increasingly, you'll find 3-in-1 credit-monitoring services. However, the lower-cost services still exist, and they don't give you enough information.

Why don't credit-reporting companies have the same information? Credit-reporting companies only hold data that their clients report. Lenders are the most common clients of credit-reporting companies, and different lenders choose to work with different companies. They might only report to one or two companies.

In addition, credit-monitoring services won't give you information on every aspect of your credit, including the factors that lenders, insurers, and employers might look at. They typically don't track information related to insurance claims, medical records, or employment history. While some of the most extensive services can keep you updated, most do not.

### *Slow Reporting*

When you purchase a credit-monitoring service, you may find that you can log in every single day and view your reports. How often does the report get updated? It's important that your reports are monitored and updated frequently. Some services only update your report weekly, monthly, or quarterly. If you need up-to-date information, don't buy a service with quarterly updates.

Keep in mind that data providers like credit card companies, finance companies, and courts may also be slow in reporting information. If you pay down a credit card balance or change your address, the credit-reporting companies might not hear about it for several weeks. You just need to know that there can be a long lag between when something happens and when you are notified.

### *A False Sense of Security*

Using a credit-monitoring service can help quite a bit. You enlist the credit-reporting companies and others to keep you informed. Computers search for problems while you sleep or go about your daily life. However, is this enough to keep your credit clean?

You really need to take an active role in monitoring your credit. While computers can do a lot, nobody knows your credit better than you do. A service can do most of the heavy lifting, but you shouldn't assume that everything is on autopilot. Check your reports manually from time to time—you'll be glad you did.

## Your Not-So-Credit Reports

Your credit is about more than just credit use. Lenders want to know about your employment, assets, and income when they make a decision. Employers want to know about your credit use and any public records. Insurers want to know how you use credit and how often you've made insurance claims in the past. You need to make sure all of the different puzzle pieces are arranged to present the most attractive picture. To do this, it's important that you know what people are saying about you.

### ChoicePoint

A company that may say a lot about you is ChoicePoint. ChoicePoint compiles information from a variety of sources to create a consolidated snapshot of who you are. Information comes from credit-reporting companies, insurance agencies, government databases, and more. Most of this information is available for you to view direct from the sources; however, ChoicePoint merges the data so you can see it all in one place.

Your homeowner's and auto insurance claims are shared among insurers. The practice started in order to detect and reduce fraud. For example, it would answer the question, "How many times has this client had his home burn down?" Nowadays, the information is used for additional purposes. If insurance companies find that you make a lot of claims, they don't want to insure you. Likewise, if the home you just bought has had a history of problems, they don't want to insure the home.

In addition to monitoring claims history, ChoicePoint issues insurance scores. These scores are based on information in your credit reports. Auto and homeowner's insurance companies will use the score to decide whether or not to insure you. Somehow, they've found a way to link your credit behavior to your claims behavior. If you've got a bad credit history or certain public records on your reports, you're likely to cost them more.

Think twice before calling your insurance company to inquire about a claim. Simply asking questions about coverage can add a record to your insurance files which may be used against you. Some states are trying to limit this practice, but it just goes to show that you have to be very careful.

Under the Fair Credit Reporting Act, you can request free annual reports on some of the information ChoicePoint keeps. However, you'll have to pay if you want to get all of your scores and files, and they have a lot of scores and files available. To get your reports, visit ChoicePoint's ChoiceTrust site (*www.choicetrust.com*). There are other companies out there that do reporting similar to ChoicePoint's, but they are not as user-friendly at the present time.

### *Medical Information Bureau*

If your credit report contains information on your credit past, your medical reports will contain history on your medical past. The main place for centralized medical reporting is the Medical Information Bureau (MIB). Many people don't even have a MIB file. You will only have information there if you have applied for individual insurance coverage.

The MIB gets information from insurers and health care providers. When you apply for insurance, you typically disclose any conditions that you've had in the past. In addition, you'll often consent to have the insurance company investigate your past with your health care providers. The information that your health care providers report can end up in the MIB files.

As with your auto and homeowner's insurance, you need to make sure that your MIB files are accurate. Any errors can be costly. For example, when you buy health, life, or long-term care insurance, your MIB history can put you into a much more expensive risk category. The insurer might even reject you altogether. Like many consumer-reporting companies, the MIB will provide you a free report annually, or if anybody has taken adverse action against you based on information held at the MIB.

## Be Your Own Consumer Advocate

This chapter just scratches the surface on some of the consumer-reporting companies out there, and what they do. By now, you should understand that organizations are constantly inquiring about you, reporting on you, and double checking your files. Based on what they find, services could cost you thousands of unnecessary dollars every year! Keeping an eye on your credit is essential. If you are unaware of negative information, it can be devastating. Yes, employers, insurers, and lenders (and who knows who else) should notify you if they take adverse action based on information in your consumer files. However, it might be too late. Imagine being left without homeowner's insurance or auto insurance while you correct errors. Perhaps you won't be uncovered, but you might have to spend a lot more in premiums while you fix your reports.

Businesses are watching you, and they make periodic checkups to see what you are up to. Watch them back, and do your own checkups. You don't have to make this your life, just make it a point to find out what other consumer advocates think is a big deal.

Lenders and others have a right to know something about you. Otherwise, how could they decide whether or not to lend to you? The appropriate extent of their knowledge and how they use it is what's up for debate. However, most consumers benefit by having some information-sharing take place. If everybody had to pay equal rates, the more-responsible borrowers (like you) would have to pay extra to cover the costs of the less-responsible borrowers.

Just like they have a right to know something about you, you have the right to know what they're saying about you. Exercise your rights. It's not always easy or pleasant, but pulling your reports and fixing errors are the only way you can make sure you get what you deserve. You have to be your own consumer advocate, because nobody knows the truth about you better than you. Keep your ears open: new consumer-reporting companies will undoubtedly appear and use information for new purposes.

# 15 A Close Look at Credit Scores

A credit score is often the only thing that will get you a loan, or prevent you from getting a loan. Unfortunately, most people don't even know their credit scores, much less understand how they work. Because of their significance in your life, you should become intimately familiar with credit scores. When you know how things work, it is a lot easier to work on them. This section will demystify the world of credit scores so that you can start improving yours.

## How to Get a Credit Score

If you have not already done so, you will need to get your hands on a credit score. This is the magic number that lenders and others judge you by. Once you know the number, you take a big step toward managing your credit. As you go looking for credit scores, you'll be inundated with offers. Go to any search engine and type in the words "credit score." Every one of the listed results will have your phrase prominently displayed and bolded.

Any time you get a loan, ask your lender for your credit score. Since they just pulled your credit reports, they will have an up-to-date credit score for you. If you don't like what you see, dig deeper. Order your credit reports and see what may be affecting your scores.

You need to be careful out there because you're working with some very sensitive information. If you give your sensitive personal information to the wrong party, you risk becoming a victim of identity theft. Stick with the big names, or ask your lender which credit score they use when evaluating a borrower.

### *Your FICO credit score*

The granddaddy of all credit scores is the FICO score. The Fair Isaac Corporation pioneered credit scoring, and is deeply entrenched as a market leader. For most mortgage loans, lenders will look at your FICO credit score. This is because selling mortgages in the secondary market has traditionally been easier if the borrower had a good credit score. The use of the FICO score for automated underwriting is beginning to shift, but the FICO credit score is still by far the dominant scoring model.

Because of its dominance, you might consider buying your credit score directly from the Fair Isaac Corporation. That way, you will be sure to get a FICO credit score, not an imitation. You can purchase your FICO credit scores directly from Fair Isaac at their consumer web site, *www.myfico.com.*

If you only need one credit score (because you know which credit-reporting company your lender will use) then you can buy a single score from a single bureau. If you want a FICO credit score from all three of the credit-reporting companies, you can buy those as part of a complete package.

While the FICO credit score is a strong market leader, the VantageScore may catch up. VantageScore is the scoring model created by the three major credit-reporting companies: TransUnion, Equifax, and Experian. To purchase your VantageScore, you can visit one of the credit-reporting companies' Web sites, or you can do so at *www.vantagescore.com*.

### Buying Other Scores

You can buy other scores, but you may not want to. There are a million different vendors out there selling credit scores of questionable value. There is so much confusion about credit and credit scores that these companies get away with selling consumers a score that a lender will never use. The major credit-reporting companies are guilty of this. However, they also sell FICO credit scores, so you have to be careful when buying from them. You might get a proprietary score, or you might get the genuine article. Read the fine print to make sure you get what you want. Other scores typically score you a little higher than your FICO credit score would be, giving you a false sense of security.

### Monitoring Services

You can also buy credit scores in conjunction with credit-monitoring services. Typically, these services might hold themselves out to be identity-theft protection services. As an added bonus, they say that they will throw in a credit score. Unfortunately, these credit scores are rarely FICO credit scores. They might move up and down similar to the way the FICO credit score will move, but they're not exactly the same.

## Managing Your Credit Score

If you're going to look at your credit score, it is reasonable to assume that you will try to increase your credit score. You want your credit score to be as high as possible. If you develop the right habits and behaviors, your credit score will follow. In other words, you don't necessarily need to focus on your credit score; focusing on the right activities will do the trick.

If you focus on your credit score, you will focus on behaviors that are intended only to improve your credit score. This may not be the most effective way to manage your credit. You may be able to force your score higher because of a few strategic actions. However, do you really have good credit?

How can I improve my credit score? There are several ways to improve your credit scores. The basic, simple way (the method of choice) is to simply improve your credit. If you do that, your credit scores will follow. How do you improve your credit? Just use credit wisely and responsibly. Follow the tips found elsewhere in this book.

Your credit should have a wide and strong foundation, and you can't build this foundation by trying to fiddle with your credit score. You build a foundation by using credit wisely and responsibly over a long period of time. You only take on debt when you need it, you make your payments on time and as agreed, and you use different types of loans for different types of things.

Of course, you might benefit in the short term by fiddling with your credit score. For example, suppose that you are buying a house. This is a huge loan, and saving a little bit on your interest rate can go a long way. If you have a quick and easy way to raise your credit score, you should do it. For example, you might pay down some debts so that you are using a lower percentage of your total available credit. This will give you an important short-term boost in your credit scores, but you need to address the issue of why you were previously using so much credit.

## Credit Score versus Credit Report

It is essential that you can distinguish between a credit score and a credit report. There is a major difference. Credit reports are just reports that have information on your credit use. They show accounts that you have used in the past, and those that you use today. They show whether or not you paid on time, and how much you have borrowed.

### *Credit List*

You will learn all of the details of your credit reports later in this book. For now, it might be wise just to think of your credit report as a credit list. Your credit report is like a big sheet of paper with a listing of your past behaviors. It also has personal information on you, such as your name, address, and Social Security Number. It is full of information, and looking through this list will take several minutes or more.

### *A Three-Digit Number*

A credit score, on the other hand, is a three-digit number. The higher the number, the better (for most lending-oriented scores). Doesn't that sound simple? Credit scores exist to simplify the lending process. Instead of spending several minutes looking for a long list of data, a person or computer can just look at a three-digit number. This makes the process go faster, which means more people can get more loans at better rates. This is a win-win for consumers and lenders: when lenders switch from using credit reports to credit scores, they end up granting loans to an additional 20 percent to 30 percent of applicants (FICO statement to the Senate Committee On Banking, Housing, and Urban Affairs, 2003).

### Just a Number

Just like your credit report, your credit score doesn't tell lenders whether or not to grant a loan. Your credit reports (or credit lists) are simply testimonials from other lenders. A new prospective lender may look through your credit reports and decide whether or not they wish to loan money to you. The report itself does not make the decision. Likewise, credit scores are just another piece of information that lenders use. A score below a certain number does not mean that you won't get a loan. It simply means that you may be more likely to fall behind on a payment.

Always remember the distinctions between FICO scores, other scores, and credit reports. Credit reports are raw data, typically from the credit-reporting companies. Credit-scoring models analyze the data. The most popular score for lending decisions is the FICO score. Other scores may be based on the same information as the FICO score, or they may incorporate additional information.

Nobody is 100 percent likely to make all of their payments on time. People may pay on time all the time, but no model in existence can claim that anything is 100 percent certain. Because of this, credit scores cannot rule you out as a borrower. Instead, lenders make decisions on how much risk they want to take. If they are unwilling to take much risk, they have to limit their lending. They can only accept customers who are least likely to fall behind on a payment. They accomplish this by setting an internal policy. Different lenders will set their limits at different credit scores, so it is the lender who ultimately makes a lending decision.

## The Secret Mathematical Formula

Credit scores are based on mathematical formulas. A computer program looks at all of the information in your credit report, categorizes it, and spits out that three-digit number. You don't necessarily need to know the details of how the math works. If you wanted to know, it would be very difficult to find out; the mathematical models are "trade secrets," or proprietary intellectual property. The Fair Isaac Corporation does not publish its mathematical formula anywhere.

*Multivariate analysis* is a method that statisticians use to see how numerous inputs affect a single output. In the case of your credit, we can use the FICO credit score as an example. The FICO credit score is designed to predict how likely you are to be more than ninety days late on a payment with any creditor within the next two years. The input data include a variety of different factors, including:

- The number of credit accounts you have open
- The average age of your credit accounts
- The number of late payments in your credit history
- If you're behind on your payments, how much you owe
- If you're behind on your payments, how long you have been behind
- What percentage of your total available credit you are currently using
- Number of revolving accounts (such as credit cards) you have
- Whether you have a mortgage account

In all, your credit score might take twenty to thirty different factors into account. Depending on how you mix and match all of these moving parts, you wind up with a good or bad credit score. To complicate matters, the FICO scoring-model groups consumers into various categories for scorecards while crunching the numbers. If your eyes are beginning to glaze over at this point, remember the three-word secret to improving your score: use debt responsibly.

### FICO Score Simulator

You might not be able to see exactly how your credit score is compiled, but there are some useful tools that can help you understand how your behavior will affect your credit score. At *www.myfico.com* you can use the Fair Isaac Corporation's Personalized FICO Simulator. You have to pay and sign up for this service, but it may be worth the cost if you need to perform major surgery on your credit score.

With the Personalized FICO Simulator, your actual credit history is used to run some what-if scenarios. The Simulator will show your balances, loans, and delinquencies. You can see what would happen if you take a variety of different actions. For example, you can find out what would happen if you were late on one of your bills. At the click of a button you can see what your current score is, and what your score would likely be after this action.

## Does Credit Scoring Work?

Credit-scoring models are extremely complex. Even if you had the time, desire, and mathematical genius to validate the scores, you would not be allowed to. Credit-scoring models are top-secret. This may lead you to wonder if they are fair and accurate. In fact, this question has been raised frequently throughout the history of credit scoring.

### *Are They Discriminatory?*

One of the major criticisms of credit scoring is that nobody except the scorer understands how they work. Because of this, consumer advocates worry that the scores could be discriminatory, or just plain useless. According to Craig Watts at the Fair Isaac Corporation, government regulators have taken a look under the hood of the FICO credit score. They have seen how the model works, and which factors pushed the score up or down. Regulators did not find that the models were discriminatory.

It is difficult to determine exactly how credit-scoring models do what they are supposed to do. Nevertheless, market forces have shown that credit scoring does something right. Lenders and insurers, even though they may not understand the exact process, are willing to pay for credit scores and base decisions on them.

While the models themselves may not be discriminatory, this subject continually sparks heated debate. It seems that some minorities may appear less favorable under certain scoring models. Is this because the model is discriminatory, or because historical discrimination still affects society? There are a number of studies on each side of the debate, all of which claim to provide a definitive answer. Because credit data is used in more and more places (like insurance scoring, for example), this debate is sure to continue.

### *Are They Accurate?*

While regulators may say the models are not discriminatory, another question remains: does a credit score accurately predict whether or not a borrower is likely to fall behind on payments? To answer this, you may expect that lenders would want to look under the hood just like regulators have. They might want to see how the various inputs affect the output.

The models are top-secret, and lenders are not allowed to look at the nuts and bolts. However, they continually use credit scores as a major part in their lending decisions. Why would this be? According to the Fair Isaac Corporation, lenders use the FICO credit score because it works. They have tested and retested this score against their own internal decision-making process. They found that the score seems to work, and that's all that matters to them.

## The Main Ingredients

The specifics of your FICO credit score are a closely guarded secret. Try as you might, you will not find out that a given action raises or lowers your score by a specific number of points. However, the Fair Isaac Corporation has offered some guidance for consumers. For starters, be aware that your credit score is based on five key factors (listed in order of importance):

- Payment history
- Amounts owed
- Length of credit history
- New credit
- Types of credit used

### *Payment History*

Your payment history accounts for 35 percent of your FICO credit score. It is the most important category. It looks at how you have paid your bills in the past. If you always pay at least the minimum required payment, and you get your payments in on time, then you are doing well in this category. When you think about it, this is the most important thing to lenders. All they want you to do is pay on your accounts as agreed.

If you need to improve your credit score, you can do so by attacking this category. Make sure that you are current with all of your creditors. If you're behind on payments, write a check to get caught up. If you can't get caught up, call them up and see if you can agree on some type of payment plan.

When evaluating your payment history, the scoring models dig into the details. If you're behind on a debt, the model checks to see how long you've been delinquent. The longer it has been, the more it affects your score. If you continually pay your bills on time, any late payments will become less and less significant.

### *Amounts Owed*

The amount of your debt accounts for 30 percent of your FICO credit score. The scoring models look to see if you are using debt, how much, and what type. In general, you want to avoid the appearance of being maxed out. Therefore, you should only use a small portion of the total available to you. Ideally, keep your credit card balances at 35 percent or less of the maximum borrowing limit.

For installment loans such as mortgages and auto loans this is not as important. The scoring models calculate the maximum borrowing limits as your original loan amount, so you will be using a high percentage of that amount in the early years of your installment loan. As time wears on and you have paid off the majority of your installment loan, you will have demonstrated that you are a responsible borrower. This can only help your score.

If you need to improve your credit score, the best thing you can do is pay down your debts. If you're using $8,000 of credit on a card with a $10,000 limit, you are using 80 percent of your available credit—that is too high. If you write a check to that credit card company and bring your balance under $3,500, your credit score should increase almost immediately.

### *Length of Credit History*

The length of your credit history accounts for 15 percent of your FICO credit score. The scoring models look to see how long you have been using credit. If you are a seasoned credit-using veteran, you are presumably more responsible (if you're not, it will be obvious in the payment history category). You can optimize your credit by keeping old accounts open.

### *New Credit*

New credit accounts for 10 percent of your FICO credit score. The scoring models check to see if you are opening too many new accounts. You should avoid opening several new credit card accounts within a short period of time. This type of activity makes it look like you're desperate for cash, and lenders are hesitant to lend to people in desperate situations.

You should have a healthy mix of credit types. You might shoot for two to six revolving accounts, and a few installment loans. Some lenders require a minimum number of accounts to offer a loan, and these numbers will keep you in the ballpark. Don't do anything drastic to get there, you should open and close credit accounts slowly and carefully.

The scoring models also look at recent inquiries into your credit. Only hard inquiries are used in the score—inquiries as a result of your request for credit. Again, if you have too many inquiries within a short amount of time, you appear desperate for money. Therefore, you should limit the number of lenders that pull your credit. If you are shopping for a home or auto loan, the models will not penalize you as long as you keep all of your inquiries within a few weeks of each other.

### *Types of Credit Used*

The types of credit you use account for 10 percent of your FICO credit score. The scoring models are looking to see if you use different types of loans. You should have a mixture of revolving debt, mortgage debt, and installment loans. While it may not hurt you if you don't have a mortgage on your credit report, having one will most likely help your score.

Your FICO credit score only uses information that is found in your credit reports. In fact, there is information on your reports that is ignored by the FICO scoring models. Your lenders may use some information in addition to your credit score. That information—such as your income or number of years at your job—might help you or hurt you.

### *"Thin" Files*

If you have a "thin" credit history, it means that there is not much information about you on file at the major credit-reporting companies. This may be because you have not used credit much in the past—perhaps you are young, recently divorced from a spouse who used credit, or new to the United States. When you have a thin file, every move you make has more impact on your credit scores. Upward and downward swings will be more dramatic.

## Average Credit Statistics

With all of this talk about credit scores, you're probably eager to look at some numbers. What is the average credit score? What does the average person's credit report look like? With this information, you can see where you fit in with other consumers.

### *What's the Score?*

The Fair Isaac Corporation publishes information on the national distribution of FICO credit scores. In the United States, here is where consumers fall:

| FICO Scores of U.S. Consumers | |
|---|---|
| **FICO Score** | **Percent of Population** |
| 800+ | 13 percent |
| 750–799 | 27 percent |
| 700–749 | 18 percent |
| 650–699 | 15 percent |
| 600–649 | 12 percent |
| 550–599 | 8 percent |
| 500–549 | 5 percent |
| 499 or less | 2 percent |

As you can see, 58 percent of the U.S. population has a FICO score above 700. This shows that a healthy portion of the population has a pretty good credit score. An additional 15 percent have a score above 650. Therefore, roughly three out of four consumers qualify for a standard loan rate or better.

In 2006, the median FICO credit score in the United States was 723. This means that half of the people had scores below that number, and half of the people had scores above that number. This number is considered a pretty good FICO score, so most people are doing a good job with their credit.

As you make improvements on your credit, it is important that you understand how you stack up. According to the Fair Isaac Corporation, credit scores rank you relative to other consumers. In other words, a relatively high score means that you are less likely to fall behind than somebody with a relatively low score. How did they decide what to measure? Why did they try to determine how likely you are to be ninety days late within the next two years? They researched what lenders wanted.

# 16 Good Credit Behavior

Managing your credit is an ongoing process. If there are errors or blemishes, of course you need to fix those. However, you can't just fix it and forget it. You have to continually follow good habits that will keep your credit in tip-top shape. This section highlights some of the most important behaviors that should become second nature to you.

## Pay on Time

The single most important thing you can do to maintain or improve your credit is pay on time. If you're not on time, lenders assume that you're having problems that could lead to a default. The longer you pay on time, the better your credit will get.

Keep in mind that the goal of credit-scoring models is to predict whether or not you are likely to pay more than ninety days late. Why so much emphasis on a late payment? It's an indicator of much more serious financial trouble and potential loss to creditors. There is an easy way and a hard way to determine if somebody will pay ninety days late. The hard way: create a complex formula that runs through their credit files and spits out a likelihood of late payments. The easy way: the person lets you know by paying ninety days late.

### *Paying on Time Pays Dividends*

Making timely payments will help your credit. According to Fair Isaac, approximately 35 percent of your FICO credit score is based on your payment history. If you can keep up with payments and avoid any delinquency items, you're helping a substantial portion of your score. Credit-scoring models look to see how many past-due items are on your report, how long since they've been reported, and how significant the dollar amounts are. If you never make a late payment, you won't have these items weighing down your score.

If you must pay late, try to get the payment in within thirty days of the due date. If you can manage this, your lenders may not report your late payment to the credit-reporting companies. If this is not possible, see if you can beat the sixty-day deadline.

Likewise, if you've got a clean payment history, it's easier to catch a break when you get into a jam. Suppose you're on vacation or you change bank accounts. The confusion could cause you to make a late payment. With a history of consistent on-time payments, this mistake won't be devastating.

Your credit history will show that you've been responsible before, and you're likely to be responsible in the future.

### *How to Pay on Time*

As with most aspects of managing your credit, you have to work a little to make sure you get your payments in on time. The easiest way to get the work done is to automate it.

Online bill-pay services can do a lot of work for you, so that you're less likely to make late payments. In their most basic form, they allow you to get your bills paid with a few mouse clicks. After that, you're done; the bill-pay service prints and mails a check. You can even schedule the payment to go out in a few weeks so that you pace yourself, or wait until you know you'll have sufficient funds in your checking account.

Keep in mind, you should always schedule your payment to arrive a week or so before the payment due date. Because you're not using your lender's preprinted envelopes and forms, they may process your payments manually, which can take more time. If you have any doubts, send a test check or call your lender to see if they'll process the payments for you.

If you want to really automate things, you can set up a system that simply pulls money from your bank account without you having to do anything. Some lenders call this an online bill pay or easy-pay system. You simply provide them with a voided check (or just your bank account number and routing information), and they get the money from your account when it's due. Of course, you have to be careful to keep sufficient funds in your bank account, and inform your lenders when you change banks.

## Keep Long-Term Relationships

Some surprises are great, but your creditors, potential employers, and insurance companies probably want to minimize surprises. They like to have contracts that explain what should happen, and when. By having a history of long-term relationships, you demonstrate predictability and consistency. If you've been consistently good, then your credit will be good.

### *We've Done Business Together Forever*

In some ways, your credit is just a bunch of lenders telling each other about their experiences with you. Your job is to have a good reputation among these lenders. One of the best ways to do this is to have a successful long-term relationship on file. In essence, you want a credit card company to be your advocate and say, "We've done business together forever." Note that if you play the balance-transfer game—transferring balances from one card to another to take advantage of introductory rates—it's harder to have long-term relationships.

Some creditors don't report everything to the major credit-reporting companies. For competitive reasons, these creditors want to keep you a secret; you're a good, profitable customer. While this helps them avoid competition, it doesn't help you manage and improve your credit. Shop around for lenders that will tell the truth, the whole truth, and nothing but the truth.

As you go through life, you should select one or two major bankcards that you'll keep forever. They should be with big name lenders that will continually report to the major credit-reporting companies. Treat these lenders as long-term partners, because that's what they are. Pay on time, pay at least the minimums, and don't jump ship just because your rate changes.

### *Staying Together*

If you are unhappy with rates or service from your older credit cards, call them and ask for a better deal. If they won't accommodate you, consider using them as little as possible. There's nothing unfair about this. The free-market system says that if they're not competitive, you shouldn't use them as often. Likewise, as time goes on and your credit improves, you become less and less of a liability for them. You're less likely to run up debts and default. They make less profit off you, but at a lower risk.

When you decide to stop using one of your older cards regularly, you should be careful. Some credit card companies will cancel your card if you are inactive for too long, because you've become unprofitable. It's a good idea to set up an automatic monthly charge on the account (examples might be your wireless phone bill, or other subscriptions or memberships), and pay most of it off in full. The card companies make a little money on each transaction, and paying a few dollars in interest each year is a small price to pay for good credit.

### *More Than Just Credit*

You can show long-term stability and predictability in several areas of your life. The major credit-scoring models take a close look at your credit accounts and how long they've been around. However, other automated credit-scoring models (and real people, too) look at other aspects of your life.

Your employment history is important in many cases. Credit applications often ask how long you've been with your current employer. They're looking to find out if you are a stable employee, and if your level of income has been somewhat stable. If you change jobs right before applying for credit, consider informing the lender how long you were at your previous employer.

Residence history is also important, and it typically shows up on a credit application. Again, stability can indicate that your payments will be more predictable. If you keep moving, creditors will wonder why—could you not afford the place you got into? A long time in your current residence can help outweigh some other blemishes on your credit if a real person is looking at the application.

## Communicate with Lenders

Communication is key. You probably know this to be true in your personal relationships, and communication comes in very handy in the professional world as well. For some reason, consumers still haven't caught on that communication with lenders can be really helpful.

### *Red Sky in Morning*

"Red sky at night, sailor's delight. Red sky in morning, sailor's warning." This ancient wisdom helped sailors know about bad weather ahead of time so that they could prepare for the worst. Like them, you should keep your eyes on the horizon to see what's coming at you. If things are going to get tough, then get ready.

You know better than any of your creditors how your financial health is. You know when you lose your job, suffer a family tragedy, incur major medical expenses, and so on. Use that knowledge to communicate with your lenders. If something happens that's going to make it hard to pay bills, be proactive and tell them up front. You might be surprised how easy it will be.

There are several ways to communicate with your lenders. One way is to make a late payment, or no payment at all. This tells them something, but the message isn't very clear. Another way to communicate with lenders is to pick up the phone, tell them what's going on, and ask if they can work with you.

### *Thinking Like a Lender*

When you miss payments, your lender doesn't know what happened. Are you unwilling to pay the debt? Are you out of money and declaring bankruptcy? Are you still alive? They want to know what's going on because they've got money at risk. If it's just a temporary thing because of some financial hardships, they'll be relieved to hear that.

Remember, lenders don't want you to default on your loans. Although it may not always seem like it, lenders will work with you to make sure you can successfully pay off your debts. Consider the alternative: if you file for a Chapter 7 bankruptcy, your debts might be liquidated. In such a case, your lender could lose money forever. If they have to constantly contact you or take more aggressive steps to collect the money, it costs them money. From a lender's perspective, it might be more efficient to just work with you and wait until you're able to pay your bills.

### *Getting a Workout*

There are a variety of ways that you can work out a deal. The most important thing to know is that you actually can work out a deal. Furthermore, it's best to take action early. By doing so, you can help keep the situation from getting worse than it needs to be, and you'll have more negotiating clout with your lenders. Consider how lenders will view these two situations:

- A borrower with a history of paying on time calls and says, "I just lost my job yesterday, and will be short on cash for the next several months. It will be hard to pay you. Is there anything we can do?"
- A borrower has not made his payments for the last three months. He has received notices to remind him and requests to call the lender. He finally calls and says, "Sorry I've been late paying. Cash flow has been tough since I lost my job. Is there anything we can do?"

Who do you think is going to have it easier? In addition, the proactive person will probably pay less in late fees, and the situation might not appear on her credit report.

### *Possible Workout Options*

When you ask for help, your lenders might work with you in a variety of ways. In general, you can ask them to waive any fees that they've charged you or would charge you in the future. Additional fees will only increase your debt load and make it harder to pay them off.

Lenders might allow a temporary forbearance, which means you can stop making payments, or make smaller payments, for a specified term. When you know your problems are temporary, forbearance makes sense. At the end of your forbearance, you might have the opportunity to pay back what you missed in one lump sum. Or, you can add the missed payments on top of the existing loan balance, and get those paid off at the back end of your loan.

Another way to get up to date with your lender is to start a repayment plan. You might add a small amount to your normal periodic payments so that you pay off any past-due balance over time. As long as you're making payments on time and settling the debt, your lenders will be happy.

Working out programs and open communication reduce the likelihood of home loss by 80 percent. Freddie Mac conducted a 2004 study to determine the value of foreclosure alternatives like repayment plans and loan modifications and determined that it was a win-win situation. Consumers avoid the stress and costs of foreclosure, and lenders avoid the hassle and loss of revenue.

Finally, you can consider changing the structure of your loan. Sometimes, agreeing to different terms can lower your monthly payments and make it easier to take care of the debt. One way to do this is to extend the term of the loan. Keep in mind that this doesn't help you out when you look at the big picture, it's more of a short-term solution. If you extend the number of years you're paying, you'll also increase the total amount of interest you pay over the term of the loan.

## Pay Now, Argue Later

Sometimes things don't work out. It's frustrating when somebody asks you for money they didn't earn or that they're not entitled to. Should you pay them or stand firm? Some common examples of this dilemma are:

- You bought a product that didn't work
- There's an erroneous charge on your credit card
- You feel swindled by a lender who got you a bad deal
- Your health insurance company is supposed to pay for a treatment, but hasn't

- You don't believe you owe the government taxes
- Your ex-spouse is uncooperative so you shouldn't have to pay child support
- Your ex-spouse racked up debt that you shouldn't have to pay

## How Much Does Principle Cost?

Have you ever heard somebody say, "It's not about the money, it's about the principle?" This is typical in a case where somebody has the money to pay for something, but they refuse to pay because they're dissatisfied or upset about how things are working. Refusing to pay can be personally rewarding, and it can sometimes serve as leverage to get things done the right way. However, refusing to pay can also damage your credit.

When you have disputes with lenders, vendors, or service providers, beware of dragging your credit into it. The costs of fighting a battle can be huge. If you're committed to sticking to your guns, know what you're putting on the line.

A bittersweet truth about the credit world is that creditors have a lot of power over customers. If they report negative information about you, you can have major problems. You can miss out on job opportunities, you may have higher interest rates or be unable to get a loan, and you might not be able to renew or purchase insurance. Of course, this power is what makes the whole system work. The system gives borrowers a compelling reason to pay off debts as agreed. The message is, "If you don't pay, you're going to have trouble elsewhere."

## A Conservative Course of Action

If you want to be careful about your credit, consider paying down any debts and settling the details later. By having the debt paid, you gain two advantages. First, nobody can ding up your credit by reporting you to the major credit-reporting companies. Second, you prove that it really is not about the money—it's about the principle.

When it comes to medical bills, make sure you know how your insurance company operates. Getting a claim covered can be more painful than surgery, and can take months or years. Find out exactly what they require to get your treatments paid. If you can pay the service provider and then work with the insurance company for reimbursement, you may get faster results. Instead of letting a bunch of uninterested parties handle the affair, you can stay on top of things and call for accountability.

If your debt has been turned over to a collection agency, you need to be very careful. In such a case, pay now and argue later may not be the best course of action. In fact, it could backfire. Pay now and argue later is a strategy to keep you out of collections and avoid damage to your credit reports.

## Charge for Long Life

To use credit most effectively, you should buy things that last. Another way of looking at this is to avoid using credit to buy things that have a very short life. A rule of thumb: you should be able to pay off the debt by the end of the item's useful life. People who follow this rule are able to stay on top of their debt. This section is not intended to lecture you about spending habits; rather, you should simply understand the concept about the lifetime value of your purchases.

### *What's a Long Life?*

Before you charge something or apply for a loan, consider how long you'll enjoy the benefits of the item. For example, consider a night out on the town—perhaps some cocktails in a classy setting, a gourmet dinner, a show, and a cab ride. It can be very tempting to use your credit card for a night of luxury. However, consider how long you'll be paying for that one night. You can't relive it except in your memories, but the debt is on your cards.

If you make the minimum payments, it can take decades to pay off a debt. Do you really want to pay for your night out for the next twenty years? What if you want to have another night out? It is okay to splurge on yourself from time to time, but borrowing for things that come and go will get you into a hole quickly.

If you're going to borrow, borrow for things that will give you value for the entire time you make payments on them. A house is a great example. Sure, you have to make payments for many years, and you might never own the thing outright, but you get to live in it and participate in any market appreciation.

### Upside-Down Cars

Another example might be your automobile. You sometimes hear that somebody is "upside down" on their auto loan. What does it mean to be upside down? It means the loan amount is greater than the auto's value. If you sold the car at current market prices, you would not pay off the loan balance. This happens when the car loses value faster than the debt is paid down. If you need another car and you're upside down, the only way to get one is to take a loss on your current car and add more debt. Again, you're not getting ahead, you're falling behind.

Now that you know the concept, look at everything you are thinking of charging or purchasing with the help of a loan. Which will last longer, your enjoyment of the item, or your debt? If the debt will far outlive the item, reconsider the purchase.

As with the night on the town, people get upside down on their auto loans due to shortsightedness. Too many auto buyers look at their monthly payment when they consider a purchase. One way to lower your monthly payment is to lengthen the term of your loan. That's fine if the auto will last at least as long as your loan. If it doesn't, your debt outlives the item you purchased.

## Be Involved

The best habit you can develop is to be actively involved in managing your credit. Don't worry, it really doesn't take that much time. You simply have to decide that you're going to take charge, and then do it.

### *Get Informed, Stay Informed*

You are already taking great steps in the right direction. By reading this book, you now know more about improving your credit than the average consumer. The world is full of inaccuracies and myths, and consumers who don't pay any attention to their credit. This is not your problem.

As time goes on, laws and lending practices will undoubtedly change. New credit-scoring models will emerge, and noncredit-related scoring will increase. As that happens, keep your ears open and find out how it works. You can only benefit by staying up to date on how your information is managed.

### *Know All of the Scores*

Starting now, find out what everybody is saying about you. There are many different types of scores floating around, and you are being graded. Be aware that you have more than just one credit score. First, there is the FICO credit score, the granddaddy of them all. This is used in the majority of lending decisions, but not all of them.

Which credit score is the most important? The one that your prospective lender is using. You can have the best score at one of the credit-reporting companies, but your lender may be pulling a lower score from a different company, or using its own proprietary formulas. Find out how your lenders will judge you.

Each of the three major credit-reporting companies issues its own scores as well. Based on differences between the information kept at these companies, your credit scores can vary. In fact, you might even purchase a credit score from a major credit-reporting company, but not know if it is your FICO score or a proprietary score. Get as many details as you can before you purchase scores.

Besides credit scores, there are a variety of privately developed scores that help businesses figure you out. They predict how profitable you will be, how likely you are to default or declare bankruptcy, how likely you are to make insurance claims, and more. These scores typically are not available to you, but you might see them become available in the future. If so, make sure you take advantage and understand how companies view you as a consumer.

### *Read the Fine Print*

You already know that agreements can contain some nasty provisions. However, most people still do not read the fine print. Instead, mail from the credit card companies goes right into the shredder (or worse, the trash can). If you don't understand what you are getting yourself into, you can get blindsided by something that you should have seen coming.

Along the same lines, you should always glance over your credit card statements for any red flags. You want to make sure the interest rate they are charging you is the same as what you expected it to be. Likewise, look for unexpected fees, especially late fees if you did not pay late. Finally, check for charges that you did not initiate. If you find anything unexpected, you should contact your card issuer immediately and get it fixed. You can save yourself expensive fees, expensive credit damage, and expensive, time-consuming identity theft.

If you can stay on top of your loans and your finances, your credit should show improvements. Develop the habits that allow you to have a strong foundation, so that when surprises pop up, your life will be a little bit easier.

# 17 Building Credit

Credit scores reflect known information about you. If nobody knows anything about you, then you're not a good candidate for credit. Unfortunately, it is a "no news is bad news" situation. There should be a healthy helping of data about you and your creditworthiness available for all lenders to see. In this section, we'll look at how you can start building your credit record, how you can rebuild bad credit, and how you can get favorable information added to your reports.

## What's the Big Deal?

How do you get credit without a strong credit history? This is one of the grand mysteries in life. Nobody wants to give you credit unless you already have a good background of using credit wisely. However, if you had that background, you wouldn't need their help.

Improving your credit might require that you simply build a credit history to spread the word about yourself. Building credit is the process of adding favorable information to your credit files, and doing the things that lenders like to see. Remember, this is a marathon, not a sprint. By pacing yourself, you will get to the finish without getting hurt.

Some people believe that paying cash for everything is the best way to manage money. While the concept of having enough cash to pay for what you buy is admirable, failing to use credit is foolhardy. If you never use credit, you might not be able to get it when you need it.

Using credit does not have to be expensive. Indeed, you can pay your credit card balances in full every month, and you will not pay a penny in interest. However, your creditors will know that you are a responsible person. They will know that they can count on you, and you'll be able to count on them in an emergency.

The skills you learn in this chapter are like powerful magic: they can be used for good or evil purposes. Once you build a nice-looking credit history, it will be really, really easy to get a lot of money. Don't go over to the dark side and misuse your powers. You will lead a much simpler life if you only use credit when you need it, and pay it off when you don't. Be sure to follow all of the good credit habits discussed elsewhere in this book. Ultimately, you should think of these techniques as "the ones that worked so well I quit using them."

## Who Needs Credit?

Everybody ought to have a decent credit history. In times of trouble, your credit may be all you have, and it can keep you from getting into deeper trouble. If you don't have a strong credit history, you should start building one now. Nobody is going to give you any substantial money if you do not have credit. Lenders are scared of losing money, so they try to make wise lending decisions.

### *Give the Kid a Chance*

There are a variety of reasons that you might not have any credit history. Many people go through this in their lives. For young adults who are just setting out on their own, there is no credit history. If you are in this position, it is now up to you to make your mark on the world. Just avoid making any negative marks.

If you are a parent, consider helping your children build credit before they leave the nest. They will have it much easier, and borrowing in their earlier years will be less expensive. Perhaps most importantly, giving your child a chance to use credit in a limited capacity can teach them some valuable lessons. When they are out in the world, unsupervised, they are going to get a lot of offers for credit. Some will be good offers, but some might fall into the category of predatory lending. If your child is educated and has a decent start on a credit history, it is less likely that she will get caught in the worst traps.

### *Welcome to the United States of America*

Recent arrivals to the United States also find themselves without credit. Not only do they have to learn customs and a new locale, not to mention a language, they have to do it without credit. Other countries often have ways of judging their citizens' creditworthiness, but those metrics do not always work in the United States. Here, most lending decisions are automated; they pull a credit score and say "yes" or "no." Because of that, new arrivals need to get into the system and play by a new set of rules. Granted, there are institutions that make lending decisions without using automated processes, but not many.

### *Till Death Do Us Part*

Some marriages do not work out. While the emotional costs are huge, there is also a great financial cost. What's worse, one of the parties might have been the sole credit user in the family. If credit cards, mortgages, and auto loans are only in one spouse's name, the other spouse probably does not have much of a credit score. Left on his own, he might have to build credit even though he's been using it for years.

A more tragic possibility is that the spouse who used credit passes away unexpectedly. A surviving spouse will have a hard time all around. Of course, one way to protect against these challenges is to make sure that everybody has some credit in their name. Keep a well-aged account open and in good standing.

### *I Had Some Credit, but It Broke*

In addition to those without credit, individuals with bad credit can use the same techniques. In such a case, you might be rebuilding your credit after some hard times. The concept is the same: by taking steps to show lenders that you're responsible, you can earn access to better deals.

Don't believe that you're stuck with the hand you were dealt. Your credit is always a work in progress. You can create it, improve it, destroy it, and rebuild it. It might take time and patience, but you will eventually earn trust if you do the right things.

Building and rebuilding credit takes time. However, you can see improvements over several months. After several years of credit-building behavior, you will find access to attractive loans and terms that you never knew were available. Keep in mind that the ugliest parts of your past will disappear from your credit files after seven to ten years. If you are building a good reputation in the meantime, your credibility should skyrocket once those items fall off your reports.

## Building Credit-Ability

As you build credit, you are building credibility. From a lender's perspective, credibility means "credit-ability." In other words, the lender is asking: "If I loan this person money, will I get it back the way I want to get it back?" Note that you are not trying to deceive anybody here. You know you can handle the responsibility, so let the rest of the world know. As you go through this process, think of your credit as a brutally honest friend who always tells the truth about you. If you have been doing well, you will know. If you made a few mistakes, you can be certain that you will hear about them.

### *Starting from Scratch*

If you do not have the bare-bones foundation in place, you will have a hard time getting anywhere. Do you have a checking and a savings account? If not, it is time to get with the program. Many lenders do not accept cash anyway, so open a free checking account at the very least.

Having money saved up is a major credibility builder, especially if you want to borrow from the institution that has your savings. Make regular monthly deposits, similar to a monthly debt payment, and you look even better. Another advantage of having a stash of cash is that you can use it for a down payment on an installment loan. Why does that help? It lowers the total amount of money they lend you, and it also lowers your required monthly payment. These factors increase the likelihood that you will be able to pay off the debt.

As always, you need to think like a lender. Consider all of the different ways you can convince them that you are likely to pay on your debts as agreed. If you have a stable employment and residence history, that might help. Before you move or change jobs, see if you can take on a little bit more credit. If you move first and then apply, you might scare them off.

### *Base Hits, Build on Successes*

The goal of building credit is to have small successes, and build on them. You are not trying to get a zero-down mortgage as your very first loan. If you do manage to get one, it will probably cost you more in fees and interest than it should. Try to apply for credit that you feel reasonably confident you can get. Otherwise, you might end up with a higher-than-normal concentration of inquiries in your credit files. When in doubt, ask the lender for their opinion. Don't always take no for an answer though, sometimes the only way to find out is to submit an application.

Offers that say "You're Preapproved" are not entirely accurate. The lender will likely make a hard inquiry into your credit to determine whether or not they wish to do business with you. Look for clues that you might or might not be able to get an account before you apply for it.

When you are just starting to build or rebuild credit, everything is just a little bit more important. The things you do have a greater impact on your credit than the same actions might have for a seasoned credit user. Therefore, be especially careful at this point. If you do not feel like you should take on additional loans, you are doing the right thing by holding back.

### Got Better? Get Better!

Don't forget to pat yourself on the back periodically. When your lenders first gave you a shot, they were taking a risk. Therefore, they probably did not give you the best possible deal available, and there's nothing wrong with that. It's only fair that lenders who take risks deserve to earn a little more. How do things look today? Are you less risky now, based on your more robust credit history? If so, speak up.

See if you can qualify for better loan terms after you've built a good reputation. If you have credit cards, pick up the phone and ask them for a better rate. You might be surprised at what you hear. If you got a mortgage, talk with a trusted mortgage broker to see if there is any sense in changing your mortgage terms. You might now qualify for a more attractive loan. Of course, if interest rates are not cooperating, it might not do you any good to change right away.

In general, don't forget that you are moving forward and improving your credit score. You should periodically see the benefits of all the hard work you are doing. Ask for better deals. Don't forget to shop around for auto insurance every few years. Your improved credit might help you in a variety of ways.

## Secured Loans

One of the most effective ways to build credit is by using secured loans. The loans are secured because you pledge some type of collateral—like money in a savings account—to the lender in exchange for using their credit card. If you should fail to pay the money back, the lender knows that they can take your collateral.

Secured loans will get your foot in the door so you can start using credit. Lenders give you a chance, and you can build on your successes.

The bank knows that you are good for the money because they're holding it in your account. They'll freeze your account so that you can't take the money out, but this is a small price to pay for the chance to get good information in your credit report.

Secured loans are not a bad thing. In fact, the holy grail of all loans—the home mortgage—is a secured loan. In exchange for your home-purchase funds, your lender has the right to take back, or foreclose on, your house if you fail to pay as agreed.

### *Secured Credit Cards*

One of the most powerful credit-building moves you can make is to use a secured credit card. A secured credit card offers the ability to use a standard credit card at little risk to the lender. To do this, you make a deposit into your bank or credit union account. Then, you apply for a secured credit card with the same dollar limit as your deposit. You must apply for the card from the same institution that has your deposit. For example, if you deposit $500 into a savings account, you might apply for a credit card with a $500 limit.

Your secured card acts just like an unsecured credit card. You can use it in all the same places, and nobody except you and the bank will know that it's a secured card. Keep in mind that the bank is taking some risk, so they'll likely pull your credit just to make sure you won't get out of hand. Even though the card has a limit, it is possible to charge more than the limit, and doing this will get you in trouble.

When using a secured loan, make sure that your institution will report the loan to the major credit-reporting companies. The whole point of using a secured loan is to build or rebuild your credit, otherwise you'd just spend the cash without depositing it first. If your bank doesn't report your loans, shop around and find an institution that will.

### Expanding the Foundation

Once you have a secured credit card, it is essential that you use it responsibly. Use it in moderation, and pay down the balance every month. Use the card even if you have the cash to pay for what you are buying—the key is to show others that you can use credit. If you do this, lenders will eventually see you as an attractive borrower.

As time goes on, you should be able to increase your access to credit. Perhaps you can have the bank raise your limit above the amount that you keep on deposit. This will improve your credit score by decreasing your credit utilization, and it will be a stepping stone to even greater loans. Ask about a credit-line increase every six to eighteen months until you have received several increases.

The best time to ask for an increase is when you are only using a small portion of your available balance. Otherwise, your lender might think you've fallen on hard times and you are becoming a default risk. Of course, you should not use your full credit line when you are building credit—you're just showing them that you can handle the responsibility.

### *Secured Auto Loans*

In addition to credit cards, you can use an auto loan to help build your credit. The concept is similar to the concept of a secured credit card. However, your deposit might not be large enough to pay the whole cost of your automobile. That's okay, because the loan is secured by your deposit plus the auto itself, the bank should be able to get its money back if it repossesses the car.

The auto loan shows up as an installment loan on your credit report, so you can add some variety and spice to the items in your history. In some cases, your financial institution might not pull your credit history if you use a secured auto loan—this is more likely at smaller institutions and credit unions. This means you can reduce hard inquiries, as well as get a loan no matter how bad your history is.

> After you open a secured credit card account, you should try to find a way to open an installment type of account, like a secured auto loan. Credit-scoring models look more favorably on installment accounts, and they also reward you for having different types of credit.

## Utilities

While they may not be in your classic credit score, your relationships with utility companies can help you or hurt you. Telephone, energy, and cable companies that you've worked with keep data on your payment history. Establishing utility accounts and paying on time will open the door to increasingly better loans and better credit.

Be sure to get utility accounts in your name if you need to build credit. If one spouse of a married couple has a limited credit history, they should put utility accounts in that spouse's name. Likewise, if you live with roommates, see if you can get the utility accounts in your name to help with your credit. Of course, having the accounts in your name means you are on the hook for paying all of the bills.

### A Different Kind of Score

Experian has a credit score developed specifically from your relationships with utility companies. Their Telecommunications, Energy, and Cable (TEC) Risk Model uses information from utility accounts to predict how likely you are to pay on time. While utility companies obviously have an interest in this score, people with little credit history are increasingly judged with the same information.

Innovations like the Telecommunications, Energy, and Cable (TEC) Risk Model allow vendors and lenders to score millions of additional consumers. Previously, these consumers were excluded from offers because nobody knew what to do with them. Imagine how many people use mobile phones and pay electricity bills, but have never used a credit card.

Likewise, the Fair Isaac Corporation uses has a credit score that incorporates information from utilities and other service providers. The FICO Expansion Score makes credit scores—and credit—available for consumers who previously could not be scored.

### Keep Your Nose Clean

Utilities are also essential in keeping your credit squeaky clean. If you've failed to pay bills you owe, your debt could be sent to a collection company. Collection items are especially damaging to your credit history, and an unpaid utility bill can leave a black mark on your credit for seven years. As always, communicating with your utility providers before a problem gets out of hand is the best route. They would rather work with you than send your account to collections.

Another reason to stay current on utility bills is that you may have an opportunity to use your payment history as negotiating clout. While many lending decisions are automated, some lenders still make decisions the old-fashioned way. If you can show them a steady history of on-time utility payments, an uncertain lender may give you a shot at a better loan.

## Using a Co-Signer

A co-signer is somebody who shares a credit account with you. If you don't have credit, or if you have bad credit, lenders will consider the co-signer's credit strength when making a decision. It's important that your co-signer has better credit than you do, otherwise using a co-signer won't help you at all.

Who should you use as a co-signer? As the old saying goes, start with friends, family, and fools. You'll need to find a close person who trusts you, has good credit, and is willing to stick their neck out for you. For younger people, parents are a good first choice. Ask your parents if they'd be willing to help you out and co-sign for a credit card or a loan. To sweeten the deal, offer to have statements sent directly to them so that they can see it if you should miss any payments.

Using a co-signer is a major responsibility, so don't take it lightly. If you fail to pay debts that your co-signer helped you get, the lenders go after your co-signer. Lenders will demand payment, and add negative items to the co-signer's credit report. If somebody does you a favor by co-signing, repay the favor by repaying your loans as agreed.

If your parents cannot or will not co-sign, look to a spouse next. Your spouse's credit might help you get your foot in the door with a good lender. Recent arrivals to the United States often establish credit when their spouse (if she is a U.S. citizen with a credit history) co-signs for them. Finally, siblings might take you under their wing and sign for you.

If you can't find a co-signer in your immediate family, you'll have to branch out and find a friend to do you a huge favor. Proceed with caution; ruining somebody's credit is a surefire way to end a friendship.

Keep in mind that financial experts often warn people not to co-sign on a loan. There is good reasoning behind this. If the lenders will not give you money on your own merit, your friends and family should have reason to hesitate as well. Don't take it personally if a friend will not co-sign—some people just can't afford to take the risk.

## Use the Big Names

You could be the best borrower in the world and nobody would know it. Being responsible and paying debts off is good, but letting everybody know about it is even better. If you're taking steps to build a strong credit history, make sure the word gets out. The best way to do this is to use large financial institutions as you build or rebuild credit. These institutions are more likely to report to the major credit-reporting companies, thereby adding positive information to your credit report.

One way to make sure your loans are getting reported is to ask. Simply find out which credit-reporting bureaus your lender uses. If they don't report their loans, see if you can find a lender that does. It may be that you can't find a lender that routinely reports loans. In that case, ask them if they'll report your loans to the bureaus; all they can do is say no.

Another way to leverage the big names is by using credit accounts at large department stores. Find out if they report to the bureaus. You will find that the older and more established stores do report on your account. Getting a credit card with a department store is usually quite easy, so take advantage if it is an establishment where you would normally shop. Of course, you should always pay your balance off in full with this type of account. The interest rates are usually not the best, and you can easily forget about department store accounts.

Finally, you can try for a credit card that works at one of the big gas stations. These cards have less-restrictive rules, so they might give you a chance. Again, you do not really want to carry balances on these cards. Instead, you simply want them to make reports to the major credit-reporting companies.

# 18 Optimizing Your Borrowing

Saving your pennies and borrowing wisely are the keys to having good credit. If you use products and services wisely, you have more money to spend as you need. If you are going to borrow, you should do it in the most efficient and effective way possible. This will allow you to minimize your borrowing costs, which keeps you out of some dangerous credit pitfalls. This section highlights some ways that you can borrow wisely and keep your credit in excellent shape.

## Zero Percent Interest Offers

If your credit is halfway decent, your mailbox may be flooded with offers for new credit cards. In many cases, these offers include a teaser rate as low as 0 percent. Teaser rates are artificially low rates that credit card companies offer to get you in the door. Typically, these rates expire after several months or a year, and then the account charges standard interest rates.

### *Free Money*

Teaser rates are extremely tempting. If you can borrow money at a 0 percent interest rate, then you use somebody else's money at absolutely no cost. However, there may be a hidden cost. The lure of free money tempts people to spend like crazy and rack up significant debts. Once the teaser rate expires, reality sets in. You have to repay those debts, and the credit card company starts to charge hefty interest rates. Likewise, any late payments will cause the credit card company to take away the teaser rate and start charging higher rates.

In general, you should use these offers only as a short-term strategy. For example, if you have a credit card balance with a high rate of interest, you may want to take advantage of an offer for a 0 percent balance transfer. As long as you completely pay off that debt before the teaser rate expires, this is a wise strategy.

### *Surfing Cards*

Unfortunately, too many people fall into the trap of surfing cards. Their intention is to use teaser rates as a long-term strategy. This is a very dangerous strategy. These people simply shift the balance from one card to the next. They open a new credit card account with a promotional rate every time their previous promotional rate expires. The problem with this strategy is that you never pay off your debts; you simply shift them from one place to another. As time goes on, chances are that your overall debt burden increases, simply because you are treating the symptom, and not the cause, and your credit only deteriorates. What's worse, a sickness or disaster could strike and you'd start missing payments. If you're going to use teaser rates, use them as a short-term strategy.

## Student Loan Consolidation

If you have student loans, you may be able to make some adjustments that will help you financially. With a little bit of tweaking, you might free up some money that you can use to manage your credit. Student loans have some unique features. If you consolidate them, you can choose among several different repayment plans (how the plans work will depend on your student loan balances, among other things). If you can extend your payments over many years, your required monthly payment will decrease.

If you extend your student loan repayments, you will end up paying more in interest over the life of your loan. You might have an attractive interest rate, but you'll pay interest for many more years. It may work out in your favor, but you should be aware of how much you are paying.

What should you do with the money you save? If you want to improve your credit—and if you have credit card balances—then you can use those extra dollars to pay down your revolving debts. Once your revolving debts are under control, you can redirect those dollars to your student loans or some other financial goal.

## Mortgage Refinancing

Your mortgage will most likely be the largest loan you ever take on. It buys you a place to lay your head, and peace of mind. Because the dollar amounts are usually so large, the interest rate that you get on your mortgage is extremely important. By shaving off a percent or more, you can save a bundle of money. If you know you can save money, refinancing your mortgage is a good move.

How can you get a lower mortgage rate? One way is to work with changing interest rates. If interest rates in general have gone down since you got your mortgage, you may be able to refinance and get a better rate. Before doing this, you need to make sure that it makes financial sense. Do the math, or sit with an honest mortgage broker. Refinancing costs money—the fees and closing costs may wipe out any potential gains. However, if all the moving parts line up correctly, it may be worth your while. If you're going to stay in the house long enough to regain those costs, refinancing makes sense.

## Home Equity Loans

Home equity loans are another tool you can use to optimize your borrowing. If you have revolving debts that you would like to reduce, you can borrow against your home's equity to pay down those debts. The two main advantages of using this strategy are lower interest costs and potential tax savings.

### *Lower Interest Costs*

A home equity loan usually has a lower interest rate than a standard credit card. This is because a home equity loan is secured by your home, and the bank can kick you out and sell your house if you fail to repay the loan. Credit cards, on the other hand, are not secured by anything. If you fail to pay them, the credit card company can sue you. However, you don't pledge any collateral when you open up a credit card account. Because the lender takes on more risk with a credit card account, the interest rate is higher. Therefore, if you shift your revolving debt to a home equity loan, the interest rate that you pay on that debt should decrease.

### *Potential Tax Savings*

You might also get some tax savings by using a home equity loan to consolidate your debts. The interest you pay on a home equity loan is tax deductible in some situations. Essentially, this means that you don't lose all of the money you're paying in interest; some of the interest payment is effectively subsidized through your tax savings. Before you take this approach, check IRS Publication 936 to make sure that you can qualify to take the deduction.

### *Pitfalls of Home Equity Loans*

Home equity loans can be dangerous, so you should not take the idea lightly. When you borrow against the value of your home, you're taking a serious risk. As mentioned above, your lender has the right to foreclose on your home if you fail to make payments on the loan. Is that risk worth it? You may only save modest amounts of money in exchange for that risk.

When you borrow against your home equity, you truly are "betting the farm." If you are unable to make your required payments for any reason, you risk being evicted from your house. Don't do it unless you are reasonably confident that you can afford the risk.

As with mortgage refinancing, home equity loans cost money. You need to take those costs into consideration before going forward. You might get a lower interest rate and enjoy some tax savings, but those savings could be wiped out by fees associated with closing the loan. When you factor in the risk of losing your home, it might not be worth considering. A home equity loan can help you optimize your borrowing in a few specific situations, but it does not work for everybody.

## Nothing Wrong with Asking

To get the most out of your borrowing, you should ask your credit card companies to work with you. If you keep balances on your credit cards, the first thing you should ask for is a lower interest rate. By keeping a balance on your card, you are a profitable customer. The credit card company should be willing to work with you and give you a deal. To get a better rate, just call them up and ask.

### *Getting a Lower Rate*

When you request a lower interest rate, let them know that you think you deserve a lower rate. If you have seen more attractive offers elsewhere, let them know. However, you probably won't make much ground by telling them specifically what offers you've seen. The customer-service representative on the other end of the line will simply try to overcome and rebut any arguments you make. State your case simply, tell them what you want, and ask them for a yes or no answer.

You should be polite, but firm when you ask for a lower interest rate. If you are thinking of leaving for a better deal, let them know. However, you will most likely talk with an entry-level employee who does not care about your business. If you don't make much progress, try again later or take your business elsewhere.

Getting a lower interest rate will be easier if you've been a cooperative borrower. In other words, you should ask for a deal only after you have made on-time payments for an extended period of time. If you have missed payments, they will consider you a risky borrower who they have no incentive to negotiate with. In addition, it will help you if you have a low balance on that credit card relative to the maximum credit limit. Again, you appear less risky, and there's always the potential that you'll increase your balance if they give you a deal.

### Getting to No

Your credit card company may reject your request. However, don't be discouraged. A no simply means that they were not ready to make a deal when you talked with them. You can always call back in a few months, or you can take your business elsewhere. If you decide to do business with a company that is more willing to work with you, don't rush to close the accounts that denied your request. As you've learned elsewhere, it helps your credit to have old accounts with low balances. If a credit card company was unwilling to give you the deal you deserve, you can simply keep a small balance on your account and let it lie dormant.

### Increasing Credit Limits

You can also ask your credit card company to increase your credit limit. This means that they will allow you to borrow more—but that's not why you would do it. Borrowing more would only mean that you have more debt to pay off in the future. Instead, you increase your credit limit so that you can increase your credit scores. By using a smaller percentage of your total available credit, you appear less risky to the credit-scoring models.

The "amounts owed" category accounts for 30 percent of your FICO credit score. In this category, the scoring models look at how much you owe relative to how much you are allowed to borrow. This category also accepts other factors, but increasing your credit limit is intended to make it look like you're borrowing less. If you keep your debt balances exactly the same, you will look better because you have more available credit.

This strategy can help even if you pay your balances off in full every month. Your credit card companies don't necessarily report that you pay your balances off every month, instead, they simply report your current balance on whatever day they happen to report to the credit-reporting companies. It is simply a snapshot in time. They might happen to report your balance the day before your check arrives to pay it off.

Having a higher available credit limit will help you show that you are not skating on thin ice. Another way to do this is to have a low balance on the days they report. If you can figure out when your lender reports your balance to the credit-reporting companies, you might want to pay down your balances a few days ahead of time.

> Your credit reports may show that you're maxing out your credit cards even if you pay your cards off in full each month. The credit card company simply takes a snapshot of your account and forwards that snapshot to the credit-reporting companies. If you use your card heavily and then pay it off each month you could be hurting your credit.

Getting a credit card limit increase is easy. All you have to do is ask. You can pick up the phone, or you can even make your request online while you're logged in to your accounts.

## Managing Fees

Having good credit means you can save a lot of money in interest costs. Unfortunately, lenders sometimes find other ways to get into your pocket. As a result, you have to be vigilant and manage the fees that you pay.

### *"Waive" Goodbye*

Some credit card companies charge an annual fee just for the right to use their card. They also make a small percentage each time you purchase something on credit. Even if you pay your balances in full each month and avoid finance charges, you can still be a profitable customer. Therefore, there's no reason that you should have to pay annual fees. If you have halfway-decent credit, you need a really good reason to pay annual fees.

Remember that it costs at least twice as much to get a new customer than it does to keep an old one. Once credit card companies have a foot in the door with you, they have an incentive to keep you around. This means that you have some bargaining power, and you can walk away if you want. You should exercise this power, and ask your credit card company to waive any unreasonable fees that they charge you. Sometimes, you only have to call once, and they will waive your annual fees indefinitely.

If the company is unwilling to completely waive the fees, they may cover half of the cost or offer you something else. Therefore, it never hurts to call them and ask. You might not get exactly what you asked for, but you may get something else to sweeten the deal. You should ask them what it takes to get an annual fee waived—are there specific criteria that you need to meet as a customer?

### *Everybody Makes Mistakes*

Some fees act as penalties. The credit card company may smack you with a fee if you send your payment in late. Likewise, you may be assessed a fee if you charge more than your maximum allowable credit limit. Just like your annual fees, you may be able to get these fees waived. If you are a good customer and you don't often make the same mistake, then you have a decent chance of getting these fees reversed. Call your credit card issuer, state your case, and ask that the fee be reversed.

> Credit card companies occasionally waive your fees without you having to ask. However, you should certainly not count on that. Find a time when you have a few minutes to sit on hold, and call the credit card company. Explain that you're a good customer, and ask them what they can do for you.

## A Healthy Mix

To have the best credit scores, you should have a healthy mix of credit. This means that you should have a variety of accounts and use a variety of credit types: revolving credit, installment credit, and real estate credit. While the specifics are a mystery, some experts recommend having two to six revolving credit accounts, and two or three installment loans.

This may make you wonder whether or not you should pay off mortgage and auto loans. If you pay these loans off and they eventually disappear from your credit reports, you may lower your credit scores. What you actually do is up to you—you may philosophically believe that you should pay off your mortgage if you have the means to do so. According to the credit-reporting companies, paying off your mortgage will not hurt your credit, but it generally helps to have a mortgage.

# 19 Protecting Yourself from Identity Theft

It takes a lot of work to build up your good name. You do what it takes to make all of those payments on time. You build a healthy mix of credit accounts to show that you are a seasoned borrower. You manage your money wisely, and you protect yourself against the unknown. Improving your credit takes years. Unfortunately, it can be stolen and ruined in an instant. If you're not thinking about identity theft, it is time you did.

## What Happens with Identity Theft

Identity theft occurs when somebody uses your identity to commit crimes. An important distinction here is that that somebody is not actually you. They lead others to believe that they are you, so you get all of the blame and consequences. Unfortunately, there are no known cases where an identity thief has committed random acts of kindness and senseless acts of beauty and left the credit to his victim. Instead, they create a variety of problems in your name. Identity theft is a serious crime, usually involving some type of fraud.

### *Who Are You?*

Identity theft can get really complicated. The problem is that businesses, governments, and organizations don't really know who you are. They have never met you, and they could not put a face to your name. The reality of the world today is that computers keep track of things for us. There are just too many people out there; even if you are really good at remembering names, you can't remember them all.

An identity thief will take advantage of this. Even though they're not really you, they lead others to believe that they are. How do they do this? They use some distinct characteristics that are supposedly unique to you, and only you. Not surprisingly, the big ones are your name, address, date of birth, and Social Security Number. Think about it: these are the characteristics that organizations ask for whenever you apply for a driver's license, credit card, auto loan, bank account, or insurance.

If any organization that you do business with asks for your Social Security Number, see if they really need it. Some places allow you to use an alternative—they may assign you a unique customer ID, or allow you to choose one. The less you use your Social Security Number, the better.

Long, long ago, these characteristics must have held more meaning. Presumably, they were top-secret information that only you and your trustworthy business partners knew. Over time, people got lazy and began to use these characteristics more and more publicly. Colleges assigned Student ID numbers that happened to be the student's Social Security Number. Driver's licenses displayed Social Security Numbers, and Internet user names were often Social Security Numbers.

### *Where To Go from Here*

Granted, there is some wisdom in using Social Security Numbers. A consumer can hardly remember twenty different user IDs, but they often remember their Social Security Number. The problem is that the Social Security Number is at the top of the information hierarchy. There is nothing more unique about you than your Social Security Number; at least, there is nothing practical and widely affordable at the present time. Your DNA is substantially more unique, but it is hard for the customer-service representative on the other end of the line to verify this.

Don't be surprised to see increased use of fingerprints, retina scans, voice recognition, DNA testing, and a variety of other sophisticated tools in the future. These methods will certainly make it harder for identity thieves to claim that they are somebody else. However, criminals are notoriously pesky and creative. For years, Hollywood movies have shown ways that a creative person might circumvent these security measures. Whether or not criminals will use the same methods is unclear, but there is no doubt that they will find a way to beat the system.

### *I Am You*

In the meantime, identity theft is relatively easy. All a would-be thief needs to do is write your name, address, Social Security Number, and birthday on an application. They are now you, and because of this, they have all of the same rights and powers that you do. They can change your address, use your credit to open accounts, withdraw your money, and more. If you are starting to get nervous, that's good.

Some identity thieves assume your identity in every sense of the word. They're not just looking to steal some money from a credit card company. Instead, they want to live an entire life under your identity. These people may be in the country illegally—perhaps they just want a shot at the American dream, or perhaps they are terrorists. Some of these folks are hiding from the past. They may not want somebody to find them, like law-enforcement officials, for example. As a result, they live their life as you. They give your name and information to employers, but they usually "forget" to pay income taxes on your Social Security Number.

## A Standard Case

A typical identity-theft case is just a matter of stealing money. The identity thief is somebody who does not have as much money as they would like to have. Instead of getting a job, the identity thief turns to fraud. Once they have your personal information, they start using accounts in your name. Sometimes, identity thieves will open brand-new accounts. They contact credit card companies and open new accounts in your name. They might also frequent stores that offer instant credit. For example, they may buy clothes at a major department store, or they may buy furniture from a rent-to-own establishment.

Do I have to pay for charges made by a thief? In most cases, you will not be responsible for debts created by an identity thief. However, you have to report the crime in a timely fashion, and alert your creditors. You may not have to pay the charges, but you will spend a lot of time and energy cleaning up the mess.

Of course, the identity thief has no intention of paying the bills. The whole point of stealing somebody's identity is that the victim is left with the bill. Therefore, in a standard identity-theft case, the victim finds huge amounts of debt that he did not personally incur.

### *Here's a Nice Account*

Sometimes, identity thieves will attack your existing accounts. If they know (or have reason to believe) that you have a lot of assets, they may try to make withdrawals in your name. Your bank account and brokerage account would be prime targets. A common tactic is to change your address on your bank and brokerage accounts. That way, statements are no longer mailed to your house for your review. Then, the thief can take out as much money as he likes. You will not notice the transactions because the mail no longer comes to your house. In recent years, financial institutions have caught on to this. Most have added safeguards so that it is more difficult to pull this off. They send a letter to the old address and the new address stating that there has been an address change. If you ever get such a letter and you haven't moved lately, you should keep a close eye on your accounts for other signs of identity theft.

### *That Explains It!*

It can take a long time to detect an identity thief. In most cases, victims are not aware that their identity has been stolen until after the thief has racked up thousands of dollars and opened several accounts. In some cases, it goes on for years. You might go several years before you apply for a new auto loan or home loan, only to be turned down because of a poor credit history. If you are not aware that you have a poor credit history, you look into your credit reports and see a jumbled mix of accounts that are not yours. Then, you have to start the cleanup process.

## How Thieves Work and How to Stop Them

Identity theft comes about in a variety of ways. The common ingredient to all cases is the fact that a thief gets a hold of your personal identifying information. Once they have that, they're ready to strike. They may sit on your information for a while, waiting for you to drop your guard, and waiting for any short-term fraud alerts to expire. Once they have your information, they can use it for many years to come.

Personal information that can be used for identity theft is all over the place. Although you are not an aspiring criminal, you should know how they operate so that you can protect yourself. Identity thieves have several tricks of the trade that they use to get the information needed for identity theft.

### Dumpster Diving

A common way to get valuable personal information is a practice known as dumpster diving. As the name suggests, dumpster diving involves digging through dumpsters with the goal of finding discarded papers that contain important information. Unlike scuba diving, you don't have to travel to exotic places to be a dumpster diver. Major cities are full of them. A good dumpster diver can easily hit a hundred dumpsters in one day. If just a small percentage of consumers are careless enough to throw away important documents, the dumpster diver has a good day.

If you live in the suburbs, don't necessarily assume that you are safe. Dumpster divers might operate at a bank, doctor's office, or other institution with which you do business. Furthermore, dumpster divers can operate out of landfills and recycling facilities. It may not even be your fault—an employee may throw out a document with your information on it, and put you at risk.

To protect yourself from dumpster-diving identity thieves, you have to make sure that there is nothing there for them to find. The easiest way to do this is to shred any documents that have important personal information in them. If you don't already have one, buy yourself a cross-cut paper shredder. When in doubt about anything, shred it. If they can't read it, they cannot use it against you.

It is difficult to ensure that others who have your personal information are protecting it. Banks and other institutions can slip up, and all the shredding you've been doing might be for naught. Ask them if they have policies and procedures for protecting customer information. If they do not, consider working with somebody else.

## *Computer Hacking*

An increasingly common form of identity theft is a result of computer hacking. Thieves might gain access to your computer, or the computers of a company that you do business with. Once they are in, they can download anything they want. If the computer happens to belong to an organization, the personal information of hundreds, thousands, or even millions of consumers may be at risk. Computer hacking is the preferred method of obtaining valuable information. As you might imagine, it is much more glamorous than dumpster diving, and the working conditions are better. When computer hackers are most successful, they get information on a large number of potential victims. This increases the likelihood that they can find somebody who has assets and good credit.

Be sure to keep all of your computer software up to date in order to keep your personal information safe. Hackers and computer experts constantly discover vulnerabilities in popularly used software. Software manufacturers often provide free security updates to fix the vulnerabilities. If you don't update your software, you make it very easy on the hackers.

To protect yourself against computer hackers, you need to protect your computer. The easiest thing you can do is have a good antivirus program and keep it up to date. You should also check to see if a firewall will do you any good. Follow some commonsense computing rules: don't open attachments from unknown senders, avoid visiting Web sites that you don't need to visit, and keep all of your software up to date.

There are a lot of free software programs out there that help you protect your information. Search around consumer-privacy Web sites, and you will find some good ideas. You might start with the Gibson Research Corporation (*www.grc.com*). You can learn about some of the threats out there, and you can even run tests to see if your computer is at risk. Another useful program is Spybot Search and Destroy. This program checks for common spyware programs running on your computer. Spyware is a type of computer program that spies on you as you use your computer. These programs can allow all kinds of shady characters to learn more about you.

Old computers can also be a gold mine for identity thieves. Since computers constantly improve, you may buy a new one every few years. What happens to that old computer? If you donate it, sell it, or give it away, you need to be sure that any sensitive information is permanently deleted. Even if you delete everything, the data may still be on your computer's hard drive. To permanently wipe the data out, you should use a specialized software program designed for this purpose. As an alternative, you could reformat your hard drive before getting rid of the computer.

### *Going Phishing*

Another easy way to get information for identity theft is to use a tactic called phishing. Scammers contact you and claim to be employees of a reputable institution. They often use the names of banks and credit card companies with this strategy. For example, you may get an e-mail from somebody who claims to be an employee (or automated system) at Bank of America. The e-mail might say that they have had technical difficulties, or that something strange is going on with your account. Then, they ask you to verify your identity by sending all of your personal details: your full name, date of birth, Social Security Number, and so on. Of course, you divulge this information to an identity thief, not the bank. Much like computer hacking, phishing is fairly easy. Scammers can send thousands of e-mails just as easily as they can send one. Much like real fishing, they throw their bait out and see if anybody will bite.

> Identity thieves can use computer-hacking techniques to get your information. However, it is probably still much safer to do things online (such as pay bills with an online bill-pay service) as opposed to the old-fashioned way. Most transactions and computer systems are secure. However, systems that aren't secure make it really easy for the scammers.

To protect yourself from this type of scam, be extremely cautious about whom you talk to. If somebody calls you or e-mails you asking for sensitive information, be suspicious. If the request comes via e-mail, there's a 99.9-percent chance that it's a phishing scam. Most organizations will never call you or e-mail you and ask for personal details. If it ever happens, you can simply state that you'd like to call them back just to be safe. Then, call a number that you know is a legitimate phone number to that organization—don't call a phone number given to you by the person requesting your information.

### An Inside Job

Most of the methods described previously are fairly anonymous and involve thieves who have no idea who the victim is. Having your identity stolen by an unknown criminal is somewhat random, but it happens all of the time. Unfortunately, some victims of identity theft have a connection with the thief. Sometimes there is a close personal connection, and sometimes it's a business relationship.

Occasionally, you see a high-publicity case where an employee sells the information about his customers. A person at a bank or credit card company can easily get a hold of the personal details of a large number of consumers. If the employee is part of the wrong crowd, he may sell that information to somebody who plans to use it for identity theft. Unfortunately, one bad apple can do some serious damage to a bank's PR.

In order to access your credit report, some thieves pretend to have a permissible purpose for obtaining your credit information. They may pose as a landlord, potential employer, or financial institution as they request your reports. Once they have succeeded, they know about most of your accounts, they know your current and previous addresses, and they are ready to strike.

Sometimes the connection is even closer; family members have been known to steal each other's identity. It may be a troubled youth, or somebody in a tough financial situation. Either way, the victim feels especially violated in these cases. When the identity thief lives with the victim, it is more difficult to uncover the crime. The thief can easily intercept mail and cover his tracks.

It is difficult to prevent a dishonest insider from doing bad things. As a consumer, you are largely at the mercy of organizations that you deal with. The greatest power you have is the power to take your business elsewhere. If you suspect (or know) that an organization is not protecting your valuable information, go somewhere else. Unfortunately, they may already have information about you in their databases—the fact that your account is closed does not mean that your personal details have been deleted.

### Stolen Property

Identity theft also happens when valuable items are stolen or lost. Your purse or wallet may have all kinds of useful information for an identity thief. Your Social Security Number, birthday, address, and account numbers fall right into an identity thief's hands. Likewise, the thief may steal a laptop or computer hard drive that contains sensitive personal information about a group of people. Traveling salespeople, human-resource specialists, and consultants all have important information on their computers.

### Skimming

There are an unlimited number of ways that identity thieves operate. Most of the methods above involve impersonating a victim, and using their accounts. However, some thieves use a much simpler form of identity theft. All they need is a credit card number, and something to buy. They can get your credit card number in all the ways listed above. In addition, there are countless other creative ways to get valuable information. For example, the technique known as skimming allows criminals to capture your credit card number as you make purchases. There might be a hidden device attached to the machine, or the thief might have a small portable device he can use while he has your card.

## How to Detect a Thief

Identity thieves can wreak havoc on your life in a very short amount of time. Before you know it, they may have opened numerous accounts, siphoned money from existing accounts, and even declared bankruptcy in your name. While they operate quickly, there are steps you can take to detect identity theft in process. The sooner you catch it, the less damage you'll suffer.

### *Has Anything Changed?*

Keep an eye out for anything unusual. Once identity thieves start using your good name, a few subtle hints may pop up. For starters, you may find that you are no longer receiving bills, statements, or correspondence from financial institutions that you do business with. This could very well mean that an identity thief has changed your address so that you won't see what's going on in your accounts. Although it may be nice to stop getting bills from your credit card company, it's probably a bad sign.

Try to minimize the amount of sensitive personal information that you carry. It is too easy to lose or misplace something. If you have an option to keep your Social Security Number off your driver's license, exercise that option. Likewise, tell your service providers that you do not want to use your Social Security Number as a customer-ID number.

### *Read those Statements*

Another sign of identity theft is a series of unauthorized transactions on your accounts. This may mean that an identity thief has started using your account number to make purchases. They might be dipping into your checking account, or they may be racking-up debt on a credit card account. It is easy to give your statements a cursory glance and miss important details. Spend the extra minute it takes to look the statement over thoroughly. You might even want to check your accounts online, that way you can see transactions as they happen.

### *Interesting Phone Calls and Letters*

There's nothing out of the ordinary about somebody dialing the wrong number—you probably do it on occasion yourself. However, make a mental note every time a financial institution calls you and it seems to be in error. In particular, you should be alert to claims that you have unpaid debts. It could be that an identity thief has racked-up bills in your name and refused to pay them, and now the collectors are calling. The same thing goes for letters about unpaid debts. You should investigate these immediately, and resolve the situation.

### *Application Denied*

If you are ever denied for credit, insurance, or employment, it could be because an identity thief is ruining your credit. Anytime you are denied something based on your credit, you should receive a disclosure explaining that this happened. In addition, you're entitled to view your credit report. Especially if you are surprised to hear that you've been denied, take a close look at your credit reports for any signs of identity theft.

Federal laws require that you be notified whenever you are denied credit, a job, or insurance because of information in your credit reports. You will receive a disclosure stating that somebody took adverse action against you. When this happens, you are entitled to view your credit reports for free.

### *Lots of Inquiring Minds*

As you review your credit reports periodically, pay close attention to the section on inquiries. This section has the early warning signs that can help you stop identity theft. If financial institutions, employers, and landlords are making inquiries that don't make any sense to you, it could be that they are inquiring for somebody other than the real you. This may mean that somebody is trying to open accounts in your name or otherwise assume your identity. If an inquiry does not make sense to you, find out more. Your credit report should have contact information for anybody making inquiries into your credit.

### *Not My Account*

In addition to the inquiry section of your credit report, you should review the accounts section for signs of identity theft. If you see accounts in there that you don't remember opening, it could be that an identity thief opened that account for you. Don't assume it's just an error on the part of the credit-reporting companies. Even if it's an error, it's important that you fix it. If it's not an error, and it is in fact identity theft, the situation is even more urgent.

## If You've Been Robbed

In an ideal world, the techniques described above will keep you safe. By following these techniques, it will be hard for identity thieves to steal your identity. Like most creatures, identity thieves choose the path of least resistance; therefore, hopefully they will leave you alone. Identity thieves will tend to steal identities that are easy to steal, and there are millions of other consumers out there who take no precautions whatsoever with their identity. Until the public better understands the severity of identity theft, that's probably how things will go. Nevertheless, you can still have your identity stolen, no matter how cautious you are.

Ingenious scammers and careless business partners can make your worst nightmare come true.

### *Fraud Alert*

If you find yourself in this unfortunate situation, you need to act fast. The faster you shut everything down, the easier your life will be in the clean-up process. One of the first things you should do is place a fraud alert on your credit reports. To do this, you simply contact one of the three major credit reporting companies—Equifax, TransUnion, or Experian. The company you contact is supposed to forward the alert to the other two companies. However, there's no harm in contacting them yourself to request a fraud alert, just to be safe. The credit-reporting company will require documentation from you to make sure you are who you say you are. Once the fraud alert is created, you should receive free copies of your credit reports.

There are two types of fraud alerts. One of them lasts for ninety days, and the other one lasts for seven years. If you have been the victim of identity theft, the seven-year fraud alert is probably your best bet. Keep in mind that while the fraud alert is active, lenders are not supposed to open new credit accounts in your name without contacting you first. If you actually want to open a new credit account, the process might go slowly. Lenders will proceed with caution, and they'll have to contact you (the real you, as defined in the fraud alert) before lending any money. As a result, you should make it as easy as possible for them to get a hold of you. If you have a cellular phone, include that number when applying for new accounts.

Will creating a fraud alert protect me from identity theft? The actual value of a fraud alert is up for debate. Whether or not it will prevent an identity thief from opening new accounts in your name is unclear. However, it is certainly better than doing nothing. Responsible lenders will do their part to help fight fraud, especially since it will affect them as well.

### Freeze Them Out

A much stronger tactic you might use is to ask for a security freeze. A security freeze blocks all access to your credit reports until you remove the freeze. This is much more dramatic than merely placing a fraud alert on your reports, and it will certainly prevent identity thieves from opening new accounts in your name. Note that a security freeze may not be available in your state—only a handful of states allow them at the present time.

### Close Affected Accounts

Next, you should close any accounts that have been affected by the identity thief. These may be accounts that you opened, or they might be accounts that the identity thief opened in your name. You can find all of these accounts on your credit reports, complete with contact information for the institution that holds the account. Call these companies and ask what the procedure is to formally report that you've been a victim of identity theft, and let them know that one of their accounts was involved. Most often, they have a special department for fraud control. If the representative you speak with sounds a bit unsure of things, ask for the fraud department.

Think carefully before you add a fraud alert to, or place a freeze on, your credit reports. Doing so can make it extremely difficult to get credit. If you are hoping to buy a house, for example, things may slow down dramatically, and you might miss out on buying your dream home.

You'll most likely have to submit written documentation of the identity theft. Even if they say that a phone call is sufficient, you should follow up in writing as a safeguard. As with every other letter you send that has anything to do with correcting errors on your credit report, you should send the letter by certified mail, return receipt requested. They may have a special form that they want you to use, and they may require copies of official documents, such as a police report. The Federal Trade Commission (FTC) has a model Identity Theft Affidavit that you can use with your creditors. This affidavit is available at *www.consumer.gov/idtheft.*

Once you are successful in closing the accounts affected by identity theft, ask for written documentation from the credit provider stating that the account was closed in good order. If the identity thief opened new accounts in your name, be sure to get written documentation from the creditor acknowledging that it was a fraudulent account from the beginning.

### *Alerting the Authorities*

Identity theft is a serious crime. It involves both theft and fraud, and it can make your life miserable. Therefore, you should report occurrences of identity theft to the authorities. First, file a police report with your local law-enforcement agency. Let them know that you've had your identity stolen, and provide documentation, including information on accounts affected by the theft. You should also try to file a report in the jurisdiction where the identity thief lives, if you have that information.

You should also inform the FTC that you are a victim of identity theft. While the FTC does not necessarily follow up on your case, they do keep records of identity-theft cases nationally. With enough information, the FTC and other regulators can better fight identity theft.

# 20 Building Your Investment Portfolio

Whether you're working with a financial advisor or a brokerage firm, you're at the wheel of your own investment vehicle. You decide the pace at which you head into the investment world, and you determine how much risk you're willing to take in order to win. However, you're responsible for more than just making investment decisions. You'll also have to do independent research. That includes due diligence on companies where you're considering parking some of your investment dollars, as well as portfolio tracking and performance monitoring to keep your investment portfolio chugging along in the right direction.

## Investment Cornerstones

Having all the ingredients for success is a good start, but you won't get too far without the recipe. If you take all the ingredients for a delicious pastry and throw them together in equal parts, you'll end up with an inedible brick. Developing the art of measuring and mixing your ingredients so that they work together to create investment perfection requires patience and diligence on your part. You need to figure out the delicate balance that will provide the most effective and productive investment portfolio for your needs.

Most investment portfolios are comprised of five or so components. Usually, they include some combination of the following: liquid assets (cash and equivalents), fixed income (bonds and annuities), equities (stocks), real estate, precious metals, and other investments.

Figuring out which stocks and bonds will comprise your portfolio isn't a difficult process, as long as you apply the tried-and-true investment tenets: knowing your risk levels, having a fixed time horizon, using some form of investment diversification, and having fixed investment goals (such as retirement, college tuition, or starting your own business). Two of the more important factors in your portfolio decision-making process are risk and diversification. Read on to learn more about these factors.

## Why Good Poker Players Make Good Investors

"Every serious choice that a man or a woman makes is a leap, more or less frightening, into contingency. Not to make those choices, not to open oneself to misfortune and the fear of misfortune, is a tempting choice, but one gives into it at the risk of never living a fully human life," says Nelson Aldrich, multimillionaire investor and author of the best-selling book *Old Money*. Aldrich is simply stating what is already obvious to legions of risk-loving Americans. Risk is at the core of many favorite pastimes, like betting on poker, and it's what makes those pastimes so appealing to participants.

PartyPoker.com, the world's largest online poker Web site, hosts more than 35,000 simultaneous players during its peak traffic time every day. That is no insignificant achievement, especially considering the site only launched in August of 2001. With the incredible upsurge in poker popularity around the world, greatly driven by televised poker tournaments, poker has undergone a renaissance of sorts, with bricks-and-mortar poker rooms experiencing a 40-percent increase from 2003 to 2004. Online gaming has jumped a whopping 500–600 percent during the same time period.

But even those numbers pale in comparison to the amounts of money pouring into Wall Street these days. According to the Investment Company Institute, mutual fund investors alone account for $7 trillion worth of assets through mid-2004. The New York Stock Exchange's "Shareownership 2000" survey estimated that there were 84 million direct and indirect U.S. shareholders in 2000, representing 43.6 percent of the country's adult population. That figure was up 21 percent from 1995's 69.3 million and up 61 percent from 1989's 52.3 million.

Risk is the reason that those who excel at poker are usually those who excel on Wall Street. Each industry rewards those participants who take matters very seriously and understand risk, just as they understand preparation, discipline, and opportunity. Good poker players, like good investors, also understand human emotion, and they leverage that information to separate other people from their money.

Consider the legendary financier Jay Gould, who made a fortune in the railroad industry and was a dominating force on Wall Street during the latter half of the nineteenth century. Gould was so good at separating people from their money that he earned the moniker "The Devil of Wall Street." Once, when Gould was attending his local church service on Monday, the minister pulled Gould aside and asked him how to invest a $30,000 windfall that had fallen into the congregation's lap. Gould advised the minister to invest the entire sum in shares of Missouri Pacific Railroad. The minister did so and watched happily for a short spell as the stock rose. But after awhile the stock slid precipitously, finally falling below fifty cents per share. The minister, distraught over losing virtually all of the $30,000, poured his woes out to Gould, who snapped open his checkbook and covered the entire loss with one sweep of his pen. Then the minister confessed that despite Gould's request to the contrary, he had passed the stock tip along to other members of the congregation. "Oh, I guessed that," Gould replied merrily. "As a matter of fact, they were the ones I was after."

Gould knew, like good poker players know, that there is little in the investment world that is more delicate and more personal than the trade-off between risk and reward. The more uncertain the investment, the greater the investment risk. The greater the investment risk, the greater the opportunity for hefty investment returns. If you're uncomfortable with too much risk and seek to minimize it, you'll be penalized with lower investment returns. You can't completely eliminate risk. If you don't take any risk, you surely won't make any money.

Investment risk is tied to market volatility—the fluctuations in the financial markets that happen constantly over time. The sources of this volatility are many. Interest-rate changes, inflation, political consequences, and economic trends can all create combustible market conditions with the power to change a portfolio's performance results in a hurry. Ironically, this volatility, by its very nature, creates the opportunities for economic benefit in our own portfolios.

## What's Your Tolerance for Risk?

Your comfort level as an investor depends on many factors, including your age, financial needs, number of dependents, and level of debt. If you're twenty-five years old, single, childless, and debt-free, you obviously have far more tolerance for risk than a fifty-five-year-old nearing retirement with two kids in college.

Trying to pin down your tolerance for risk is an uncertain process that's forever susceptible to second-guessing. You can never be quite sure what your tolerance for risk will be from year to year. But the following test, developed by Lincoln Benefit Life, a subsidiary of Allstate Life Group, can help clear things up. Simply choose an answer from the choices given for each question and assess your results at the end.

1. If someone made me an offer to invest 15 percent of my net worth in a deal he said had an 80 percent chance of being profitable, I'd say:

   A. No level of profit would be worth that kind of risk.
   B. The level of profit would have to be seven times the amount I invested.
   C. The level of profit would have to be three times the amount I invested.
   D. The level of profit would have to be at least as much as my original investment.

2. How comfortable would I be assuming a $10,000 debt in the hope of achieving a $20,000 gain over the next few months?

   A. Totally uncomfortable. I'd never do it.
   B. Somewhat uncomfortable. I'd probably never do it.
   C. Somewhat uncomfortable. But I might do it.
   D. Very comfortable. I'd definitely do it.

3. I am holding a lottery ticket that's gotten me to the finals, where I have a 1-in-4 chance of winning the $100,000 jackpot. I'd be willing to sell my ticket before the drawing, but for nothing less than:

   A. $15,000
   B. $20,000
   C. $35,000
   D. $60,000

4. How often do I bet more than $150 on one or more of these activities: professional sports gambling, casino gambling, or lottery tickets?

   A. Never.
   B. Only a few times in my life.
   C. Just in one of these activities in the past year.
   D. In two or more of these activities in the past year.

**5.** If a stock I bought doubled in the year after I bought it, I'd:

A. Sell all my shares.
B. Sell half my shares.
C. Not sell any shares.
D. Buy more shares.

**6.** I have a high-yielding certificate of deposit that is about to mature, and interest rates have dropped so much that I feel compelled to invest in something with a higher yield. The most likely place I'd invest the money is:

A. U.S. savings bonds.
B. A short-term bond fund.
C. A long-term bond fund.
D. A stock fund.

**7.** Whenever I have to decide where to invest a large amount of money, I:

A. Delay the decision.
B. Get someone else, like my broker, to decide for me.
C. Share the decision with my advisors.
D. Decide on my own.

**8.** Which of the following describes how I make my investment decisions?

A. Never on my own.
B. Sometimes on my own.
C. Often on my own.
D. Totally on my own.

**9.** My luck in investing is:

A. Terrible.
B. Average.
C. Better than average.
D. Fantastic.

**10.** My investments are successful mainly because:

A. Fate is always on my side.
B. I was in the right place at the right time.
C. When opportunities arose, I took advantage of them.
D. I carefully planned them to work out that way.

Give yourself one point for each answer **A**, two points for each answer **B**, three points for each answer **C**, and four points for each answer **D**.

If you scored nineteen points or fewer, you're a conservative investor who feels uncomfortable taking risks. You probably realize that you will have to take some calculated risks to attain your financial goals, but this doesn't mean you will be comfortable doing so.

If you scored twenty to twenty-nine points, you're a moderate investor who feels comfortable taking moderate risks. You are probably willing to take reasonable risks without a great deal of discomfort.

If you scored thirty or more points, you're an aggressive investor who is willing to take high risks in search of high returns. You are not greatly stressed by taking significant risks.

Typical behavior indicates that most investors either don't understand risk or choose to ignore it. Here's how we know. When the market is rising, money floods into stocks and mutual funds, even as each upward move in price increases risk and reduces potential returns. In a bear market, many investors engage in near-panic selling, even though each drop in price decreases risk and increases potential returns. For most investors, the two most effective ways to manage risk are to limit your aggressive exposure to a small part of the whole portfolio and to stick with your program once you have embarked on it.

## Different Types of Risk

There are many different types of risk, and some are more complicated than others. The risk classifications you'll learn about here are the primary forms of risk, which aren't as complex as some. You'll likely run into some of the following five risking categories when investing in your separate account plan.

There are a lot of details that go along with determining risk. But one of the biggest mistakes an investor can make is to sell the impact of investment risk short—whether the investment is in a separate account or not. Spend some time thinking about your tolerance for risk, and then invest accordingly. If you're working with a personal financial advisor, make sure you discuss risk before deciding on the securities that will comprise your separate account portfolio. And never underestimate the power of an exit plan. When you're prepared to react to a drastic change in the markets, your portfolio will have a fighting chance at self preservation.

### Stock Specific Risk

Any single stock carries a specific amount of risk for the investor. You can minimize this risk by making sure your portfolio is diversified. An investor dabbling in one or two stocks can see his investment wiped out; although it is still possible, the chances of that happening in a well-diversified portfolio are much more slender. (One example would be the event of an overall bear market, as was seen in the early 1990s.) By adding a component of trend analysis to your decision-making process, and by keeping an eye on the big picture (global economics and politics, for example), you are better equipped to prevent the kinds of devastating losses that come with an unexpected sharp turn in the markets.

### Risk of Passivity and Inflation Rate Risk

People who don't trust the financial markets and who feel more comfortable sticking their money in a bank savings account could end up with less than they expect. Because the interest rates on savings accounts cannot keep up with the rate of inflation, they decrease the purchasing power of your investment at the same time—even as they preserve your core investing principle of avoiding risk. For this somewhat paradoxical reason, savings accounts may not always be your safest choice. You may want to consider investments with at least slightly higher returns (like inflation-indexed U.S. Treasury bonds) to help you combat inflation without giving up your sense of security.

A close relative of passivity risk, inflation risk is based upon the expectation of lower purchasing power of each dollar down the road. Typically, stocks are the best investment when you're interested in outpacing inflation, and money-market funds are the least effective in combating inflation.

### Market Risk

Market risk is pretty much what it sounds like. Every time you invest money in the financial markets, even via a conservative money-market mutual fund, you're subjecting your money to the risk that the markets will decline or even crash. With market risk, uncertainty due to changes in the overall stock market is caused by global, political, social, or economic events and even by the mood of the investing public. Perhaps the biggest investment risk of all, though, is not subjecting your money to market risk. If you don't put your money to work in the stock market, you won't be able to benefit from the stock market's growth over the years.

### Credit Risk

Usually associated with bond investments, credit risk is the possibility that a company, agency, or municipality might not be able to make interest or principal payments on its notes or bonds. The greatest risk of default usually lies with corporate debt: Companies go out of business all the time. On the flip side, there's virtually no credit risk associated with U.S. Treasury-related securities, because they're backed by the full faith and credit of the U.S. government. To measure the financial health of bonds, credit rating agencies like Moody's and Standard & Poor's assign them investment grades. Bonds with an A rating are considered solid, while C-rated bonds are considered unstable.

### *Currency Risk*

Although most commonly considered in international or emerging-market investing, currency risk can occur in any market at any time. This risk comes about due to currency fluctuations that may affect the value of foreign investments or profits, or the holdings of U.S. companies with interests overseas. Currency risk necessarily increases in times of geopolitical instability, like those caused by the global threat of terrorism or war.

### *Interest Rate Risk*

When bond interest rates rise, the price of the bonds falls (and vice versa). Fluctuating interest rates have a significant impact on stocks and bonds. Typically, the longer the maturity of the bond, the larger the impact of interest rate risk. But long-term bonds normally pay out higher yields to compensate for the greater risk.

### *Economic Risk*

When the economy slows, corporate profits—and thus stocks—could be hurt. For example, political instability in the Middle East makes investing there a dicey deal at best. This is true even though much of the region is flush with oil, arguably the commodity in greatest demand all over the planet.

## Diversification

Diversification simply means dividing your investments among a variety of types. It's one of the best ways, if not the absolute best, to protect your portfolio from the pendulum swings of the economy and the financial markets. Since a separate account portfolio may invest in many different securities, a decline in the value of one security may be offset by the rise in value of another.

Diversification can take other forms as well. For example, you could diversify your common stock holdings by purchasing stocks representing many different industries. That would be safer than concentrating in a single sector. Or you could diversify your bond holdings by buying a mixture of high-quality bonds and some lower-rated bonds. The high-quality bonds would tend to reduce the overall risk associated with the bond portfolio.

No matter how diversified your portfolio, you can never completely eliminate risk. You can *reduce* the risk associated with individual stocks, but general market risks affect nearly every stock, so it is important to also diversify among different assets. The key is to find a medium between risk and return; this ensures that you achieve your financial goals while still getting a good night's rest.

Another important form of diversification is obtained when you invest in different types of securities—stocks, bonds, real estate, and money market instruments, to name the major investment types. Diversifying your holdings over several asset classes, particularly among those that tend to perform differently under the same economic circumstances, adds an extra layer of protection to your portfolio.

## Understanding Asset Allocation

Investors often find the concept of asset allocation confusing or intimidating when they're initially structuring their portfolios. But it's actually quite simple. Asset allocation is nothing more than determining where your investment capital should be placed. This determination is based on variables like net worth, time frame, risk acceptance, and other assets the investor owns. Generally, properly allocating your investment dollars means assembling a portfolio from the three major asset categories: cash, fixed income, and equities. Cash includes money in the bank, short-term investments such as U.S. Treasury bills, and money market mutual funds. Fixed-income investments include bonds, guaranteed investment certificates, and other interest-generating securities. Equities are stock market investments. Equities can be further subdivided into more specific categories, such as value and growth.

Anywhere on Wall Street, the goal of asset allocation is to achieve the best possible return while reducing the risk. But how do you determine what the best performing sectors are and what your asset allocation mix should be? Here are some good questions to ask yourself to determine your investor profile:

1. Do market fluctuations keep you awake at night?
2. Are you unfamiliar with investing?
3. Do you consider yourself more a saver than an investor?
4. Are you fearful of losing 25 percent of your assets in a few days or weeks?
5. Are you comfortable with the ups and downs of the securities markets?
6. Are you knowledgeable about investing and the securities markets?
7. Are you investing for a long-term goal?
8. Can you withstand considerable short-term losses?

If you answered yes to the first four questions, you are most likely a conservative investor. If you answered yes to the last four questions, you are more likely an aggressive investor. If you fall somewhere in between, you could call yourself a moderate investor.

It is a tricky business to achieve the right mix of stock types (small, mid, and large caps, as well as internationals) and bonds (short, medium, and long-term) for maximum return on your volatility tolerance while also maintaining adequate diversification. Even a lot of brokers and fund managers get it wrong. For that reason, considering whether to consult a qualified financial planner or advisor should be at the top of your investment to-do list.

Many financial advisors say, quite sensibly, that your asset allocation plan depends on where you are in life. If you're just starting out, a long-term strategy that emphasizes stocks is advised. This strategy tends to emphasize growth to build assets by investing in more aggressive stocks. In order to moderate risk, it may also include a commitment to income investments, such as bonds. An example of a portfolio that employs a long-term strategy may include 70 percent equities, 25 percent bonds, and 5 percent short-term instruments or cash.

If you're nearing or are in retirement, advisors often advocate a short-term strategy that relies more heavily on bonds to place more emphasis on capital preservation. This strategy is designed to emphasize current income, capital preservation, and liquidity, while maintaining a smaller portion of the portfolio in stocks for growth potential. An example of a portfolio that employs a short-term strategy may include 50 percent bonds, 20 percent equities, and 30 percent short-term instruments or cash.

When establishing an asset allocation strategy, there are a few things you should do. For one, determine how long you'll be investing. Then decide how much risk you can take. Next, pick a target mix that's right for you, and select investments that will help you achieve that mix. Finally, adjust your investments gradually. Start with your future deferrals to match your asset mix, and gradually redirect existing balances to fit into your overall plan.

There are two primary ways of allocating assets. The first method is to use a stable policy over time. Based on your income needs and risk tolerance, you might pursue a balanced strategy. This might require putting 25 percent of your dollars in each class of assets, such as stocks, bonds, cash, and real estate. Then, each quarter or year, you rebalance those dollars back to your original allocation of 25 percent in each class. This forces you to sell off some of the best-performing assets while buying more of the weakest performers. This allocation system eliminates the need to make decisions on the expected return for each class and instead allows for more stable returns over long periods of time.

The second means of allocating assets is through an active strategy. With this method, you first determine your tolerance for risk and your long-term goals. Then you allocate the range of your total portfolio you will invest in each class. Thus, if you need a good mix of growth and income, you might allow your investment in stocks to range from 35 percent to 65 percent of your portfolio, based on the market. You would develop these ranges for each asset class.

An active strategy involves making a prediction of where you expect each class of asset to go. If you believe we are in a fast-growing equities market, for example, you would put the maximum amount of dollars into common stocks or common stock mutual funds. Therefore, you would be lowering the amount of dollars invested in other asset classes. Likewise, if you believe that we are in a period of great risk for the markets, you would put more dollars into cash as a means of protecting your portfolio.

Obviously, an active strategy requires a lot of homework and a good knowledge of the financial markets and what impacts them. You'll have to track your investments at least weekly and adjust your holdings based on your revised expectations—as well as on their actual performance. You'll also have to take into account greater market forces and trends, changes in the global political and economic scene, even seasonal differences in sector performance as you examine your holdings, deciding which to hold on to and which to cut loose. It is a higher-risk strategy. If you make the wrong choices, you put your portfolio at a greater risk than if you had pursued a stable strategy. But if you consistently make the right calls (an outcome that becomes more frequent as you gain experience and insight), you can make substantially higher returns.

Organizing your asset allocation campaign is a fairly straightforward process, once you get the hang of it.

## Investor Profile

Managing your own expectations is a big part of your investment planning process. You've probably heard about buy-and-hold investing and why it doesn't really matter what the market's doing when you get in, as long as you stay in. There's a great deal of truth in that line of thinking. Studies show that stocks can grow (on average) up to 10 to 12 percent annually, and bonds can grow at a rate of up to 6 to 8 percent per year, for longer term U.S. Treasury instruments. Combined with the miracle of compound interest (your accumulated investment returns rolled over year after year), a long-term outlook coupled with a solid, disciplined investment strategy can yield big bucks over twenty, thirty, and especially forty-plus years.

The trick is in staying in the markets and not missing its sharp upturns. People who engage in market timing—market timers, those Wall Street daredevils who try to get in and out of the stock market at the most optimal moments—risk missing those market spikes by weaving in and out of the financial markets. And that's money that's hard to make back.

Market timing in funds used to be viewed as a nuisance, an arcane practice by a handful of cunning investors. But timing is now under the microscope of regulators in Massachusetts and New York, who say the practice is unfair to individual investors—and illegal, in some cases.

Market timers also generally experience higher transaction costs compared to a buy-and-hold strategy. Every time an investor sells or buys securities, a transaction fee is incurred. Even if the market timer achieves above-average returns, the transaction costs could negate the superior performance. Plus, trying to time the market can create additional risk. Take the time period from 1962 to 1991. An investor who bought common stocks in 1962 would have realized a return of 10.3 percent with a buy-and-hold strategy. If that same investor tried to time the market and missed just twelve of the best-performing months (out of a total of 348 months), the return would have been only 5.4 percent. There's a flip side to this theory, it must be admitted. If the investor had jumped out of the market during its worst periods (like the 1987 crash and several subsequent bear markets), the returns would have been even higher.

One additional negative aspect of using market-timing techniques is tax reporting complications. Going in and out of the market several times in one tax year (sometimes several times in a month) generates numerous taxable gain and loss transactions, all of which must be accounted for on your income tax return.

# 21 All About Stocks

It's time to become familiar with the different types of stocks available and what they can mean for your portfolio. The stocks of companies that have stood the test of time are always in great demand. Finding these companies poses the real challenge to investors. Traders, on the other hand, take a more active approach to investing, placing as much or more emphasis on stock price movement than on the solidity of the company. Regardless of which strategy or combination of tactics you apply to your holdings, the same underlying rule applies. Know what and why you're buying (or selling) before you make any trade.

## Buy What You Know

One of the side benefits of being a consumer is that you are constantly exposed to products and services that you are probably evaluating every day. This exposure breeds a level of familiarity that takes a lot of the anxiety out of picking stocks. It also gives you valuable insight about honing in on a specific company. Did you recently try out a new gadget at an electronics show that you found intriguing? Have you come across a certain brand of car wax that does wonders for your vehicle's finish? These are experiences you can put to work when you're making your investment decisions.

In addition to your own experiences, observations are another way to gain valuable insight. During your recent trip to Japan, did you notice people consuming huge quantities of a new Coca-Cola product? While waiting to pay for dinner at the local restaurant, did many of the patrons pull out American Express cards? Part of doing your homework as an investor is noticing the companies whose products and services are prominently displayed.

Putting serious thought into your investments early on will most likely pay off in the long run. Unfortunately, many people are introduced to the world of investing through a hot stock tip from their barber, buddy, or bellman. There's really no way to make an easy buck, and by jumping into a stock because of a random tip, you'll probably end up losing income. Remember: The idea of an easy buck in the stock market is a mere fantasy.

You need to understand the difference between investing and trading. Investing is a proposition for the long term, where you buy stocks for income and growth. Trading is a much more active practice in which today's price—and what you hope it will hit tomorrow—is the number to follow. Investing can help you reach long-term goals; trading is much more immediate and much more risky. Buying stock as a means to purchase a house or to attend college within a year's time is also not advisable. Holding quality stocks for long periods of time, as in a *minimum* of five years, is the recommended course. This provides you enough time to ride out any bear markets (the term used to describe the market when it is down) or other downturns that might come about. Could your investments be in a down period right at the time you need to sell? Yes. But with a longer time frame, you're less likely to end up with an overall loss. When it comes to investing in stocks, patience is a virtue, and staying in the market for the long term has proven to be the most successful way to invest.

No matter what type of stock fits your strategy, it's important that you have some just-in-case emergency money set aside (preferably enough to cover expenses for six months) in a risk-free investment. Even the most prestigious blue-chip stocks come with inherent risks. After you've set aside an emergency fund and have reached the conclusion that you are not entirely adverse to risk taking, you can devise your own personal investment strategy.

If you had purchased 200 shares of General Electric at the end of June, 1995, for $5,640, your investment would have been worth more than $20,000 by July of 2002. General Electric is a fairly stable stock; other companies, especially smaller, less-established companies, can fluctuate significantly more in the short term.

The earlier in life you start investing, the longer you can keep your money in the market. Although past performance is no guarantee of the future, history shows that time will probably work in your favor when it comes to investing. Most analysts agree on this one universal truth: Market fluctuations, appearing in varying degrees, are inevitable, and are merely part of the entire investing process. As with most things in life, no ride is completely smooth.

## Stock Basics

Purchasing shares of stock is a lot like buying a business. That's the way Warren Buffett, one of the world's most successful investors, views it—and his philosophy is certainly worth noting. When you buy stock, you're actually buying a portion of a corporation. If you wouldn't want to own the entire company, you should think twice before you consider buying even a piece of it. If you think of investing in these terms, you'll probably be a lot more cautious when singling out a specific company.

It's important to become acquainted with all of the details of the company you're considering. What products and services does the company offer? Which part of the business accounts for the greatest revenue? Which part of the business accounts for the least revenue? Is the company too diversified? Who are its competitors? Is there a demand for the company's offerings? Is the company an industry leader? Are any mergers and acquisitions in the works? Until you understand exactly what the company does and how well it does it, it would be wise to postpone your investment decision.

Let's say you want to buy a convenience store in your hometown. You've reviewed such factors as inventory, the quality of the company's employees, and customer service programs. In addition to selling staple grocery items, the company also rents videos and operates a gas pump. The grocery side of the business may only account for a small percentage of the overall revenue. It would be in your best interest to value each part of the business separately in order to get a complete and accurate picture of the company's profit potential. Many companies may have traditionally been associated with a specific business, yet that same company may have expanded into totally new venues.

The Altria Group, formerly known as Philip Morris, is commonly associated with tobacco products though it has many other holdings as well. The company also profits from food and beer subsidiaries, including 84 percent of Kraft (featuring popular brands like Jell-O, Oscar Mayer, and Post) and 36 percent of SABMiller Brewing (home of Miller beers).

Disney, for example, has historically been associated with the Disneyland and Disney World theme parks. The reality is that Disney is also involved in a host of other ventures. Among other things, the multifaceted company also has interests in television and movie production, including Touchstone Pictures and Buena Vista Home Entertainment. Disney's ABC, Inc., division includes the ABC television network, as well as numerous television stations and shares in various cable channels like ESPN.

As with any other career, making money through investing requires work. The more research and thought you put into your strategy, the more likely you are to reap rewards. Although there are no guarantees in the world of investing, the odds will be more in your favor if you make educated and well-informed investment decisions. When you make an investment, you are putting your money into a public company, which allows you—as part of the public—to become an owner or to have equity in the company. That's why stocks are often referred to as equities.

## Types of Stocks

Common stocks are securities, sold to the public, that constitute ownership in a corporation. They come in all sizes. You can invest in a mega-company or a micro-cap company that has just begun to soar. While some individuals prefer to invest in well-established companies, other investors prefer investing in smaller, growth-oriented companies.

No matter what type of company fits in with your overall strategy, it's important to research every potential stock you buy. Just because a company has been around for decades doesn't mean it's the best investment vehicle for you. Furthermore, companies are always changing, and it's important to make sure that the information you are reviewing is current. Mergers and acquisitions have practically become commonplace. It's essential to know if a company you are considering buying is undergoing, or is planning to undergo, such a transaction.

What is an SPDR? Nicknamed "spiders," Standard & Poor's Depositary Receipts are a relatively new type of investment called exchange-traded funds (a single investment holding several securities, like a mutual fund, that trades in real-time, like a stock). SPDRs are traded on the American Stock Exchange under the ticker symbol SPY. They track the S&P 500, and trade at 1/10 of its value. Dividends are paid to owners of SPDRs every quarter.

It's also a good idea to research a company's market capitalization. The market value of all outstanding shares of a particular stock is synonymous with its market capitalization (or cap). Market capitalization is calculated by multiplying the market price by the number of outstanding shares. The number of outstanding shares refers to the number of shares that have been sold and that now are therefore shares outstanding. Larger companies usually have a lot more outstanding shares than their smaller counterparts. Shares that are issued are outstanding until they are redeemed, reacquired, converted, or canceled.

A public company with 20 million shares outstanding that trade at $40 each would have a market capitalization of $800 million. Although there are no concrete rules to categorize stocks, they can be differentiated as follows:

- **Large cap:** $5 billion and over
- **Mid cap:** Between $1 billion and $5 billion
- **Small cap:** Between $300 million and $1 billion
- **Micro cap**: Below $300 million

There are also different categories of stock to suit almost every personality. The variety includes blue chip, growth, small cap, large cap, cyclical, defensive, value, income, and speculative stocks, and socially responsible investments (SRI).

## Blue Chip and Growth Stocks

Blue chip are considered to be the most prestigious, well-established companies that are publicly traded, many of which have practically become household names. Included in this mostly large-cap mix are IBM (which trades on the NYSE under the acronym IBM), Disney (NYSE: DIS), and Coca-Cola (NYSE: KO). A good number of blue-chip companies have been in existence for more than twenty-five years and are still leading the pack in their respective industries. Since most of these organizations have a solid track record, they are good investment vehicles for individuals leaning to the conservative side in their stock picks.

Morgan Stanley created a new way to invest in blue chips called Blue Chip Baskets. Basically, instead of using your money to buy one or two stocks, you buy one share of a basket that includes tiny portions of stock in several blue chip companies. For example, a $50 basket may include 1/10 of a share of Microsoft, 1/5 of a share of Disney, 1/8 of a share of Coca-Cola, and so on. This allows you to spread out your investments without having to choose the specific companies.

As the name suggests, growth stocks comprise companies that have strong growth potential. Many companies in this category have sales, earnings, and market share that are growing faster than the overall economy. Such stocks usually represent companies that are big on research and development; for example, pioneers in new technology are often growth stock companies. Earnings in these companies are usually put right back into the business.

Growth stocks may be riskier than their blue-chip counterparts, but in many cases you can also reap greater rewards. In recent years, growth stocks have outperformed value stocks (defined later in this section), though that has not been the case at times in the past, and the trend may well turn around in the future. A word of caution: Beware of stocks whose price seems to be growing faster than would make sense. Sometimes momentum traders will help run growth stock prices to sky-scraping levels, then sell them off causing the stock to plummet.

## Small-Cap and Large-Cap Stocks

The small-cap stock category comprises many of the small, emerging companies that have survived their initial growing pains and are now enjoying strong earning gains, along with expanding sales and profits. Today's small-cap stock may be tomorrow's leader—it can also be tomorrow's loser. Overall, such stocks tend to be very volatile and risky. A safer way of adding these to your portfolio can be through a professionally managed small-cap fund. That way, you'll have exposure to potentially explosive profits without the added risk of investing in a particular company.

Large-cap stocks are a broad subset of the stock market. Generally considered integral to an investor's diversified portfolio, they tend to have fairly similar characteristics and so are grouped together. As a whole, large-cap stocks are an important part of the economy and therefore essential to asset allocation.

Larger companies tend to have a more established business presence and less uncertainty in sales or profits than smaller companies (that is, the small-cap stocks). Although there are exceptions, larger companies often have slower growth rates, but they are less risky investments than many smaller companies. Large-cap stocks are considered long-term investments, and fifty-plus years of historical market returns yield slightly lower than short-term returns, but with less volatility.

## Cyclical, Defensive, and Value Stocks

Companies with earnings that are strongly tied to the business cycle are considered to be cyclical. When the economy picks up momentum, these stocks follow this positive trend. When the economy slows down, these stocks follow, too. Cyclical stocks would include companies like DaimlerChrysler (NYSE: DCX), United Airlines (NYSE: UAL), and Phelps Dodge (NYSE: PD)—the copper mining and smelting company considered the bellwether of the cyclical sector.

Defensive stocks, on the other hand, are relatively stable under most economic conditions, no matter how the market is faring. Stocks with this characteristic include food companies, drug manufacturers, and utility companies. For the most part, you can't live without these companies' products no matter what the economic climate at any given time. The list of defensive stocks includes General Mills (NYSE: GIS) and Johnson & Johnson (NYSE: JNJ).

Value stocks, finally, look inexpensive when compared to earnings, dividends, sales, or other fundamental factors. When there is a big run on growth stocks, value stocks may be ignored. However, many investors believe that value stocks are a good deal given their reasonable price in relation to many growth stocks. Warren Buffett would probably vouch for that.

## Income and Speculative Stocks and Socially Responsible Investing (SRI)

Income stocks, which include real estate investment trusts (REITs), may fit the bill if generating income is your primary goal. One example of an income stock is public utility companies; such stocks have traditionally paid higher dividends than other types of stock. In addition, preferred stocks make excellent income vehicles, typically providing steady dividends and high yields. As with any stock, it's wise to look for a solid company with a good track record.

Diamonds aren't just a girl's best friend anymore! When you buy a share of a Diamond (symbol DIA), you are buying a fraction of each of the stocks in the Dow Jones Industrial Average. Like SPDRs, Diamonds are exchange-traded funds bought and sold on the American Stock Exchange.

Bewared of speculative stocks. Any company that's boasting about its brilliant ideas but doesn't have the earnings and revenue to back them up would be classified as a speculative stock. Since these companies have yet to prove their true worth, they make risky investments.

Another investment strategy that is growing in popularity is socially responsible investing (SRI). Here, investors put capital into companies that represent their personal values. Such individuals may avoid tobacco or liquor companies or any company whose products or services damage the environment. Socially responsible investors favor companies that have a positive influence on society.

## Preferred Stocks

Preferred stocks have as much in common with bonds as they do with common stock. Essentially, this type of stock comes with a redemption date and a fixed dividend the income received has nothing to do with the company's earnings. If the company has financial difficulties, holders of preferred stock have priority when it comes to dividend payments.

Think plastics are going to go sky-high this year? Maybe you're interested in the bio-tech sector? Holding company depositary receipts (or HOLDRs) allows you to invest in entire market sectors, as opposed to individual companies. This form of investment, originally created by Merrill Lynch, serves as a nice tool for those hot on a particular industry who don't want to do all the work of researching specific companies. HOLDRs are traded on the American Stock Exchange.

As the owner of preferred stock, you normally have none of the ownership rights that come with common stock ownership (like voting). However, preferred stock can be a good portfolio addition for income-oriented investors. This book focuses on common stock because, like its name, it's the far more common choice for stock investors.

## Penny Stocks

Penny stocks are stocks that sell for $5 or less, and in many cases you're lucky if they're worth even that much. Most penny stocks usually have no substantial income or revenue. You have a high potential for loss with penny stocks. If you have a strong urge to invest in this type of company, take time out to follow the stock to see if it has made any headway. Learn all you can about the company, and don't be tempted to act on a hot tip that may have been passed your way.

Penny stocks trade in either the pink sheets, a forum operated by the National Quotations Bureau, or on the NASDAQ small-cap market. Pink sheets, in brief, are listings and price information literally printed on pink sheets of paper that go to select brokers.

The companies behind these stocks are thinly capitalized and are often not required to file reports with the SEC. They trade over the counter, and there is a limited amount of public information available. This in itself is reason for concern. How many astute investors want to put their money into an investment offering little to no information? Nonetheless, people do invest in these stocks.

One of the most interesting—and alarming—aspects of penny stock dealing is that brokers are not always acting as a third party but instead set prices and act as the principals in the transaction. In other words, the broker selling the stock owns large chunks of it. Penny stocks most often do not have a single price but a number of different prices at which they can be purchased or sold. Like bonds on the market, penny stocks have asking and bidding prices. Unlike bonds, you often cannot find the price listed that is being quoted to you by a penny stock dealer.

Okay, so there's little information about the company, the price, or anything else to investigate. But the guy on the phone—making a cold call—says it will be the next Starbucks! This is where they get you. Thanks to the Internet and the selling of phone lists, penny stocks dealers can reach out far and wide. They use high-pressure sales tactics and armies of callers to tell you anything to make you buy the stocks. Beware!

The U.S. Securities and Exchange Commission (SEC) offers on its Web site (*www.sec.gov*) the opportunity to investigate any questionable activities. They also offer a host of services, including free literature, complaint tracking, and a toll-free information line at 1-800-SEC-0330.

Typically, unscrupulous brokers hype up and promote companies that have either no assets or minimal assets. Called "pump and dump," these hard-selling wheeler-dealers hype the stocks, making outrageous claims about the company that are substantiated by absolutely nothing. They bring the price up so that they can cash in on an artificial price that is high for a company that is worth nearly nothing, or not in business at all. Fraudulent practices by brokers also include unauthorized trading, churning, bait-and-switch, and other methods of pulling the wool over the eyes of unsuspecting new investors. Their goal is to convince naive investors that these stocks are an incredible bargain, so cheap that nobody should pass them by. And, when they become the next Lucent, you'll be rich!

All of this is not to say that there are no low-priced legitimate stocks on the market. There are. They are usually small grassroots companies that can grow over time—if you pick the right one and wait a while. You should invest cautiously and conservatively at first. Look for a new company with good leadership in an industry where you see growth potential. It's also advantageous to find a company that holds the patent on a new product. If the product takes off, so could your stock. You must seek out all of this information—it will not come to you via a cold caller.

## Stock Options

A stock option is a specific type of option, with a stock as the underlying instrument (that is, the stock is the security that the value of the option is based on). An option is a contract giving you the right, but not the obligation, to buy or sell shares of stock, at a predetermined or calculable price. (When you buy options, you exercise what is known as a call contract; to sell is to exercise a put contract; and the predetermined option price is called the strike price.) Options trade over exchanges, just like the underlying stocks.

For example, you could own an option to buy a share in XYZ Corp. for $100 one month from today. If the actual stock price in one month is $105, then you would exercise (use) your option and buy a stock from whoever sold you the option for $100. You could then either keep the stock, or sell it on the open market for $105, netting a profit of $5.

However, if the stock price in a month is only $95, you would not exercise your option. If you really wanted a share in XYZ Corp, you would be much smarter to buy it in the open market for $95 rather than using your option to buy it for $100. If you have an option, you have virtually unlimited profit potential, and your losses are limited to what you paid for the option. A stock option's value is determined by five principal factors: the current price of the stock, the strike price, the cumulative cost required to hold a position in the stock (including interest and dividends), the time to expiration (usually within two years), and an estimate of the future volatility of the stock price. Also available are longer term options called long-term equity anticipation securities (or LEAPs), which typically don't expire for two to three years. Other than that distinction, LEAPS trade like regular options.

You have probably heard of employee stock options. Stock options for a company's own stock are often offered to upper-level employees as part of their compensation package. Non-executive employees are occasionally offered options, especially in the technology sector, in order to give all employees an incentive to help the company become more profitable and to lure quality employees to work. Employee stock options differ from the options that are traded on exchanges as securities primarily in the time frame under which they can be exercised. Employee stock options can typically be exercised over a time frame of up to ten years.

# 22 Choosing the Right Fund Combination

There's an old joke that the key to success is setting aside eight hours a day for work and eight hours a day for sleep and making sure they are not the same hours. This is especially true with your investments. Investment gurus agree that finding the right mix of funds for you is a combination of feeling comfortable with your investment goals and tolerance for risk, and finding funds that meet those objectives and limitations. If you're losing sleep over your investments, something isn't right.

## Risk Tolerance and Your Fund Portfolio

Chapter 21 directed you to think long and hard about your personal tolerance for risk in your investment strategy. By now, you have decided whether you are a conservative, moderate, or aggressive investor. Now it's time to apply what you've discovered about your risk tolerance to your fund portfolio objectives.

A fund's beta is the measure that compares a mutual fund's volatility with that of a benchmark (usually the S&P 500). The beta should give some sense of how far you can expect a fund to fall when the market takes a dive, or how high it might climb if the bull is running hard. A fund with a beta of greater than 1 is considered more volatile than the market. A beta of less than 1 means less volatility than the market.

Identifying individual risk tolerance is one of the basic factors in determining your optimum investment strategy for a mutual fund portfolio. Regardless of whether a strategy applies to a total portfolio, a portion of a portfolio, or a qualified retirement plan, risk tolerance can affect both asset allocation and the selection of fund categories: small company growth, global, growth and income, corporate bond, government bond, and so on.

Risk in mutual funds usually refers to the fluctuations in the price of a fund, as opposed to the dividend risk and market risk associated with stocks. As risk increases, both price volatility and total return potential increase proportionately. As risk decreases, price volatility and total return potential decrease proportionately.

If you've decided that you have a conservative level of risk tolerance, you will accept lower returns on your investments in order to minimize price volatility. If you're an aggressive investor, you'll seek out the highest returns regardless of price volatility.

Regardless of your risk tolerance level, you can achieve your investment goals with mutual funds—whether they're categorized as growth, balance, or income—as long as you keep your money invested over the long term. The shorter your investment, the fewer options are available to you in the mutual fund market that will allow you to achieve your end goals.

Risk tolerance can be the most important element in determining mutual fund selections. Two investors with the exact same investment objectives and investment capital will enter into two dramatically different portfolio scenarios if they have different tolerances for risk.

## Using Diversification to Minimize Risk

Diversification in an investment portfolio is absolutely necessary to achieve a well-rounded investment strategy. Ideally, diversification spreads an investment portfolio among different fund categories to achieve not only a variety of objectives, but also a reduction in overall risk.

Different fund types (growth, growth and income, corporate bond, etc.) offer distinct risk/return objectives. Diversification increases as the combination of different risk/return objectives increases. Here are some guidelines to help you master the diversification process:

- **Define your investment objectives.** Your personal time horizon, return objectives, risk tolerance, and portfolio amount all contribute to the focal point for your investment strategy. If your selected funds accurately represent your objectives, you have an effective investment plan.
- **Choose quality over quantity.** What is important is how distinct your funds are and how they fit your investment strategy, not how many funds you own. Don't think of diversification as a challenge to buy as many funds as possible or you'll end up with a portfolio that does not match your strategy.
- **Value fund category above fund style.** A fund category defines its objectives; the fund's style is the method used to pursue those objectives.

- **Avoid duplication.** It is a waste of your investment monies to own multiple funds with identical objectives. It's best to own just one fund in any particular fund category.
- **Fewer is better.** Use the fewest funds possible to accomplish your goals. Most funds are comprised of fifty to 150 separate stocks or bonds, so you do not need to buy a huge number of funds to meet your diversification objectives.

Regardless of the number of funds in your portfolio, the key to effective diversification is to make sure that each fund serves a distinct purpose toward meeting your investment strategy.

## Investing for Your Family

It's important that your investing strategies be tailored to your family situation, whether you're investing as a family or as a couple. While children generally do not have a say in the family's investments as they grow up, explaining that Mommy and Daddy own a very tiny piece of Disney through shares of stock is a way of teaching them about money and, in time, about investing. Investing is a way of building toward a brighter future for your children. It can open the door to a college education as well as give them some financial backing to pursue their own goals and dreams. It also teaches them by example that saving money can bring you more money.

The Internet has democratized Wall Street. Online features have opened up a plethora of information to retail investors that was previously only accessible by professionals. There's easier communication between IPOs and shareholders, and investors can access the entirety of their account, from research to portfolio—all at the click of a mouse.

Couples often find that money is their most significant cause of discord. In fact, it is listed in survey after survey as the top reason couples fight or break up. Money can be, and is, very easily equated with power—and that can spell trouble in a relationship. If one person uses his or her income or savings as a means of control, the other party can, and often will, become disenchanted. For other couples, money is a source of pressure or tension if one party does not feel the other is earning enough. When it comes to investing, the problem that often arises is lack of full disclosure, when one party makes investment decisions without telling the other.

The road to harmonious investing in a relationship is an open line of communication, starting with determining your goals and dreams as a couple. If one person has a greater aversion to risk than the other, this too must be discussed, and a compromise needs to be reached. The handling of finances in the home also needs to be addressed. One couple may be satisfied with letting one party make the investment decisions, while another couple might discuss all money matters, including investments. It's important that no matter what approach a couple takes, it is discussed and established early on in the relationship. Communication and honesty are important in all relationships and especially when it comes to money—which is often at the root of many other problems.

## Your Lifelong Fund Strategy

Everyone's attitude toward investing is different, and people have very distinct long-term financial goals that they are trying to achieve with their portfolios. One investor might be looking solely at producing maximum retirement income, while another may be focused on how to send his six kids through college. Even so, most investors share some common situations throughout their lives. Where you are in your life cycle certainly affects how you invest for retirement, but other life stages aren't so closely related to age.

Let's say you're forty and expecting your first child. You'll need to decide how to balance your finances to account for the additional expenses of a baby. Perhaps you'll need to supplement your income with income-producing investments. Moreover, your child will be entering college at about the time you're ready to retire! In these circumstances, your growth and income needs most certainly will change, and maybe your risk tolerance will too.

### *Major Events*

The following are some major life events that most people share, along with some investment decisions that you may want to consider when thinking about your fund portfolio:

**Getting your first "real" job . . .**

- Start a savings account to build a cash reserve.
- Start a retirement fund and make regular monthly contributions, no matter how small.
- Start to think about long-term financial goals.

**Every time you get a raise . . .**

- Increase your contribution to your company-sponsored retirement plan.
- Invest after-tax dollars in municipal bonds that offer tax-exempt interest.
- Increase your cash reserves.
- Re-evaluate your financial position to determine how much of your income you can afford to invest. Invest more whenever possible.

**When you get married . . .**

- Determine your new investment contributions and allocations, taking into account your combined income and expenses.

**When you buy your first house . . .**

- Invest some of your nonretirement savings in a short-term investment specifically for funding your down payment, closing, and moving costs.

**When you have a baby . . .**

- Increase your cash reserves.
- Increase your life insurance.
- Start a college fund.

**When you change jobs . . .**

- Review your investment strategy and asset allocation to accommodate a new salary and a different benefits package.
- Consider your distribution options for your company's retirement savings or pension plan. You may want to roll money over into a new plan or IRA.

**When all your children move out of the house . . .**

- Boost your retirement savings contributions.

**When you reach fifty-five (or near your target retirement age) . . .**

- Review your retirement fund asset allocation to accommodate the shorter time frame for your investments.
- Continue saving for retirement.

**When you retire . . .**

- Carefully study the options you may have for taking money from your company retirement plan. Discuss your alternatives with your financial advisor.
- Review your combined potential income after retirement.
- Reallocate your investments to provide the income you need while still providing for some growth in capital to help beat inflation and fund your later years.

> Many funds allow an exchange of shares for the shares of another fund managed by the same advisor. Look at the first part of the fee table to find out if there's an exchange fee for your fund—you might be able to make a move that would benefit your portfolio for free.

Building your mutual fund portfolio is a long process. The sooner you start, the better off you'll be in the long run. It's best to start investing as soon as you start earning money, even if it's only $10 a paycheck. The discipline and skills you learn will benefit you for the rest of your life. But no matter how old you are when you start thinking seriously about your investment strategy and how mutual funds fit into it, it's never too late to begin.

## Past Performance

Judging past performance of a fund can be trickier than it might seem by glancing at five- and ten-year returns. Sectors or industries that are in vogue during one period may not be during the next. One spectacular year of 90-percent growth, followed by four years of 10-percent growth, will average 26-percent growth per year. This average would not be a good indicator of how that fund is performing at the end of the fifth year, when you are thinking about buying. Also, a sector that has not fared well over a stretch of time may be on the upswing due to new products, consumer needs, or public awareness (as with the socially responsible stocks). This won't show up in past performance.

The same holds true for the large- and small-cap companies. A fund that invests in small companies will not see large returns when the trend leans toward the large corporations, as it did in the late 1990s. The best you can do is look at each measure of past performance, read up on future expectations, and try to make an informed decision. Remember this: Long-term five- and ten-year returns are important, but they are only part of the larger picture.

Over the long-term, the success (or failure) of your investment in a fund will also depend on factors such as these:

- The fund's sales charges, fees, and expenses
- The taxes you may have to pay when you receive a distribution
- The age and size of the fund
- The fund's risks and volatility
- Recent changes in fund operations

As for selecting a fund family, it is often suggested that you look for one that has been around a while, unless you're going with an emerging industry such as tech stocks, in which the newer fund families may all have been around for about the same length of time. The better-established fund families can show you ten-year returns, which you can compare against comparable funds in other fund families. They can also give you an indication of how the fund has fared during the bear markets and how long it took them to recover. Naturally some of this will depend on the fund manager, but you have a better chance of finding a fund manager with ten years of experience at the helm of a fund at an older, more-established company. Look at the ten-year returns and see if the same fund manager was there over that time period. If you look at ten-year returns and see that the current manager has only been on board for three years, those ten-year returns won't mean as much. It's like looking at the last ten years of a baseball team that only acquired its superstars in the past three years; management experience makes a big difference.

Additionally, you should compare the mutual fund that interests you with other comparable funds. If the fund you like had a 10-percent return last year and other similar funds were also around 10 percent, then the fund is performing as expected. However, if the fund is bringing in 10 percent, and comparable funds in the same category are bringing in 12 and 15 percent, you can do better without changing your goals or choosing a more (or less) risky fund. All you have to do is find another fund in the same category.

Once you finally make a decision, expect to be in the fund for at least one year, usually five or more. Mutual funds are not generally thought of as a short-term investment, but sometimes market conditions can dictate change earlier than you had planned. If you've invested in a fund that was on the upswing, and now it's heading back down (or "correcting"), you may be better off selling before share prices drop lower. You'll almost always have the opportunity to revisit the fund after it stabilizes, when you'll have a chance to benefit from the next round of growth.

## Reading the Prospectus

Examining a mutual fund's prospectus will most likely not be the highlight of your week, even if returns are spectacularly high. A prospectus can be dense and wordy, even hard to decipher, with little consideration for the information needs of the average investor. Important information is in there, somewhere, but it can be hard to find in the midst of the legal jargon. In this highly competitive market, however, some funds are actually trying to soften the legalese in which the fund's prospectus is written. In fact, many now publish easy-to-read newsletters to supplement the information in the prospectus—or at least translate some of it. However you get it done, it's to your advantage to read the prospectus with an eye for specific areas of importance. There are certain details that deserve particular attention. (Obtaining a prospectus, by the way, should be as easy as calling the fund's toll-free number.)

### *The Fund's Objective*

The fund should have a clear statement of the objective. Is it aggressive growth? Current income? While it may be far more clear-cut in bond funds, a fund's objective is not always as obvious when reading the prospectus of a stock fund. If the objective is unclear, the mutual fund manager has more leeway. It also means your intentions in choosing that particular fund may not be carried out. If the fund objective is not clear, either seek out a fund that is more clearly defined, ask someone in the fund's investment information department, or follow the old rule of thumb and do your homework. Look up the fund's current holdings.

One of the most common errors investors make when buying mutual funds is simply buying at the wrong time. Don't invest in a mutual fund before it makes its annual capital gains distribution—even if you buy the fund just one day before gains are distributed, you'll owe taxes as if you owned the fund all year.

### *The Investment Risks*

The mutual fund prospectus should discuss the level of risks the fund will take in conjunction with its objective. Stock funds should discuss the types of stocks they are buying. Are they talking about speculation? Are they telling you about the volatility of particular stocks? Look at the warnings they're giving you. Are they telling you about the currency and political risks involved with their international holdings?

The prospectus should specify the risks associated with its portfolio. As an investor, you should be aware of the risks of investing and how those risks mesh with your risk tolerance. To make the best possible investment choices, it's important to understand how different investments perform under different economic scenarios. For example, aggressive growth stock funds typically perform best as the market is emerging from a long downward trend. Bond funds, on the other hand, often do well during periods of slow growth, as interest rates fall and bond prices climb. By combining your knowledge with the information in the prospectus, you'll be able to make better, and better-informed, investment choices.

### *Investment Breakdown*

The fund should clearly lay out the percentage of holdings they are committed to in each asset group. They should say, for example, that the management is required to hold at least 70 percent of U.S. bonds, or 80 percent in common stocks, or no more than 20 percent in international investments. The breakdown and parameters of the fund give you an idea where your money will be invested. Other types of investments, such as cash instruments, may also be included.

A fee table should outline all the fees associated with that fund. Read them carefully, and make sure you are left with no surprises. Operating costs, loads, and any other fees should all be included.

### *Financial History*

A prospectus will also give you the history of that mutual fund. The financial information should provide the per-share results for the life of the fund—or for funds that have been around for a long time, at least the past ten years. You can gauge the annual total return of the fund on an annual basis. You can also look at the year-end net asset values, the fund's expense ratio, and any other information that will help you gauge how the fund has performed over time. You can check on dividend payments, if it is an income fund, or see the types of holdings the fund has sold and purchased.

## Building Your Fund Profile

If you've targeted a fund that looks appealing to you, you need to build a profile for the fund so that you can make the best decision when it comes time to pull the trigger and buy. You should be able to construct an accurate profile of your fund from the prospectus or one of the leading financial magazines (or both). This process simply involves identifying the key features of the fund. Many of the leading financial magazines do this all the time, but rather than waiting for them to highlight the fund you're interested in, you can do it yourself. Here's an example of such a profile:

- Name: ABCD Fictitious Investment Fund
- Symbol: ABCDIF
- Category: Small-cap, aggressive growth
- Assets: $21.5 million
- Expense ratio: 2 percent
- Load fund? No
- Minimum investment: $500
- Fund manager: James B. James
- Tenure: 3 years
- The fund generally has a minimum of 70 percent of its assets in small-cap companies, with market capitalization under $250 million. 10 percent of the investments may be in foreign securities.
- Composition as of 4/15/05:
    - Domestic stocks: 87 percent
    - Foreign securities: 8 percent
    - Cash: 5 percent
- Sector breakdown:
    - Technologies: 41.3 percent
    - Financials: 19.7 percent
    - Services: 21.5 percent

- Retail: 10.0 percent
- Health: 7.5 percent

Add to these statistics the fund's three-month rate of return plus its one-, three-, and five-year rate of returns, and you have a basic idea of what can be put together to profile a specific mutual fund. You can then examine the individual segments.

Liquidity is another benefit of mutual funds. Funds can be sold on any business day at that day's closing price—or at the following day's close if the sell order is placed after the market closes.

You might, for example, want to look more closely at the track record of the fund manager. If the direction and category of the fund appeals to you, you may want to look at the specific stocks held by the fund to see their P/E ratio and performance in recent months and recent years. Essentially, the prospectus will help you determine your level of interest in the fund. Building a profile, or reading a profile in one of the leading financial publications, will allow you to organize the vital information and determine what additional details you may want to learn about the fund.

## Six Fund Investment Strategies You Can Swear By

As you head into the world of mutual funds, here are six strategies that will help steer you through the murky depths of what can sometimes be a confusing investment genre. Don't let yourself become overwhelmed; simply take your time and cover your bases.

- **Start early.** There's no substitute for getting a good start on your financial future. All the studies on the subject conclude that the earlier you get going with your investment strategy, the more money you'll have in retirement. That's because the earlier you start, the earlier compound interest goes to work for you.

- **Max out.** The more money you invest, the faster you'll become a successful investor. Put as much money as you can possibly afford into your investment plan, even if it means sacrificing some of life's luxuries.
- **Learning is earning.** Knowing enough about your investments to become the master of your financial future is priceless. Read all you can on finance and investments, and make sure you read every word of the prospectuses that come your way from the mutual fund each year. The payoff for spending an hour or two per week boning up on the ways of Wall Street is potentially huge. Don't be left behind.
- **Be aggressive.** Prudence is the proper course if you're an airplane pilot or a brain surgeon, but it's a drawback for investors. Studies show that to beat inflation and to make your money grow faster, a good chunk of your plan should be earmarked for higher-performing stock funds. That doesn't mean you should be reckless. But if you stick to conservative investments like bonds or bank savings accounts, your chances of developing a successful investment portfolio will be low to nonexistent.
- **Keep the money working.** Don't be tempted to take money out of your investments or borrow against them in order to meet short-term financial crises at home. It's important that the money you've invested be allowed to do its job over time so that you can meet your long-term financial objectives. If you hit a financial stumbling block, try to find other ways to get over it before you even think about tapping your investment monies. The government wants you to keep that money invested, and they've set up expensive traps if you don't.
- **Keep an eye on the market.** Don't ignore market trends as you're evaluating your holdings or making new investment choices. No matter how well a fund is managed, or how well it's performed in the past, changes in the overall geopolitical and economic climate can turn the markets upside down. Wise investors keep an eye on the overall trend of the markets, and accordingly on their investments.

# 23 Saving for Retirement

This chapter gets you started thinking about saving for retirement, but because of space constraints, it only scratches the surface. After reviewing this chapter, dig deeper by reading books that are devoted to the topic of retirement planning, take seminars on the subject, and/or meet with a financial planner.

## Figuring Out How Much You'll Need

This is the $64,000 question: How much money will you need in retirement? Unfortunately, there is no set answer. How much you'll need depends on your expenses during your retirement years. If, for example, you won't have a house payment or rent, you may be able to live on a lot less than if you continue to make those payments. On the other hand, if you move to a much older house in retirement than you're living in now, you may also encounter more repairs than you have now. You may want to belong to a country club in retirement, but get rid of your expensive car.

Use **Worksheet 23-1** as a way to begin to determine what your expenses will be during your retirement years.

No one has the ability to look into a crystal ball and know exactly what your expenses will be. The best you can do is estimate, make adjustments, estimate a little more closely, make more adjustments, and on and on!

**WORKSHEET 23-1 Retirement Expenses**

| Expense | Monthly Costs |
|---|---|
| | $ |
| | $ |
| | $ |
| | $ |
| | $ |
| | $ |
| | $ |
| | $ |
| | $ |
| | $ |
| | $ |

## Finding Ways to Set Money Aside Now

The main reason people put off saving for retirement is that they think they have plenty of time to do that later. (You don't.) The second most popular reason for putting it off is that most people don't know how to come up with money to put into savings. If you've read any of the chapters in the first third of this book, though, you can probably come up with a variety of ways to find $50, $100, or $200 a month for retirement savings. Use **Worksheet 23-2** to brainstorm ideas, and review the following sections for some creative ways to save more for retirement.

WORKSHEET 23-2 **Ideas for Reducing Your Current Expenses**

| Expense | Idea for Reducing or Eliminating | Potential Monthly Savings |
|---|---|---|
| | | $ |
| | | $ |
| | | $ |
| | | $ |
| | | $ |
| | | $ |
| | | $ |
| | | $ |
| | | $ |
| | | $ |
| | | $ |
| | | $ |
| | | $ |
| | | $ |

### *Stop Eating Out*

If you eat out twice a week, and you pay $12 for a meal that you could make for $2.50 at home, you could put about $82 a month into your retirement savings. Over twenty years at 8 percent, that's $48,621.68.

### *Cut Your Clothing and Shoe Budget in Half*

If you spend $1,000 per year on clothing and shoes, can you cut that amount in half and put $500 a year ($42 per month) into a retirement account? Thirty years of that at 8 percent, and you'll have $63,012.40 to retire on.

### *Move to a Smaller House*

If you're currently living with two other people in 2,400 square feet, could you move to a house with 1,800 square feet and still be comfortable? If so, your mortgage payments might go down by anywhere from $300 to $1,000 per month—money that you could put into a retirement fund. In just fifteen years at 8 percent, your $600 per month will equal a whopping $233,874.33

### *Drive Your Car Twice as Long*

If you currently get a new car every three years, pay it off, and get another new one, you can continue to pay off your car in three years but drive it for six. Put the amount of your car payment into a retirement account for three years. You'll only contribute to your retirement account three years out of every six, but you'll have found a creative way to save.

> Another way to get more money for retirement is to refinance your mortgage when interest rates decline. For the cost of closing the loan (which ranges greatly), you might be able to find an extra $50 to $150 per month for your retirement savings. Just don't increase the length of the loan, though or you'll sacrifice your long-term financial health.

### *Start a Part-Time Business*

Instead of looking only at potential expenses to cut, consider working a few extra hours per week, perhaps at your own business, and putting that income toward your retirement savings. Chapter 11 has some tips on how to earn a bit more money than you're making now.

## Looking at Tax-Deferred Ways to Save

When most people think of retirement and the government at the same time, they think of Social Security, the government program that collects money from you throughout your working life and gives it back to you, one month at a time, during your retirement years.

If you're nearing retirement, you can probably count on quite a bit of Social Security income for your retirement. If you haven't already, you will soon receive a statement that explains how much you'll receive each month, based on exactly what age you retire. (You can contact the Social Security office at *www.ssa.gov* or 1-800-772-1213.)

If you're forty or younger, however, you have little chance of using Social Security to fund your retirement. That's because instead of taking income from you, investing that income, charging a small administrative fee, and then paying you benefits from the investment, as you may have expected the federal government to do, the system actually works quite differently. The money you paid in isn't there anymore—what you paid in ten years ago was used to pay benefits to other people ten years ago; what you paid in last week was used to pay benefits to other people last week. And that worked pretty well when the largest generation in American history (the baby boomers) were working. But as they near retirement, the government will probably not be able to collect enough in Social Security income to offset the benefits being paid to boomers.

As a result, the government is taking two steps: increasing the age at which you can begin to draw Social Security benefits, and encouraging you to invest more money in your own retirement accounts to use when you retire. The following sections give you some examples of how they hope to encourage you to do that.

As you investigate all of your options (including employer-sponsored plans, which are covered in the "Letting Your Employer Help You" section), use **Worksheet 23-3** to keep track of what's available to you and how much you're legally allowed to contribute.

WORKSHEET 23-3 **Possible Retirement Savings**

| Type of Account | Possible Contribution | Employer Matching Amount |
|---|---|---|
| | $ | $ |
| | $ | $ |
| | $ | $ |
| | $ | $ |
| | $ | $ |
| | $ | $ |
| | $ | $ |
| | $ | $ |
| | $ | $ |
| | $ | $ |
| | $ | $ |
| | $ | $ |

### *Traditional IRA*

An individual retirement account (IRA) is a voluntary retirement savings plan. Up to certain limits, you can contribute to an IRA every year and deduct the amount of your contribution from your federal income taxes. Starting at age fifty-nine and a half, you can withdraw funds from your IRA each month. At that time the money you withdraw is taxed, but because you'll probably be at a lower tax level, you'll still save tax dollars. Withdrawing the money before that age results in substantial penalties. In addition, you must begin receiving disbursements from your traditional IRA at age seventy and a half.

As long as you're making money doing something, in 2002 you can deposit $3,000 into a traditional IRA. That number goes up to $4,000 in 2005 and $5,000 in 2008. However, if your income exceeds a certain level, you may not be eligible to take the tax deduction. Consult IRS documents (or visit their site at *www.irs.gov*) to determine those income levels for this year. You may also be limited in traditional IRA contributions if your company sponsors a retirement plan for you (even if you don't participate).

### Roth IRA

A Roth IRA is a variation of a traditional IRA, but the tax benefits of the plans are in total opposition. With a Roth IRA, instead of getting a tax deduction for your contribution now and paying tax on the amount distributed to you in retirement, you get no tax deduction now, but you pay no tax on the money distributed to you later.

Like a traditional IRA, you can contribute $3,000 per year in 2002, rising to $5,000 in 2008.

Also like a traditional IRA, however, you can't contribute if you earn too much money ($110,00 for single incomes; $160,000 for joint incomes), and if you earn between $95,000 and $110,000 for singles ($150,000 to $160,000 for joint filers), the amount you can contribute is less than the full allowable amount.

A Roth IRA does have a couple of benefits over traditional IRAs, though. One is that you can continue to contribute as long as you'd like and do not have to begin taking distributions at age seventy and a half. The other is that you can contribute to a Roth IRA even if your company sponsors a retirement plan.

### SEP-IRA

A Simplified Employee Pension (SEP) IRA works like a traditional IRA, but it's set up by an employer for its employees (including by you, if you're self-employed). As long as the employer does not offer another retirement plan, the employer can contribute up to 15 percent of your income (up to $30,000) into the SEP-IRA every year. You can take the account with you when leaving the company to take another job. All of the money contributed comes from your income, but it's not taxed until you receive it during your retirement years.

Looking for a fairly safe way to invest for your retirement? Look into Treasury Inflation-Protected Securities (TIPS), which currently pay around 3.5 percent, *plus* they're adjusted for inflation. Although you'll pay tax on the interest if you use them for anything other than retirement, you can buy them for your tax-deferred retirement account(s).

## Letting Your Employer Help You

For most of the twentieth century, companies paid the retirement incomes of their long-term employees, so the employees didn't have to worry about saving for their retirement years. How times have changed! Most employees do not stay with companies long enough to be considered long-term, and most companies do not provide any of their own money to fund retirement accounts. There are a few exceptions, however, discussed in the following sections.

### *Pension Plan*

Your company places money into a retirement account (the amount contributed on your behalf depends on your income, age, and years of service), manages that account, and pays benefits to you from that account when you retire. When you receive distributions from a pension plan (either monthly, annually, or in a lump-sum payment), you're taxed on the income.

### *Profit Sharing/401(k)/403(b)/457*

In this type of plan, your company contributes money, tax-free, into an individual account on your behalf based on how much you ask to have contributed (the IRS sets limits, but they're a little too detailed to include here!). Some companies match all or part of these contributions, making your potential annual contribution quite high. Distributions at retirement are taxed. 401(k) plans are used at for-profit companies; 403(b) plans are used at religious, educational, and charitable organizations; 457 plans are used for employees of state and local governments.

### SIMPLE-IRA

A Savings Incentive Match Plan for Employees (SIMPLE) IRA is similar to a traditional IRA and a SEP-IRA. A SIMPLE-IRA is set up by a business with fewer than 100 employees (including yours, if you own a small business). Contribution limits to a SIMPLE-IRA were $6,500 in 2001, ramping up to $10,000 in 2005.

The employer then matches a portion of your contribution, based on how much you make in income, up to a maximum amount. The 2001 maximum employee-employer contribution was $13,000. This means that the company is essentially allowed to give you up to $6,500 per year without asking for anything in return.

### Employee Stock Ownership Plan

An Employee Stock Ownership Plan (ESOP) is retirement account made up mostly of company stock paid for by your employer and, potentially, added to with purchases of company stock that you make. ESOPs can be difficult to take with you if you leave the company, but they can often be transferred into company stock or cash.

Keep in mind that your ESOP is worth only what your company's stock is worth. If you have any doubts about whether your company will still be in business when you retire, don't count on the money from your ESOP as retirement income.

### Other Plans

Several dozen other types of employer contribution plans exist, but many are no longer in existence except at a few companies. For a complete list, visit the Motley Fool's Foolish Retirement Plan Primer at *www.fool.com/Retirement/RetirementPlanPrimer.htm*. You can also visit your local library and ask for help in researching employer contribution plans.

In addition, SIMPLE-IRA plans, discussed in the preceding section, can take advantage of an employer's contribution on your behalf.

To find out what your company has to offer, visit the human resources department and ask questions about what's available. You won't have to commit to a plan at that point, but you can use the information to see how much you can save for your retirement with a contribution that's automatically withdrawn from your paycheck.

## Investing on Your Own

In addition to putting away retirement savings in tax-deferred or company-sponsored plans, you can always save and invest on your own. Remember, however, that you should first take advantage of any free money your employer might be offering in retirement matching plans, then take advantage of tax-deferred retirement plans, and only as a third choice begin a simple savings account or a more complex investment portfolio for your retirement income.

Saving money in a savings account is quite simple and doesn't require any particular knowledge or skill. You may want to periodically shift your savings to a long-term CD or to savings bonds to earn a higher interest rate.

Investing, which is significantly more complicated, requires some knowledge of the markets, company documents, and trading rules. If you're interested in learning more about investing, do it—if you're conservative in your investments and take time to read all the available financial documents on companies in which you're investing, the risk is far smaller than most people believe. If you have no interest in doing this, hire a stockbroker or financial consultant to invest for you.

Once you begin investing, you'll probably want to have an accountant figure your taxes every year. You may owe tax on your earnings, and figuring out exactly how much is a pretty complicated procedure.

## Starting Young

The absolute best way to save for retirement fairly painlessly is to start young. If you start saving $100 per month when you're twenty-five, and you invest that in an account that sometimes earns 18 percent interest and sometimes loses a bunch of money (most investments do go up and down this way), averaging 8 percent over the next forty years, you'll have $351,428.13 for retirement. To get the same amount of retirement savings if you start at age forty, you'll have to put away about $367 per month. Use the Savings Growth Projector Calculator at *www.finaid.org* to run these numbers for yourself.

## Making Up for Lost Time

Regardless of how old you are, you can still save some money for your retirement.

### *Using the Catch-Up Provision*

If you're over fifty, you're allowed to put away more tax-free income per year than your younger counterparts. For example, while the standard contribution to both traditional and Roth IRAs is $3,000 per year (subject to income limits, of course), anyone over fifty can contribute $500 more than that. This extra $500 deposit continues until 2006, when those over fifty can contribute $1,000 more, tax-free, than younger contributors. Your company's 401(k) plan has similar provisions, allowing you to contribute $1,000 more than younger workers. This is called a catch-up provision, and it's meant specifically for people who started saving for retirement later in life.

### *Using Your House to Help You Retire*

If you haven't made many provisions for your retirement and can't seem to find the money to do so, you may be able to tap the value of your house for your retirement. Suppose you're forty-five years old and have fifteen years left to pay on your house. You bought the house fifteen years ago, and home prices have risen significantly since then. Your house is worth $240,000 now and will likely be worth over $350,000 (based on the rate that home prices are increasing—you can get this information from any experienced Realtor or appraiser) when you turn sixty and the house is paid off.

Rather than staying in the house, you can sell it and move to a smaller house or condominium that costs far less. If you can sell your house for $350,000 and buy a condo at that time for $200,000 or $250,000, you'll have $100,000 to $150,000 to add to your retirement account.

If mortgage interest rates drop to one point or more lower than the rate on your mortgage, consider refinancing. You may be able to get a shorter loan length (say, fifteen years instead of thirty) for the same monthly payments. This can enhance your ability to use your house as part of your retirement plan.

On the other hand, you can stay in the house and get a reverse mortgage on it as soon as you begin needing income (say, when you turn sixty-five or seventy). Essentially, a bank buys the house back from you, except that you continue to own it and live in it. You must be at least sixty-two and own the house free and clear (without a mortgage). The bank then either sends you monthly payments or gives you a lump sum. You'll pay a fee for this service because if you live longer than the bank thinks you're going to live, they may actually lose money on the deal. Still, many lenders offer this interesting option.

# 24 Choosing Your Retirement Plan

In Chapter 23, you figured out the amount of money you need to save for your retirement. Now, you need to know which retirement savings strategy and plan will work best for you. This chapter offers an assortment of savings tools and programs—some individual and some provided by employers—to make it all happen, and a few important retirement planning tips to help you along the way.

## The Tax-Free Advantage

You have now observed the challenges in providing needed financial resources for retirement. If your savings and returns were continually taxed, the task would be a lot more difficult. Fortunately, the U.S. govern-ment is also well aware of the challenges and has furnished a wide assortment of tax-preferred savings vehicles to help you.

Deferring taxes helps a lot, for two reasons. First, compounding is allowed its full effect, since the money that would have been lost on taxes is retained for growth. Second, when you do withdraw funds in retirement, you're likely to be in a lower tax bracket and pay less in taxes.

Tax preference is the underlying characteristic of all retirement savings vehicles. With most of them, both you and your employer can exclude the amount of money used to fund savings from your current income. Further, the investment earnings inside these savings plans are tax-deferred, which means that the money you save in these plans is not taxed until you withdraw the funds, usually during retirement.

## Retirement Plan Classifications

When it comes to retirement plans, you have many options to choose from. Retirement savings plan provisions are defined by the U.S. Internal Revenue Code. As such, they have evolved into a patchwork of ideas and amendments, and the rules are detailed and complex. This chapter will provide you with an overview of what's available. Once you decide what type of plan will work best for you, make sure you do more research on the rules and restrictions of each plan.

### *Individual and Employer Plans*

Some plans are set up, funded, and managed entirely at the individual level, while others are provided and managed by employers. Traditional and Roth IRAs are set up and managed by individuals. Employer plans—pensions and profit-sharing plans, including the popular 401(k) plan—are set up and managed according to stringent guidelines on behalf of the employee. Amounts contributed by the employer into these plans are tax-deductible for the employer and are tax-deferred for the employee. In defined benefit plans, employers manage the assets themselves (more often through third parties); in defined contribution plans, your employer provides the platform for you to manage the assets yourself.

Falling in between employer and individual plans is a small assortment of self-employment and small-business plans. These include Keogh, SIMPLE, and SEP-IRA plans.

### *Pension and Profit-Sharing Plans*

Pension and profit-sharing plans are both employer plans. Pension plans are structured to promise a specific sum to be paid at retirement, and they require mandatory employer funding to do so. That is, the plan must be funded even if the employer does not make money in a given period. Pension plans thus place more burden and risk on the employer; on the other hand, if the employer invests wisely, the pension recipient won't get the full benefit of the investment. Pension plans include traditional defined-benefit pensions, plus a small group of defined-contribution plans known as "money purchase" plans, where the employer buy-in amount is fixed each year.

Profit-sharing plans, on the other hand, have flexible employer contributions, often based on a percentage of profits generated. The legal promise of the profit-sharing plan is to defer taxes, not to provide a specific retirement benefit.

### *Defined-Benefit and Defined-Contribution Plans*

Defined-benefit plans have a specific and promised retirement payout. A defined-benefit pension plan usually promises to pay a contractual portion of your terminating salary, regardless of the amount of money set aside or its investment performance. As an employee, you don't have a specific account or balance in a defined-benefit plan—rather, you get a promised share of a larger investment pool or trust fund upon retirement. The amount deposited by the company is determined by actuaries and is of no consequence to you, since the payout is guaranteed.

Defined-benefit plans are becoming more rare, as they are gradually being replaced by defined-contribution plans. Employers are getting out of the guaranteed-retirements business because with a defined-contribution plan, the employer transfers the investment-performance risk to the employees.

The defined-contribution plan, on the other hand, depends on the success of the investment choices you make. In this case, the employer guarantees what goes in but not what comes out.

## Some Retirement Plan Basics

It's a good idea for you to become familiar with the principles and common terminology of basic retirement savings plans. For instance, it is important to understand the vesting period of the retirement plan. Vesting is your entitlement to retirement funds (that is, the effective ownership of those funds), which prevails regardless of whether you switch jobs. The "vesting period" is mandated by the federal government: for most plans, all funds must be fully vested in either five years ("cliff vesting") or on a sliding scale in which increasing percentages are vested in years three through seven of your sustained employment. Vesting periods can be shorter than these government mandates—and it's a good thing if they are. Note also that eligibility to begin participating in the retirement plan can vary up to one year.

### Contribution Limits

All retirement savings plans have annual contribution limits to qualify for tax-preferred status. (The limits are in place to avoid giving huge tax breaks to high-income workers and corporate executives.) These limits vary widely—many profit-sharing plans allow up to $40,000 to be set aside each year. In 2001, the popular 401(k) allowed a maximum employee contribution of $11,000 (a number that increases each year, under the 2001 EGTRRA tax act), while IRAs were increased to $3,000 each year (and more for taxpayers age fifty and over.) Pension plans, while not faced with contribution limits per se, allow pension benefits to be based on salaries up to $160,000 each year—a generous sum.

### Salary Deferral and Employer Match

Some plans are built around employee salary deferrals, with a corresponding employer match. The 401(k) is the prime example. Employees are allowed to set aside a portion of their salaries before taxes—up to 17 percent—and the employer matches a percentage, usually up to 3 percent. This way the employee enjoys reduced taxes on current earnings *and* gets additional funds from the employer added into the retirement fund. Again, the employer contributions are tax deferred.

### Required Withdrawals

Many retirement savings plans require a certain amount to be withdrawn as income each year once you have turned seventy and a half. Why? Because the government has generously granted tax deferral, but it wants to collect its taxes eventually! You aren't supposed to use a retirement plan to build an estate for your heirs. A notable exception is the Roth IRA, which requires no withdrawals and can be used to pass tax-deferred savings to your heirs.

## Individual Retirement Plans

In this and the next section, employer-sponsored and individual retirement savings vehicles are discussed in more detail. It's impossible to cover all plans or all the details involved. If you need more information about a specific plan, you need to do some basic research. Fortunately, that information is readily available from the pension plan providers.

When it comes to individual retirement plans, the two that most people rely on are traditional IRAs and Roth IRAs. Let's examine these more closely.

### *Traditional IRAs*

IRA stands for "individual retirement arrangement," and it is just that—a retirement plan you fund yourself and manage yourself, all the way to retirement. IRAs are set up through any bank or brokerage house, and funding and investment choices are entirely up to you. Basic features of a traditional IRA include the following:

- You can contribute $4,000 each year, with that limit to increase to $5,000 in 2008; you can contribute somewhat larger amounts if you are fifty years old or older.
- The amount contributed is tax deductible if you're not covered by another qualified employer plan and if your AGI is less than $52,000 (single) or $83,000 (married filing jointly).
- The working spouse may open a spousal IRA account for the non-working spouse, effectively doubling the couple's annual IRA contribution.

### *Roth IRAs*

A Roth IRA is a special type of IRA set up in the early 1990s. Contributions to Roth IRAs are never tax-deductible, but earnings from a Roth IRA are tax-free (not just tax-deferred, like in most other plans). Additionally, original principal can be withdrawn with no penalties or taxes, and there is no requirement to withdraw funds at age seventy and a half. As a result, many planners recommend Roth IRAs as a way to accumulate tax-free wealth, particularly if you aren't eligible for a tax-deductible IRA.

A Roth IRA is also a better option for those of you who aren't sure you can set aside savings permanently. If you contribute to a tax-deductible IRA and then are forced to withdraw before age fifty-nine and a half, you will not only pay income taxes on the amount withdrawn (which you deducted earlier), but you will also pay a 10 percent penalty. This can be expensive. With a Roth IRA, such deductions of original principal carry no penalty and no taxes. Regardless, it isn't a good idea to kill the goose that lays your golden retirement eggs, so these "emergency" withdrawals should be avoided regardless of the type of IRA you have.

## The 401(k) Plan

The number of employer plans far exceeds the number of individual plans, particularly when self-employment and small-business plans enter the picture. The basic plan offered by employers is the 401(k). (For those of you working in the public sector, the 401(k) has a virtual equivalent known as a 403(b).)

The 401(k) allows you to defer a percentage of your salary, always within the government's maximum limit (for example, the 2008 contribution limit was $15,500 and the catch-up limit for those fifty and older was $5,000), and is usually matched up to 3 percent by the employer. The 401(k) is clearly the most popular "self-reliant" employer plan. Employers have migrated to this plan to minimize their risk (as it carries no pension payout requirements). Employees benefit from the high annual contributions, size of pretax savings, and employer matching. It is possible to accumulate sizable wealth even with no salary increases and with relatively small employee outlays.

Employees do, however, take the burden of managing their own investment portfolios. Usually they receive a fairly wide assortment of aggressive and conservative investment choices, like stock and bond mutual funds. Employees often have a chance to invest in their company's own stock, but the "all eggs in one basket" risk is high—if your company fails, your retirement savings will lose their entire value.

### *Wealth Accumulation with a 401(k)*

Suppose you earn $60,000 a year. You're thirty years from retirement, and you decide to set aside 8 percent of your salary in a 401(k). Further, your employer matches 3 percent, and you invest with a goal of earning 6 percent on your money. Effectively, your annual contribution will be $5,400 (6 percent of $60,000 plus 3 percent of $60,000). Once again, looking at the accumulation annuity table (Figure 4-3), the factor for 6 percent at thirty years is 79.1. So you take the annual contribution ($5,400) and multiply by 79.1 to get accumulated wealth of $427,140 on the first day of retirement. Do a little better on your investments—say, 8 percent—and the factor rises to 113.3, giving you $611,820 upon retirement. Wealth accumulation will be greater with higher contributions and/or higher investment returns.

What about inflation and its effect on 401(k) wealth accumulation? Earlier we discussed moderating investment returns to account for inflation, but here you don't need to, because your salary and annual deferral should rise with inflation. So the 8 percent rate of return figure used in the example is more realistic.

## Retirement Savings Strategies

You can read books and magazines or talk to financial advisors and brokers to learn more about retirement savings and savings plans. Some brokers offer excellent literature explaining these plans, and there are resources on the Web. This chapter concludes with a list of strategies and tactics to help you finance your retirement plans most effectively:

- Take advantage of what is available to you in terms of what your employer has to offer. If your company matches your contributions to a 401(k), make sure you are enrolled and are putting in as much as you can to get the matching funds.
- Contribute to your retirement plan as much as you can, and do it consistently. Remember, you can't borrow your retirement, so retirement savings should normally come before other financial goals.
- Manage your retirement investments. Wealth accumulation depends on investment returns, particularly over the long haul (because of compounding). Although they are long-term investments, retirement assets should be managed well and actively. Particularly while you're young, these investments can be more aggressive. If there's a reason to switch investments, go ahead and do it. There are no tax consequences, and negative returns in a tax-free environment are particularly unfavorable.
- If you're older and have insufficient savings for retirement goals, use the new "catch-up" higher IRA contribution limits to build your retirement base.
- Pay off your mortgage so that when you retire, you find yourself living in a house that you own, with no monthly mortgage payment to worry about.
- Plan to supplement your retirement income. Set yourself up to work in some capacity—it will keep you busy, keep your mind fresh, extend your contributions in your field or profession, and help out a lot financially.

# 25 The Five Steps of Creating an Estate Plan

Sometimes you don't start a project such as estate planning because it seems overwhelming. It is easier to approach any challenge if you have step-by-step instructions. Creating a plan for your family and loved ones is a five-step process that you needn't fear.

## Step One: Learn the Rules

Learning the rules can be fun if you have the right attitude. However, most don't view this as fun, rather they see it as a chore to do when they are ready to die. But what these people don't realize is that they are actually doing estate planning every day.

You make decisions all of the time about where you are going to work, how much money you make, how you spend your money, and how your money makes you and your family happy. As you make your daily decisions, you are probably thinking about what your children are going to do when they grow up. You may be considering how you are going to save money to help your children with college or assist them with their career choices. At the same time, you are planning for your own retirement. When you make everyday decisions for yourself and your family, you are engaged in the process of estate planning. As you will see, there is more to estate planning than making your final decisions.

### *Several Options Available*

When you learn the rules about probate, wills, trusts, joint property, and taxes, you are working on a plan that will continue after you are gone. While you are doing your everyday planning, start thinking about how you would want your property managed for the benefit of your family if you were gone. You may decide that if something happened to you, it would be best to have your property distributed as soon as possible to your spouse. If this is your plan, you may choose a simple will, or upon further research, you may decide that joint property is the best plan.

If you have young children, you may think about who would manage your property and money for your children if something happened to you and your spouse. As you've learned, you can name a guardian for your minor children, but you may decide that the person you've chosen to raise your children isn't the best person to oversee their financial property. In which case, you could name one person to physically take care of your children and a different person to manage your children's money and property.

If you are concerned about who would manage your property and money for your children if something happened to you, you should consider creating a revocable trust. A revocable trust allows you to name a trustee who will manage your property according to the instructions you put in your trust document.

Perhaps during the planning process you discover that your family would need more money if something happened to you. This may lead you to investigate some life insurance to provide for their security. As you can see, one thing often leads to another. It helps to know the rules and be aware of all the options available to you.

### *Life Is Like Monopoly*

Planning is like playing the game of Monopoly. Your life is like a Monopoly game board. Every year you travel around the board. You buy properties that make sense for you. You probably play the game differently than your neighbor or even the other members of your family. We all make different choices about the same things. You might like the steady income stream of properties like the railroad properties. Or perhaps you want to buy one piece of expensive property and build on it. But, like the game of Monopoly, life has chance cards. You don't know when you are going to land on that chance card, or what that card is going to make you do.

When you play Monopoly there are other players. Your family is like the other players in the game. If you quit the game, the other players can understand how you played and are more prepared to play the game without you.

Estate planning is a dynamic process. It can be exciting to learn the rules and keep your plan current and ready. It's important to learn about all the options available to you before setting forth with one specific legal document or estate plan. In the following chapters, you will learn everything you need to know about your options. It's a good idea to keep a pencil handy. You may want to jot down notes on each, naming the advantages and disadvantages, as well as how it may fit in with your family's needs.

## Step Two: Organize Your Assets

It is important to keep the information about your property and the debts you owe current. If you are organized, you will be able to have a plan in place that is ready for your family. You will be able to save money now as well as save your family an enormous amount of money if something happened to you.

### *Organizational System*

You should develop a system to organize the information about your property. In your three-ring notebook, you should have a separate piece of paper for each property you own. Each property should include information such as the value of the property, what you paid for it, the cost of any improvements you made, the debt against the property, and how it is owned. When you organize the information and keep it current, it will help you make the best choices while you are alive. It will also allow you to evaluate all of your property together and to have a plan in place should you pass on. It's best to review your plan on an annual basis.

> You should think about each piece of property you own from two perspectives: whether you are currently making the best choices about that piece of property and what would happen to that property if you were gone.

### *Evaluating the Information Gathered*

Evaluating the information about each piece of property you own can reap tremendous benefits for you now, as well as after you are gone. For example, assume that you have a piece of paper that describes your car. If you think about the costs associated with your car, you might take the time to evaluate whether you are paying too much for insurance. Shop around!

You might save money by keeping track of when your car has been serviced—tires, oil change, brakes, etc. And of course, you can plan for what you want to happen to your car if you are gone.

You might discover that you owe more on your car than the car is currently worth. Or, if you lease your car, you may discover that your family would owe money on the lease if something happened to you. These discoveries might lead you to make choices now about your property, as well as what will happen to your property when you are gone.

Let's say you have a sheet of paper that describes your home. One of the pieces of information about your home would be how much you owe and the interest rate you are paying on any loans against it. When you are organizing your notebook for your estate plan, you should evaluate the interest rate you are currently paying. If there are interest rates available that are less than when you financed your home, you may find you can save money now by refinancing your home. And of course, while you are evaluating all of the current costs associated with your home, you can decide who would receive your home if you were gone and whether he or she could afford to maintain it.

If you can drop your interest rate by 1 percent on a thirty-year mortgage, this saves you $69 per month for every $100,000 of debt. If you owe $200,000 on your home and you can drop your interest rate by 1 percent, you will save $138 per month!

If you have life insurance, describe the attributes of the life insurance on a piece of paper. You may discover that there are new life insurance products available that will pay a larger death benefit for less annual premiums. This can help you now with the cash flow. And, you can also evaluate who will receive the life insurance benefits when you are gone. You may discover that your life insurance will cause your estate to owe federal death taxes. You will learn how to make changes to your plan to avoid any federal death taxes on your life insurance.

### *Planning Inventory*

You may not be the notebook type of person. Or, you may feel that you do not need to organize your assets this way to create a plan that meets your needs. Another way to get organized is to complete a planning inventory. A planning inventory is a form that gathers the information you need to evaluate the property you own, assesses whether your estate would be subject to federal death taxes, and prepares you to create the documents you need. The inventory guides you through the steps to gather the information you need to plan, and it also brings all of the information together in one place for your family to access easily if something happens to you. Take a moment and review the information requested by the inventory.

When something happens to you, your family is full of grief. It is heart wrenching for your family to have to go through all of your papers trying to gather the needed information. You can avoid this crisis for your family by being prepared. Sometimes even when a person chooses to organize their information in a three-ring notebook, they like to also complete the inventory, because the inventory summarizes the information in the notebook.

If you do not organize the information about your property either by filling out an inventory or preparing a three-ring notebook, your family probably will not know how to find the needed information.

## Step Three: Decide Who, What, and When

An old journalism adage applies here: You get the right story when you tell who, what, where, when, and why. Your family is a story. It is a story that changes all of the time. Who are your loved ones? What are your goals for them? Where are your loved ones living? When would you want your loved ones to receive your property and why? Get ready to tell your story.

Think about your three-ring notebook. If you haven't already, take out a separate piece of paper and write down the name of every person you would include in your plan. Then begin to ask yourself what that person is currently doing.

Which piece of property or properties would you like that person to have? Put the piece of paper that describes that property under the piece of paper describing the person to whom you would leave that property. Develop little stacks of paper under each person's name. Then when you look at the stacks, you can ask the next question. When would you like that person to receive the property? You might find yourself beginning to think about things like:

- Would that person be able to take care of the property if something happened to you tomorrow?
- Would it promote maturity if that person received the property tomorrow?
- Would it be better if that person received the property later in life?
- If something happens to you, should the property be sold?
- How much income taxes or death taxes would it cost if you leave that piece of property to the named person?
- Is your plan fair?

When you think about your property and the persons who would enjoy your property if something were to happen to you, you may discover that the goals you have now for your loved ones and family are very different from the goals you had ten years ago.

You need to look at your plan to see if your plan meets your family's needs today and re-evaluate your plan regularly. The answers to the questions who, what, and when will change over time. And since you don't know when something might happen to you, it's best to try to keep up with changing times.

Your plans and goals change over time, so don't prepare a will or trust and hide it safely away to be forgotten. Be sure to keep your plan current with the changing needs of your family.

Most people do not keep their plans current because they don't understand the planning tools that are available or how they work. They don't know how to change their plan to meet the changing needs of their family. And last but not least, they don't want to spend a lot of money keeping their plan current every year.

The beauty of learning the rules is that it allows you to do most of the work. Many times, you can make the necessary changes yourself, without the help of a lawyer. But, even if you do need the help of a lawyer, when you understand the planning tools available and how they work, it will be much less expensive for you to have your plan tweaked.

## Step Four: Choose Your Planning Tools

There are so many fun planning tools available. When you understand your options and how the planning tools work, you can become an involved player in your plan rather than a passive observer. It is always scary to have someone tell you what you need to do, without explaining why you should do that particular thing. In the same way, it can be disturbing when you don't understand the planning tools or what the consequences will be if you don't plan. When something scares you, it's natural to try to avoid it.

You don't need to be nervous and scared. And there's certainly no reason to avoid these planning tools. You simply need to figure out how they can work for you. Once you do, you suddenly don't have to be a passive participant in planning for your family. You can make decisions that may help you save money now and provide for the security of your loved ones later.

### *Planning Tools Available*

There are numerous planning tools available. You will soon learn the rules regarding:

- Wills
- Trusts
- Joint property
- Annuities
- Life insurance
- Retirement plans
- Taxes

### *One Tool Affects Another*

You will probably have or need more than one planning tool. When you create anything, there are typically parts that are combined to make a whole finished product. When you make a decision about one planning tool, it may change what you do with another planning tool. For instance, let's say you have an IRA, and you learn how the IRA is taxed when you die. You aren't happy with this outcome so you conduct more research. What you find allows you to change some of your IRA elections to reduce the tax impact.

Or perhaps you already have a will in place, but you learn that it has no impact on how or to whom your insurance, annuities, IRA, or joint property are paid and distributed. You might have thought that if you put instructions in your will about how these items were to be distributed, that your will would control. As you know, this isn't true, so you will probably want to re-evaluate your plan to make it coincide with your wishes.

Most families have different types of property and need multiple planning tools to accomplish their goals. When you understand what each of the planning tools can do for you, you will be in a position to play the game, participate in the choices, and create a plan that you can maintain and change as the needs of your family change.

Every person should have a will or trust. Even if all of your property is in joint name with your spouse, you should have a document that will direct how your property passes in the unlikely event that both you and your spouse die in a common accident.

## Step Five: Implement Your Plan

A plan is no good unless you take the steps that are necessary to implement it. Many people sit around and think about plans, but don't do anything to set them in motion. This failure to implement a plan is even more common with estate planning. The reason is that most plans you make result in something you look forward to. Let's face it, it's unlikely there are people out there that jump out of bed in the morning and say, "I can't wait to do my estate planning today, because I'm really looking forward to passing on!" But when you think about estate planning as part of your everyday life and consider the benefits you can enjoy today by creating and implementing a plan, you may have a little more motivation to get started.

A good estate plan is not set in motion in one hour. It's probably not accomplished in one day or even one week. In order to implement a plan, you need to be organized, understand your options and planning tools, and think about how your property should be distributed or managed if you are gone. This all takes time and effort.

If you follow the steps recommended in this book, you will be well prepared to implement your plan. Implementing your plan is not about having a lawyer draft documents. It is about knowing your story—who, what, where, when, and why. When you understand your story, you can walk through the steps to determine which planning tools meet your needs. Then, you can either prepare the necessary documents yourself, or you can make an appointment with a lawyer who will be able to draft the documents for you. And remember, your plan will probably change regularly, as your needs and the needs of your family change.

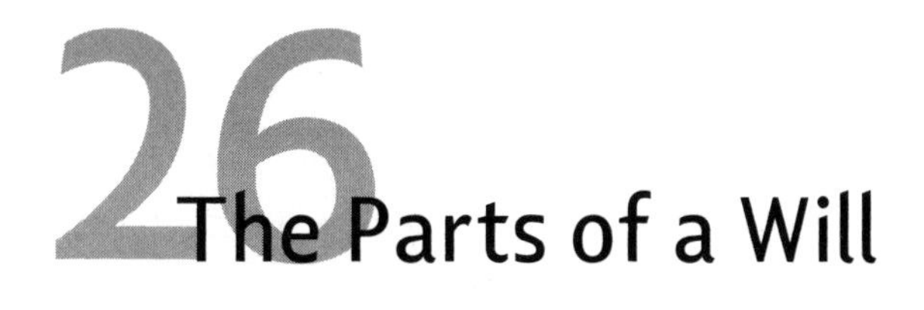

# 26 The Parts of a Will

A will is the legal document that provides instructions on how property that is titled in your name will be distributed when you are gone. Each part of your will serves a different purpose. Once you understand the parts, you can make the decisions needed to begin a draft of your will.

## An Overview

A will is a piece of paper that is presented to the probate court after you are gone. The probate court judge needs to be able to read that piece of paper and determine that it is in fact your will and that you signed that will. The judge then issues a court order to distribute your property per your instructions. This all sounds very simple. However, you are not available to testify that the will is in fact yours. The judge has to make sure that no one changed your will without your permission. The judge also needs to determine by reading the will who you wanted to receive your property and what you wanted each person to have. All of these decisions are made without the testimony of the one and only person who really knew what he or she wanted: you! Therefore, your will must speak for itself.

### *A Will Is Divided into Parts*

The more specific you are about what you want, the easier it will be for the probate court judge to make the right decisions about your property. Each part of your will is designed to help the probate court judge interpret your intentions. A will has parts, often referred to as the *articles*. Each article is designed to accomplish a purpose.

### *Don't Be Intimidated by Fancy Words*

Words are intimidating when you don't understand what they mean. For instance, let's say you take your car to a mechanic. The mechanic starts talking about the lifters, pistons, plugs, serpentine belt, and catalytic converter, and you become nervous because you have no idea what he or she is talking about. When your will includes phrases like "descendants by right of representations" or "property passing per stirpes," that same sense of panic fills your body. Don't be intimidated! When you finish reading this chapter, you will understand those fancy words.

The words in a will are confusing because the law on wills came from our English heritage. Unlike most areas of law where more modern terms have been incorporated into the law, the terminology associated with wills has not changed much for centuries.

## Declarations

The first part, or Article I, of your will identifies you and your heirs. This part is referred to as the declaration section. An heir is any person who would receive your property if you died without a will. If you think about a ladder, it will help you understand the heirs you should list in this first part. If you have living heirs at the first step of the ladder, you don't need to go to the second step. If you have no heirs at the first or second step, you need to list your heirs at the third step.

### *The Ladder of Heirs*

The first step, or level, of heirs is your spouse and your children. If you have no spouse, the only heirs at this first step are your children. If one or more of your children have died and are survived by one or more children, the child or children of the child who is gone is included as an heir on the first step of the ladder. If any of these persons are living, you can stop here.

If there is no one living at the first step, you must go to the second step, which includes your mother and father. If your mother is gone, your father is your only heir, and vice versa. If your mother and/or father are living, you can stop. If your mother and father are gone, go to the next step.

The third step is your siblings or their children. If one of your siblings is gone, the child or children of the deceased sibling will become an heir, and should be listed. If you have no spouse, children, grandchildren, parents, siblings, or children of siblings, you need help from a lawyer to define your heirs.

It may seem silly to spend so much time teaching you about your heirs, but the probate court judge wants to be sure that you knew who your heirs were. Then, if you decide not to leave any property to an heir, later in your will you can explain why you have excluded that heir.

Remember, the probate court judge's job is to issue an order to distribute your property to the persons you name in your will. If you don't identify your heirs in the declaration portion of your will, you run the risk that an excluded heir will contest your will, alleging that you forgot about him or her.

### *Defining Children*

The next part of the declaration section of your will defines the words *child, children,* and *descendants.* The most important thing for you to understand is that the word child (or children) will not include stepchildren or foster children. If you want to make a distribution to a stepchild or a foster child you can do so in Articles III or IV, but you will need to be very specific. As you read on about how to distribute your property, you will learn about the significance of the word *descendant.*

## Payment of Debts

The next part of your will, Article II, directs that all of your debts, obligations, and taxes be paid. Any person or entity to which you owed money when you died is called a creditor. You've learned that when you die, one of the first jobs of the executor is to hire a lawyer to file the necessary papers with the probate court. The lawyer will also tell the executor what he or she needs to do to administer your estate. One of the jobs of your executor is to pay the debts and obligations you owed when you died.

If your executor does not pay the creditors, an unpaid creditor is allowed to file a claim against your estate demanding payment. If there are not enough assets to pay all of your debts and obligations, there is an ordering process to determine which debts will be paid in full and which debts will either not be paid or will be partially paid.

### *Secured Debt*

There are certain types of debts that are secured. When a debt is secured by property you owned while you are living, that piece of property can be sold to pay the debt. The best example of this type of secured debt is the debt you owe on your home.

When you borrowed money to buy your home, you signed two types of legal papers. The first was a promissory note. The promissory note made you and whoever else signed the promissory note personally liable for the debt. The second type of paper you signed gave the lender, typically your bank, a security interest in your house, known as a mortgage. If you don't make your payments, the lender has two choices. The lender can sue you and whoever else signed on the promissory note, or the lender can take the house back and sell your home under the terms of the mortgage.

Don't forget that your will has no effect on joint property, nor does it have an effect on IRAs, annuities, or life insurance, where someone other than the estate is named as the beneficiary.

### *Lenders Have Rights When You Die*

When you die, if you owed money on a promissory note, secured by a mortgage on your home, the lender typically has the right to demand that the debt be paid in full. Anytime you own property secured by a mortgage, that property can be sold to pay the debt. Lenders typically don't exercise this right as long as someone continues to make the monthly payments.

Article II may include an excerpt such as the following:

*If any property owned by me jointly, or individually, passing under this will or otherwise, shall be encumbered by a mortgage, pledge, security interest, loan, lien or unpaid taxes, the indebtedness secured by such encumbrance shall not be charged to or paid by my estate but such property shall pass subject to all encumbrances existing at my death.*

This language is merely telling your executor that if there is a secured loan against a particular piece of property you owned, the executor is to distribute that property without paying off the loan against the property.

Please understand these instructions are not binding on the lender. The lender will have the right to be paid in full before the property is distributed to your heirs, if the lender chooses to exercise its rights under the loan documents. A lender may choose to exercise its right to demand that the property be sold if your estate has more debts than it has assets, and the lender is not comfortable that the other person who signed the note, if there is one, is capable of making the payments.

Before you prepare your will it is a good idea to analyze the property you own, the debt against the property, and how that debt is secured. If your family would not have enough money to pay the outstanding bills, you might consider purchasing some life insurance.

## Specific Devises

*Devise* is the term that is used in a will to describe the fact that you are leaving property to someone. The person to whom you devise property is called a *devisee.* When you make a specific devise, you are describing a piece of property and giving specific instructions to give that property to a named person.

### *Specific Devise of Tangible Personal Property*

Tangible personal property is any property other than real estate that you can feel or touch. Tangible property does not include bank accounts, shares of stock, certificates of deposit, bonds, partnership interests, or any other financial interests. These items are known as intangible personal property.

Most wills include a separate article telling the executor what to do with your tangible personal property. For example, let's say a will specifies that all of the tangible personal property is to be left to the spouse, and if the spouse is not living, to the children. If the children cannot agree on how to divide the tangible personal property within six months, the will states that the executor shall decide how to divide the tangible personal property, and the decision of the executor is final and binding.

Even if your will states that the decision of the executor shall be final and binding, someone could file a contest with the probate court, alleging that the executor is breaching his or her duty. It will be tough for that person to win, but it is expensive for your estate to spend money on a lawyer to defend the contest.

### *Avoiding Conflict*

If you think your children or heirs are going to fight about what each one receives, you can specifically describe each piece of tangible personal property and who should receive that property. Heirs typically fight about jewelry, crystal, china, furniture, cars, boats, and collectibles. It takes time and thought on your part to include specifics in your will, but it can avoid hard feelings after you are gone.

Or, you might consider putting a clause in your will that says "if my children can not agree on how to distribute the rest of my tangible personal property within six months after my death, I hereby instruct the executor to sell the disputed items and divide the proceeds equally between my children." It would be almost impossible for any child to contest this language.

### *Who Pays Expenses*

You should include instructions about who pays the expenses incurred in storing, packing, or moving the tangible personal property. A will may state that these expenses are not to be charged against the devisee that receives the tangible personal property. In plain English this means that if there are expenses in storing, packing, or moving any tangible personal property, those expenses are to be paid from other assets or property in your estate, and are not charged to the one who receives the property. If this is not your intention, you should instruct your executor that any expenses for storing, packing, or moving will be charged against the devisee that receives the property. Sometimes it's not fair if one child lives 3,000 miles away that the other heirs must bear the expense of packing and moving the property!

## *Specific Devises of Other Property*

There is no magic number of how many articles there will be in your will. If you want to make specific devises of any other property, you should have another article titled "Specific Devises of Other Property." You should number each paragraph. In each paragraph you should describe in detail each piece of property and who is going to receive that property. For instance:

1. I leave the property located at 7301 Chase Drive, Sarasota, Florida, to my daughter.
2. I leave my brokerage account held at X Company to my son.
3. I leave the balance of my savings account held at X Bank to my daughter.

There are two points you should consider regarding specific devises. First, if you don't own the described property when you die, the devise is ignored, and the devisee does not get other property unless it is already specified. Second, you should specify what happens to the property if the devisee you name is not living. For example, if you leave your daughter 7301 Chase Drive, that provision should continue and state that if your daughter is not living, the property shall pass to her children, or to her brother, or according to the residual clause of your will. These are choices you need to make when you include specific devises in your will.

When you leave a specific devise of property to a named individual in your will, make sure that the property you are attempting to leave to the named person is actually titled in your individual name. The property could be very clearly described, but if the property is owned in joint name, the will has no effect.

## *Per Stirpes*

There are two legal terms you should understand. The first is *per stirpes,* and the second is *per capita.* Let's first take a look at per stirpes. Whenever you leave property to a person per stirpes, this has a very definite legal effect. It means that if the named person is dead, the property passes to the lineal descendants, by representation. The best way to understand this concept is with a diagram.

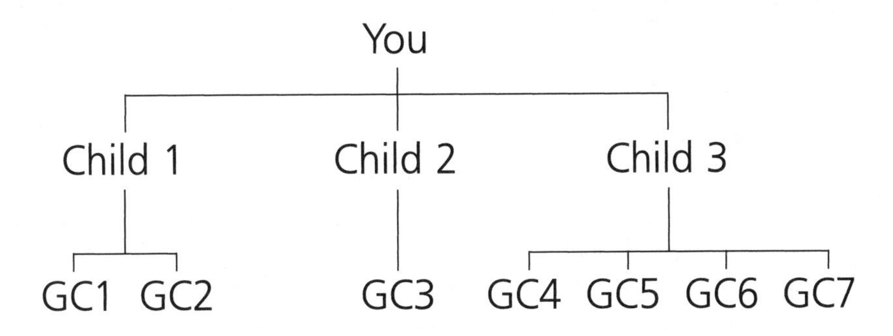


Per stirpes means that if Child 1 is dead, Child 1's share will be divided equally between GC1 and GC2. In other words, Child 1's ⅓ share will be divided equally between GC1 and GC2, who will each receive ⅙ of the property. If you would rather have Child 1's property distributed to your other two children, Child 2 and Child 3, you don't want to use the term *per stirpes.*

Assume that all three of children are gone. Because you have left the property per stirpes, Child 1's children will each receive ⅙ (½ × ⅓); Child 2's child will receive ⅓ because Child 2 had only one child; and Child 3's children will each take 1/12 of the property (¼ × ⅓). This may not be what you intended. If your children are all gone, you might want each of the seven grandchildren to take equal shares. In which case you shouldn't use the term per stirpes.

### *Per Capita*

Another option is to use the term *per capita.* If you leave the property to a group per capita, and a member of the group is gone, the property goes in equal shares to the other persons in the group. For instance, if you leave your property per capita to your three children and one child dies, then the property will pass to your two living children, and not to the children of your deceased child.

If you don't define who will take a property (if the specific devisee is gone) with the term per stirpes or per capita, you can specifically name who should receive the property and in what share. It makes your will longer, but ensures that your property will pass the way you want.

## Residuary Devise

This is the clause that distributes the rest of your property. This may also be the clause that will distribute specifically devised property if the person to whom you specifically devised property is not living, and you put in a provision that reads "If this person is not living, the property shall be distributed according to the terms of my residual clause."

You can direct your executor to divide the residual of your property to one or more persons. If you include very few specific devises in your will, most of your property will pass according to the instructions contained in the residual clause.

### *Testamentary Trusts*

You have the option of creating a complete trust in the residual clause of your will. Your residual clause will then read "I leave the rest and remainder of my property to John Doe, Trustee. John Doe shall administer the trust as follows." The trust you create inside of your will is called a *testamentary trust.*

The testamentary trust is identical in every single way to a revocable trust that you might have created while you were living, with two very important distinctions. First, the trust is not created until after you are gone. The trust becomes alive after you are dead and is funded and created by the residual clause of your will. Second, the trust document will not include provisions about how to administer the trust property while you are living, because the trust won't be created until after you are gone.

### *Advantages and Disadvantages*

You might create a testamentary trust in your will because you don't want to go through the trouble of transferring all of your property into your name as trustee while you are living as you have to do when creating a revocable trust. But, you still want the benefits of creating a trust plan for your family that will govern after you are gone.

It is very important for you to understand that if you create a testamentary trust, your property must be probated. Once the testamentary trust is created in your will, it will be governed by the same rules as a revocable trust, except a testamentary trust remains under the annual supervision of the probate court, because that is where the trust was created.

A revocable trust you create while you are alive only comes under the supervision of the probate court if someone files a complaint with the probate court about how the trust is being operated.

## Taxes

Your will instructs your executor to pay all taxes that are owing—local, state, and federal taxes. The most common taxes owing when a person dies are income taxes or estate and gift taxes.

Your executor will be responsible for filing your final federal and state income tax returns. Most of the rules about how to compute the final income tax returns are the same whether you are living or it is your final return.

If your estate is required to file a federal death tax return, there are elections to take certain deductions on the federal death tax return versus your final income tax return. You should ask the accountant or lawyer who prepares the federal death tax return about these elections.

If you choose to use a will as your planning document, the probate courts will not allow your executor to close your estate until the executor has verified that all tax returns have been filed. In most cases, this means that your estate cannot be closed until after January 31 following the year of your death. This is because payers are not required to send the forms and statements that you need to compute the return until January 31. Also, the federal death tax return, if one needs to be filed, is due no later than nine months after the date of your death. Preparing this return may delay the closing of your estate.

## The Powers of Your Executor

Your will names the executor, who will be in charge of administering your estate. In some states, the executor is called a personal representative. Your executor is legally responsible for doing everything necessary to probate your estate. The only document that allows you to appoint an executor is your will.

If there are certain assets or property you definitely don't want sold or encumbered, you can place a limited restriction on your executor as it relates to that piece of property.

Your will also defines the powers of your executor. You typically want to give your executor all of the powers to deal with your property that you would have had if you were still alive. You can't anticipate how long it will take to probate your estate. It is difficult to complete the probate process more quickly than six months, and because your executor can't close the estate until all claims have been resolved and all tax returns have been filed, it is quite common for an estate to be open for at least one year. If you restrict the powers your executor has to buy, sell, mortgage, loan, or deal with the estate property, it may hurt your heirs. For example, if you placed a restriction on the executor that he or she cannot sell your property, and your estate holds a particular stock, if the value of the stock begins to decline, your executor will not be able to sell the stock.

## How to Sign

Almost all states require that you sign your will in your own handwriting in the presence of two witnesses and a notary. Some states require that the witnesses be over the age of majority.

### *Physical Presence Is Mandatory*

Although signing your name seems easy enough, there are a couple of things that could create problems. As you know, you must sign in the presence of two witnesses. This can be tricky. You should make sure that you sign the document in the physical presence of the two witnesses who sign in your presence and in the presence of each other. In some states, a will can be found invalid if it is established that the witnesses signed in your presence, but signed at different times. For example, let's say you sign your will in the presence of Witness Number One. And then two hours later, Witness Number Two stops by to sign his name. Because these witnesses did not witness your will in the presence of each other, the will may be invalidated. If you sign your will in the presence of two witnesses, and then the witnesses go to the room next door and sign your will, the witnesses did not sign in your presence, and, again, the will might be invalidated.

### *It's All in the Signature*

It is best that you sign your legal name. If the way you normally sign documents is different from your legal name, the probate court judge will usually require testimony from someone who can prove that the way you signed your will is the way you normally sign legal documents. There have been cases where a person signed his will with an *X*, and the will was valid because the person always signed his name with an *X*. It is not the time to be tricky or unusual when you are signing your will. Again, it is highly recommended that you sign your legal name.

# INDEX

## D



## E



## F

## G



## H



## I



## J



## L



## M



## N

## O



## P



## R



## S



## T